SERMONS ON THE LOVE OF GOD
AND COGNATE THEMES

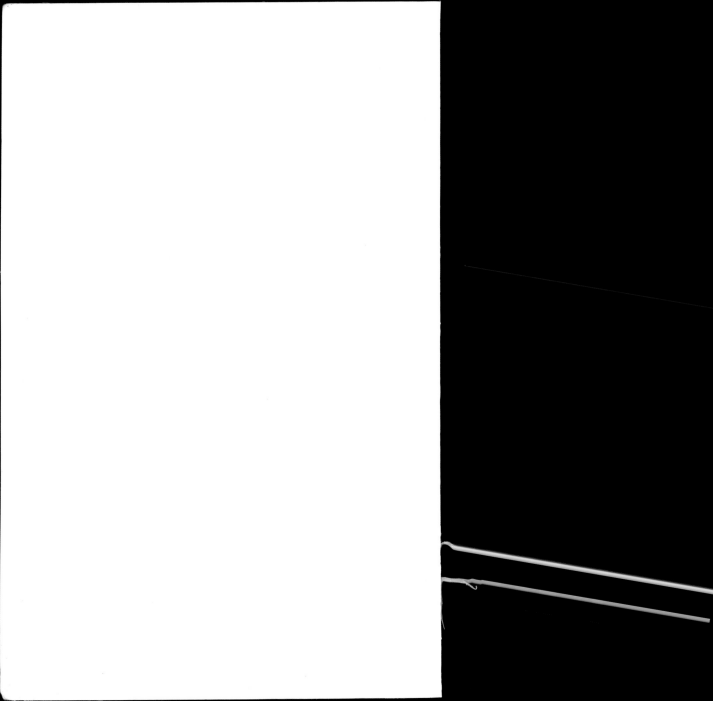

SERMONS

BY

REV. DONALD MACFARLANE

(Originally published under the title *Sermons on the Love of God and Cognate Themes* by Rev. Donald MacFarlane, Dingwall)

FREE PRESBYTERIAN PUBLICATIONS

FREE PRESBYTERIAN PUBLICATIONS
133 WOODLANDS ROAD
GLASGOW G3 6LE

First Published 1918
This Edition 1986
© Free Presbyterian Publications 1986

ISBN 0 902506 20 X

Printed in Great Britain by
Bell and Bain Ltd., Glasgow

PREFACE

AT the urgent request of friends, in whose judgment I
have confidence, I have, in the evening of my ministerial
labours, ventured to give publicity in this form to a
selection of sermons, the greater number of which were
preached within the last two or three years.   I have
to thank Mr Kenneth MacIver, Strathpeffer, for his
invaluable help in having these sermons committed to
manuscript, and the Rev. John R. Mackay, M.A.,
Inverness, for kindly reading the proofs for me.
Readers will find the sermons constituting this volume
simple in their construction, but I am confident that
they are in harmony with the Scriptures, and issue
them with the prayer that the Lord may use them for
the salvation of the lost, and for the building up of
His people.

DONALD MACFARLANE.

F.P. MANSE,
DINGWALL, *August*, 1918.

Introduction

REV. DONALD MACFARLANE OF DINGWALL

Rev. Donald Macfarlane was born in 1834 in the island of North Uist. In 1856, while listening to the renowned preacher, Rev. Alexander MacColl, he was arrested and deeply impressed by the question, fervently asked by Mr MacColl, "Is there any young man in the audience that will come to Christ?" That impression was deepened and, under a thorough conviction of the sinfulness of his nature, he was enabled eventually to close in with Christ as the only Saviour of sinners.

After teaching in some schools in his home island, and also having studied in Glasgow, in the University and Free Church College there, he was licensed to preach. His first charge, to which he was inducted in 1876, was Strathconon. Thereafter he was minister of Moy and Raasay congregations.

"During this time", records one biographical sketch, "the Rationalistic Party in the Free Church was making every effort to overthrow the Westminster Confession of Faith as the doctrinal standard of the church. Their efforts culminated in the passing of the infamous Declaratory Act which altered the Constitution of the then Free Church. Thereupon, Mr Macfarlane laid his protest on the table of the Assembly in 1893, and thereby separated from that body. Thus began the movement which took the name of the Free Presbyterian Church of Scotland."

In 1903 he accepted a call from Dingwall Congregation and continued there until his death in 1926.

"As preacher," wrote his biographer, Rev. Donald · Beaton, "Mr Macfarlane had a place in the estimation of the Lord's people that can only be accounted for by the fact that he was feeding them with the very finest of the wheat. It was not his oratorical gifts that captivated them, for, in the accepted sense of the word, he was no orator. Neither was it his lively manner in delivering his message that kept up their attention, for in presenting the truth he did so in a quiet, calm, deliberate way. But there was something in the message that excelled all these, and that was the unction that accompanied the truth delivered. It fell like the gentle dew from heaven upon the hearts of those who delighted in the message of the everlasting Gospel ...

"He shunned not to declare the whole counsel of God. He believed the Bible to be the Word of God with all his heart; he received its truths unhesitatingly, and whether these were popular or unpopular with men never weighed with him as a servant of Christ ... He never forgot in his preaching that he was only a servant in the Master's house, that the message was not his, but that of Him whom he served ...

"Mr Macfarlane excelled as an expository preacher. He had a special gift in getting at the meaning of the passage he was expounding, especially in its relation to its context. No preacher we ever listened to excelled him in this gift ... This gift enabled him to keep up the interest of his hearers while it instructed them. His preaching had always a sound doctrinal foundation even in his most experimental and practical discourses ...

"As an experimental preacher he knew the different phases of sin in his own heart, its deceitfulness, its depravity, its deadening effects, its determination to gain the mastery. Added to this was his knowledge of Satan's devices. The result was, when he preached to the tried and tempted heritage of God they felt they were listening to one who had been in deep places himself and who could tell them the way he got deliverance...

"Mr Macfarlane was careful as a preacher to make pointed application to his hearers of the doctrine and experience he preached. He did not leave them with the impression that it was a matter of indifference whether they practised what was set before them or not...

"It was with no cold and indifferent heart he delivered his message, but as one that yearned that Christ would be formed in the hearts of his hearers as the hope of glory...

"A feature of Mr Macfarlane's sermons which is worthy of notice is their remarkable clearness and simplicity... It was not the result of paucity of thought or mental poverty, but rather the reverse... The writer recalls a sermon he heard from Mr Macfarlane, preached in St Jude's, on the doctrine of justification by faith. It was one of the simplest sermons as far as the language and the treatment were concerned that he ever heard, but it was listened to with entranced interest by the congregation..."

Free Presbyterian Publications has great pleasure in issuing this new edition of his sermons. First published in 1918, it met with wide acceptance then, and we believe that it will be warmly welcomed by not a few today. Our prayer is that the Lord, who alone "giveth the increase," will bless these sermons to the spiritual benefit of many.

N.M.R.

CONTENTS

		PAGE
I.	God's Love to His People—Ps. cvi. 4	1
II.	Creation—Heb. xi. 3	9
III.	The Giving of the Law—Exod. xxiv. 12	18
IV.	The Fourth Commandment—Exod. xx. 8-11	28
V.	Grace Abounding—Rom. v. 20	38
VI.	God's Name Proclaimed—Exod. xxxiv. 4-7	43
VII.	The New Covenant—Heb. viii. 10-12	52
VIII.	Jacob's Dream—Gen. xxviii. 12, 13	62
IX.	The Fulness of the Time—Gal. iv. 4, 5	72
X.	His Name, Jesus—Matt. i. 21	80
XI.	The Sword Smiting the Shepherd—Zech. xiii. 7	88
XII.	Christ Seeing of His Travail—Is. liii. 4	99
XIII.	A Free Salvation—Rev. iii. 18	113
XIV.	The Gospel the Power of God—1 Cor. i. 18	125
XV.	Natural Unwillingness—John v. 40	134
XVI.	The Gospel Invitation—Matt. xi. 28-30.	146
XVII.	Christ Drawing all Sorts—John xii. 32	156
XVIII.	The Gospel Day—Zech. xiv. 6, 7	168
XIX.	Prisoners of Hope—Zech. ix. 12	178
XX.	The Strait Gate—Matt. vii. 13, 14	187
XXI.	The Good Work Begun—Phil. i. 6	198
XXII.	Justification—Rom. iii. 24, 25	209
XXIII.	Christ made Wisdom, etc.—1 Cor. i. 30	220
XXIV.	The Bethrothal—Hos. ii. 19, 20	230
XXV.	The Feast of Fat Things—Is. xxv. 6	238
XXVI.	The Shepherd and the Flock—John x. 27, 28	247
XXVII.	Arise, my Love—Song ii. 10-12	257
XXVIII.	Job's Complaint—Job. xxiii. 3-10.	270
XXIX.	Saving Faith—Heb. xi. 1	284
XXX.	The Ransomed of the Lord—Is. xxxv. 10	292

SERMONS

God's Love to his People

"Remember me, O Lord, with the favour that Thou bearest unto Thy people."—Ps. cvi. 4.

HERE we have one of the prayers of the Psalmist. It is a very large prayer; the largest which a mere man ever offered up to God for himself. Some may ask for some particular blessing, such as reconciliation with God, pardon of sin, or other such blessings. But the psalmist, taking a wide view of the favour, or love, of God, opens his mouth wide, to drink in of the infinite ocean of that love. The love of God is compared to a fire, that hath a most vehement flame (Song viii. 6). When you come home cold, how are you to get warm? By sitting near a big fire. The love of God is such a big fire that although you would be shivering and freezing with cold, if you get near it, you will soon get warm. It was when the psalmist drew near to the love of God that he prayed, "Remember me, Lord, with that love which Thou bearest to Thine own."

In speaking from these words, as the Lord may enable me, I shall call your attention to four things:—

1

I. The love of God.

II. The objects of His love.

III. The fruits of His love, and

IV. The prayer—Remember me with that love which Thou bearest to Thine own.

I. *The love of God.*

(1) We note that the love of God is everlasting, without a break from eternity to eternity. As it is infinite, we cannot get at the beginning of it, nor shall we see the end of it. It is like God Himself, from everlasting to everlasting. From the past eternity it runs on without a break through time and continues to all eternity. It cannot be broken. Did not the sin of man break it? If anything could break the love of God, sin would do it; but sin did not break it. God still loved His people, notwithstanding that they sinned; but, although sin did not break the love of God, it put a stop, for a short time, to its flowing forth to its objects. Before it could flow forth, a new way would require to be opened up, and that way was to be the way of blood—that is, the blood of Christ. The bloody sacrifice which Abel offered up was a type of the blood of Christ, and, as soon as this way by blood was opened, the love of God began to flow forth, and it continues to flow to its objects ever since, and shall continue to flow for ever and ever.

(2) The love of God is unchangeable. The love of His people to Him is, during their time in this world, changeable. It is like the sea that flows and ebbs, but the love of God is like Himself, Who says, " I am Jehovah, I change not." Did He love His people with unchangeable love, when they were unconverted? Yes.

It was His love that surrounded them in their unconverted state, and protected them from death coming
near them, till they were changed by His grace. There
is such a thing in God as a love of complacency, and He
did not then love His people with that kind of love; but
He loved them with the love which is the source of
salvation. The love which is the source of salvation
sees nothing in sinners why God should love them.
But, in the case of believers, there is something in them
to draw forth a love of complacency, and that is His
own image in them. With regard to this love of
complacency, God loves some of His people more than
others of them. Amongst men, parents love some of
their children more than others of them, and although
they love all their children, they love with a greater
love those of them that are obedient to them, while they
cannot love so much those that are disobedient.

(3) God loves freely. That is, you cannot buy or
merit His love. Love is of such a nature that it cannot
be bought. " If a man would give all the substance of
his house for love, it would utterly be contemned "
(Song viii. 7). Did not Christ's death buy God's love?
No. Christ's death was not the cause of God's love, but
the effect of it, as Christ Himself told us: " For God so
loved the world, that He gave His only begotten Son "
(John iii. 16). If Christ did not buy God's love, how
can we expect to buy it? Although Christ did not buy
the Father's love, He, as already stated, opened up a
way for it to flow forth to its objects.

(4) God's love is sovereign. He loved some of the
human race, and did not love the rest of them. This is
a solemn thought, but it is a fact. He was not under

any obligation to love any of the human race.   He
might have left them all to perish, as He left the angels
that kept not their first estate.   It depended upon His
own sovereign will, and those whom He loved shall be
under unspeakable obligations to Him for loving them,
while He left others of their fellow creatures to perish
in their sins.

II. *The objects of His love.*

These, before their conversion, are known to God
alone.   They are unknown to men, and to angels, until
they are effectually called, and, when they are effectually
called, they are known not only by God's people, but by
the unconverted.   " All that see them shall acknowledge them, that they are the seed which the Lord hath
blessed " (Isai. lxi. 9).   In a certain parish in the
Highlands there was a godly man of the name, little
Lauchlan.   A minister met a boy from the district in
which that man lived.   The minister asked the boy,
" Are there good people in your district ?"   The boy
said, " There is one good man there."   The minister
asked, " Who is that man ?"   The boy answered,
" Little Lauchlan."   (He was little in stature, but
great in grace).   The minister asked the boy, " How do
you know that little Lauchlan is a good man ?"   " The
boy said, " I see him every morning, when he sends his
cattle to the hill, kneeling down to pray beside a dyke,
before he returns home."   Then the minister asked
him, " Are there good women in the district ?"   The
boy said, " No."   The minister asked how he knew.
The boy said that almost every day he heard them
quarrelling among themselves.   That boy, though not

converted himself, could make a distinction between good and bad people. By their fruits they shall be known.

Another mark by which they are known is that they love God, and their love to Him is the effect of His love to them, as they themselves declare : '' We love Him because He first loved us '' ; and as God manifested His love to them in such a wonderful manner as to give His Son to be the propitiation for their sins, so they manifest their love to Him in keeping His commandments. These are called, justified, adopted, and sanctified in this world. They love God's word ; His people, with brotherly love ; and they love their fellow sinners, with compassionate love.

III. *The fruits of His love.*

(1) One great fruit of God's love is His eternal purpose of salvation. Although His purpose of salvation is as eternal as His love, we deem it proper to give the precedence to His love, because it is the great source from which salvation flows.

(2) Another great fruit of God's love is the revelation which He has given us of His purpose. We have that revelation in the Scriptures of the Old and New Testaments. Although God purposed to save sinners of the human race, we would be ignorant of it, if He had not revealed it.

(3) Another great fruit—the greatest—is His sending His only begotten Son to the world, in our nature, to execute the Father's purpose, and especially to work out everlasting redemption by His obedience unto death.

(4) The preaching of the Gospel, by means of which sinners are saved, is another precious fruit. The Gospel

is the power of God unto salvation to every one that
believeth, whether Jew or Gentile.

(5) The gift of the Holy Spirit to convince and con-
vert sinners, is another great fruit. The Gospel is a
means, but the Spirit is an agent that works effectually
by means of the word of the Gospel.

(6) Ministers of the Gospel are another fruit of God's
love. They are spoken of as gifts from God. The
psalmist, addressing Christ, regarding His ascension to
heaven, says: " Thou hast ascended on high, Thou hast
led captivity captive: Thou has received gifts for men ;
yea, for the rebellious also, that the Lord God might
dwell among them " (Ps. lxviii. 18). The Apostle Paul
speaks of ministers as a gift from God. He gave some,
apostles ; and some, prophets ; and some, evangelists ;
and some, pastors and teachers ; for the perfecting of
the saints, for the work of the ministry, for the edifying
of the body of Christ : till we all come in the unity of
the faith, and of the knowledge of the Son of God, unto
a perfect man, unto the measure of the stature of the
fulness of Christ " (Eph. iv. 11-13). Gospel ministers
are a gift from God, and a fruit of His love, howsoever
much they are despised and persecuted in an evil age.
The greatest Preacher was despised and rejected of men,
and He told the Apostles : " If they persecuted Me, they
will also persecute you " (John xv. 20). But they
count the reproaches of Christ greater riches than the
treasures of this world.

(7) Divine chastisements are another fruit of God's
love. " Whom the Lord loveth He chasteneth, and
scourgeth every son whom He receiveth . . . . . But
if ye be without chastisement, whereof all are partakers,
then are ye bastards and not sons " (Heb. xii. 6-8).

(8). The means of grace are a fruit of His love. In New Testament times these means are few—the word, the two sacraments, and prayer, all which are made effectual unto salvation to the elect.

(9) The fellowship of saints on earth is a fruit of God's love, together with their fellowship and felicity throughout eternity.

IV. *The prayer:* '' Remember me, O LORD, with the favour [or love] that Thou bearest unto Thy people.''

The psalmist would be quite content if God remembered Him with the love which He bears to His people, for he was sure that that love would bring him to heaven. He would have nothing to do with the love of God, according to the Arminian view. According to that view some, yea many, whom God loved are lost in hell. Even Arminians admit this. According to their view the love of God is not everlasting, yet Scripture says it is. The psalmist was made a partaker of God's love before he uttered this prayer, but he felt his need of being remembered with that love again, for he was still imperfect, and poor and needy, as all the Lord's people are, during their time on earth, and, as all spiritual blessings flowed from that great love, there was room for this prayer.

In conclusion. Some of you, who are the Lord's people, may be in doubt as to whether God loved you or not; but if you cannot say that God loved you, you may pray with the psalmist—'' Remember me with the favour [or love] that Thou bearest to Thy people,'' and even the unconverted may pray the same prayer, and, if you are sincere in uttering this prayer, you will use the

next petition, " O visit me with Thy salvation." The
two petitions are intimately connected. God's love is
the efficient cause of salvation, and salvation is the effect
of God's love. As God is rich in mercy, so He is rich
in love. The late Rev. Donald MacDonald, Shieldaig,
used to say, when speaking of God's love, " There are
many tons of it in heaven." He experienced what he
said; for the Lord poured down into his soul a large
quantity of that love from heaven. He often fainted
under its weight, but, now in glory, he is full of it, and
there is no room or need for this prayer in the place of
perfect felicity. Although many professing people, and
even ministers, speak of God's love to the exclusion of
His other attributes, they are as ignorant of it in their
own experience as the moles which live under the earth.
The Apostle John was so full of God's love that he
exclaimed in admiration: " Behold, what manner of
love the Father hath bestowed upon us, that we should
be called the sons of God " (1 John iii. 1). The love of
God, shed abroad in the heart, is the motive power
which actuates His people to obey Him, and to serve
Him with their bodies and spirits, which are His (1
Cor. vi. 20). AMEN.

II.

Creation

"Through faith we understand that the worlds were framed by the word of God; so that things which are seen were not made of things which do appear."—Heb. xi. 3.

In the 38th verse of the preceding chapter the Apostle says: "Now the just shall live by faith," and he begins this chapter by giving a definition or description of faith. "Faith," he says, "is the substance of things hoped for, the evidence of things not seen." In reading this definition one would be apt at first sight to think that the Apostle thereby only made it more difficult to understand what faith is; but the truth is that he made the matter in hand as plain as possible. You cannot **see the being of faith.** It can only be seen and known by its fruits, and its effects. It is in this way that the Apostle speaks of it, and explains it in this chapter. He gives many examples of how faith manifested itself in the lives and actions of Old Testament believers. Faith, according to the definition given of it, gives substance or reality to things hoped for, and the strongest evidence or assurance to things not seen by the bodily eye. The creation, and framing of the world, belong to the things not seen. We see the world, and cannot deny that it exists, and that on the testimony of our eyes. But it is by faith we know and are sure that the world was created by God. "Through faith we understand that the worlds were framed by the word of God." Our warrant to believe this is, God's testimony concerning the work of creation in the chapter we have read (Gen. i.).

In speaking from our text, as the Lord may enable me, I shall notice : —

    I. That it was God who created the world.

    II. That He created it out of nothing.

    III. That He created it by His word.

    IV. That He created it in the space of six days.

    V. The marks of design in the work of creation.

I. It was God who created the world. Among men there are and there have been many theories as to how the world came to exist. Even heathen philosophers had their own views on this. Some held that the world was eternal—always existed. Others were of the opinion that it was by mere chance the world began to be as it is now. But these philosophers had not faith : if they had they would come to see that God was the Creator of all ; as the Apostle says here, " Through faith we understand that the worlds were created by the word of God." Now, how does faith arrive at this ? You will observe that he says we understand, or we know, we are sure, we are convinced, we have the strongest evidence that the worlds were framed by the word of God. Well, faith has to do with testimony, and especially with the testimony of God's word, and we have that testimony in the chapter we have read— the first of Genesis. Heathen philosophers had not the word of God, and therefore they could only make guesses from conjectures as to how the world came to exist ; but those who have faith have the right kind of evidence for their beliefs in these matters. Although we see the world, we did not see it come into existence, but faith has to do with the testimony of God's word, and we are bound to believe all that is written in His word. Where there is faith the word is believed—the true believer has no doubt about it. The first chapter of Genesis gives an account of the creation of the world by God. " In the beginning God created the heavens and the earth." The word God there is plural (Elohim), denoting, not that there are three Gods, but that there are three Persons in the one Godhead. In Heb. ii. 10, God the Father is spoken of as " He by whom are all things." In John i. 10, it is said that the world was made by Christ, the second Person ; and in Psalm xxxiii. 6, it is written that God made the heavens (and the earth also) by the breath of His mouth, or by His Spirit. The world was not eternal ; it could not create itself, no creature could create it, not even the least atom of it. No finite power, infinite power alone could create it. Faith believes this ; it believes all that is written in the Bible concerning the creation.

II. He created it out of nothing. This is declared in our text—" So that things which are seen were not made of things which do appear." When a man builds a house, he needs material to do so. It is beyond his power to build out of nothing. But God, who is infinite in power, as He is infinite in all His attributes, created the world out of nothing. To create is the prerogative of God. Man cannot create the least atom of matter, nor can he destroy it—reduce it to nothing. We have heard of some men who, before their death, gave orders to have their bodies, after their death, cremated. These must have been influenced by Atheism. The word of God told them that if they died without a saving change, their bodies after the resurrection would be punished along with their souls in hell for ever. By burning their bodies in this world they imagined that their resurrection would be made impossible! But they have not succeeded in reducing their bodies to nothing, and God will gather their ashes at the last day—raise them up complete bodies at the resurrection to be burned once more (but not consumed) for an endless eternity.

III. He created it by the word of His power. He spoke and it was done. He said, " Let there be light, and there was light "—let the world be, and the world sprang into existence. When the Son of God was in the world, in His state of humiliation, He by His mighty word healed the sick, raised the dead to life again. He had only to say, " Lazarus, come forth," and he that was dead came forth out of the grave. Were a mere man to call to the dead, would they rise to life? Ah, no ; but the word of God is quick and powerful, and can call into being that which had no previous existence. And as this is true in the natural creation, it is also true in the spiritual creation, for in speaking to the dead soul He makes use of His word, and restores it to life. It is the voice of God, who created the world by His word, that shall raise to life the dead at the last day (John v. 28, 29).

IV. He created it in the space of six days, as we have an account of it in the book of Genesis. While all who profess to believe the Scripture account of the work of creation agree as to the number of days in which the work was done, there is a difference of opinion as to the length of these days. Some hold that each of these days was a long period of time, probably a thousand years. Others assert that each day was of the same length as what is now called day. My own belief is that in Genesis i. we should take the term day in the sense of twenty-four hours. The repeated formula—" the evening and the morning "—with each of the first five creative days seem to me to demand that interpretation.

Man was the last part of the creation and the crown of it. Not only did God create the world, but He created man also, after He had created all other creatures and things for the use of man; for He provided for man before He created him. Man had his table spread before him when he appeared in the world. We have seen that when God created the world He created it just in the fulness in which we see it to-day. And in like manner, when He created man, He created him just in the full stature of a grown up man. The Higher Critics do not accept the testimony of God's word concerning this. Why? Ah, because they have not the faith of the just. " Faith is the evidence of things not seen." We did not see God creating man, but we have the testimony of Scripture for it, and through faith we are sure, we are certain, that it is so. Evolutionists say that man has evolved. Well, after our first parents, who were created at once in their full stature, all their posterity are born as little babes, and they certainly evolve to this extent, that, if spared, they grow up to the full stature of men and women. But this was not the case with the first man. Of course it would be vain to speak to a little baby. It could not be made to understand anything. But we read that

God spoke to Adam, and told him that He gave him
dominion over all the world and over all creatures.
Surely that is convincing proof that God created Adam
not as a little child, but in the full stature of a perfect
man. Evolutionists go further, and say that mankind
have descended from the monkeys. That is a very
common opinion, and is held even by so-called ministers
of the Gospel. I heard of a minister who, on hearing
that the evolution theory about the descent of man was
held by many of the young ministers in our day,
remarked, '' Their congregations should be composed of
monkeys, and not of human beings.'' These evolutionists are led by science, but it is '' science falsely
so-called,'' as the Apostle says.

I remember, and shall now refer to, what the great
Dr Hugh Martin said in combatting those theories of
the evolutionists, who go by science, as did Hugh Miller
when he wrote that book, '' The Testimony of the
Rocks,'' the main object of which is to discover how
long a period of time it would take for the rocks to
grow, from their first beginnings until they arrived at
their present dimensions. Dr Martin put it in this
way : If a scientist were to meet Adam as he came forth
from God's hand, and were asked to estimate Adam's
age, he would calculate according to the usual time it
takes for man to come to full growth, and would
probably put Adam's age at about thirty years. But
if Adam himself were asked, he would correctly say he
was but one day old. Thus we see that unless people
keep to the Scriptures they are sure to go wrong. We
cannot be sure of anything, but through faith ; for
faith has to do, not with the testimony of mere
creatures, but with the testimony of the eternal God.

Through faith, then, we know that He made the worlds. Unless we believe that, we are just infidels, or atheists, as evolutionists are. Man can do nothing without some material to work upon, but God had nothing. He called the world out of non-existence into existence.

V. Marks of design in the works of creation:

Not only have we an account of the time God took in putting the world into the order in which it now is, we have also to note the beautiful design or order in which it now is—the land, and sea, and firmament; the heavenly bodies, sun, moon, and stars. The world was to be inhabited by human beings and other creatures. If all were dry land, there would be no sea, and we all know how useful the sea is. If it were all sea, there would be no dry land, and man and other creatures could not live in the sea. But God ordered both sea and land to their appointed places, so as to be useful for man and beasts and all things that He created. Then, if it were always dark, people could not see their way to go about; so God created light, the sun for the day and the moon and stars for the night. Another design to be observed in the creation is that the earth brings forth liberally fruit for the use of man; but God had in view other creatures besides man, so He commanded the earth to bring forth grass and herbs fit for the use of cattle and other beasts which he created. Ah, these were not the works of chance. Everything upon which we look has a well ordered design impressed upon it. Take even the colour of the grass. If it were all white, our eyes would be hurt and dazzled, as is the case when the ground is covered with snow; but the grass is green,

and green is known to be a very restful colour for the
eye.

Philosophers and atheists do not take the word of
God as evidence of the divine creation, but it is no
difficult matter to meet them in argument, even upon
their own ground. They say that the world had no
intelligent creator at all. Well, let us take some
familiar object, such as a dwelling-house, and let us
suppose that it is approached by a person who had
never seen a dwelling-house. He first notices the door,
which he sees is to allow people in and out, and he
concludes that an intelligent person made it, because it
is built with an object—a design. He goes inside and
observes a window. That is to let in the light. He
says that was not made by chance. He goes forward
and sees a fireplace, the work of a reasoning being. He
says that is for a fire to give warmth and heat. No
work of chance here. He examines the house further,
and finds a chair, a bed, and so on. He cannot come
to any other conclusion than that the whole was
designed by an intelligent person, for these articles were
made for resting upon. He knows it would be the
greatest folly to suppose that all these merely happened
by chance, and that there was no designer and builder
of them all. Yet atheists pretend to believe that the
whole universe with its great and beautiful marks of
well ordered design came into existence by chance, and
not by Almighty Power and Infinite Wisdom. Thus
you see that, without resorting to Scripture at all, you
may by ordinary reasoning meet the atheist on his own
ground. But while this is so, Scripture remains our
proper testimony that " the worlds were created by the
word of God." We cannot be sure of anything but

through faith, for faith has to do, not with the testimony of mere creatures, but with the testimony of the eternal God. Through faith, then, we *know* that He made the worlds. Unless we believe that, we are just infidels. Man can do nothing without some material to work upon, but God needed not that antecedent material. He called the worlds out of non-existence into existence.

III.

The Giving of the Law

" And the Lord said unto Moses, Come up to Me into the mount, and be there; and I will give thee tables of stone, and a law, and commandments which I have written; that thou mayest teach them."—Exodus xxiv. 12.

In this chapter we have an account of the giving of the law by God to Moses, that he might teach the commandments of God to the people, in order to regulate them in the performance of their duty to God, and in their duty to one another, in their several relations, as superiors, inferiors, and equals. In this book of Exodus, and in other books of Moses, we find that the Lord gave three kinds of laws to the people of Israel—the moral, the ceremonial, and the judicial. It is of the moral law we are to speak now. In doing this we shall notice:—

      I. The time and the place when and where the the law was given.

     II. The manner of its promulgation.

    III. The ends for which the law was given.

    I. As to the time, it was at the end of three months, after the people had been brought out of Egypt. (Ex. xix. 1). As to the place, it was at Mount Sinai, in the wilderness of Arabia. It was at that mount that the Lord appeared to Moses when He sent him to deliver His people out of their bondage in Egypt. Before He sent him, He assured him that he would be successful in his work of deliverance; telling him that he and the people would worship God at that mount (Ex. iii. 12), and this was now fulfilled. The moral law was first given verbally, or was spoken by God to the people, as you may see in the 20th chapter of this book; but now it is given in writing, that it might be the more permanent. What is spoken is soon forgotten, but what is written is more permanent, and lasting. Speaking generally, one may say that the word of God in the Bible was largely at first spoken, and afterwards written in order that it might continue in the world from generation to generation to the end of time. The law also thus came to be written by God Himself on two tables of stone, and was given to Moses to teach it to the people. For this purpose the Lord called Moses to come up to the mount, as we have it in our text. Aaron and his two sons, Nadab and Abihu, and seventy of the elders of Israel, were ordered to accompany him to the foot of the mount, to worship the glorious Lawgiver afar off. Then, it is said, they saw Him, and, notwithstanding their sinfulness, they were not consumed. " Upon these nobles of Israel He laid not His hand in judgment." They might truly say, " It is of the Lord's mercies that we are not consumed."

After finishing worship, they all returned to the congregation, except Moses, and Joshua, his minister, who was to succeed him as a leader of the people. Joshua accompanied Moses to a certain place near the top of the mount, where both remained for six days till Moses alone was called to the top of the mountain on the seventh day to receive the law. It would appear that it was on the Sabbath day the law was given, which adds to its sacredness and importance. A cloud

covered the top of the mountain, and yet the glory of
the Lord as it shined forth through that cloud was like
devouring fire, and of that glory the children of Israel
were spectators, stationed as they were at the foot of
the mount (xxiv. 17). Moses remained on the mount
for forty days and forty nights. Some might ask, why
was it necessary for him to remain there for such a long
time, seeing that the moral law was already prepared
for him by the Lawgiver? The answer to this is, that
although the moral law was prepared by the Lord Himself, Moses had to write the ceremonial and the judicial
or civil law, and the instructions to be in this connection
given to him required of Moses all this time.   It is
mentioned that Moses neither ate or drank anything for
the support of his body during that long period.   How
did he manage to fast so long? He enjoyed so much of
the gracious presence of God, that he did not feel any
need of food for his body.   When the Lord's people
enjoy much of the presence of the Lord they can do
without food for their bodies for a long time, though
not always.   Moses, sustained in body for so long a
time, is an instance that helps us to understand how
the redeemed, after the resurrection, will live throughout eternity without material food for their bodies.   It
is not mentioned in Scripture that they shall need
material food for their bodies.   Their bodies shall be
sustained by the full enjoyment of God to all eternity.

II. *The manner of its promulgation*:

The moral law was written on two tables of stone.
These tables were written or engraven on both sides of
the two tables.   The ceremonial law was not written on
tables of stone, but on parchment, as it was to be only

temporary, and was to be abolished after it had served the purpose for which it was given. But the moral law was written on tables of stone, and, as already mentioned, it was written on both sides of the two tables, so that nothing could be added to it and nothing could be taken from it without breaking the tables, for it was engraven or cut into the tables. The two tables were filled on both sides, so that there was no space left to add one iota to it. If men made any addition, they would require to do so on a material different from the tables containing the law. Although the Jews were very strict in holding the Scriptures pure and entire, yet Christ charges the Pharisees with adding to them the traditions of men. In the book of Revelation there is a curse pronounced upon those that would add to or take from the word of God. Such would be visited with awful plagues on their minds or bodies, or both—plagues have fallen on many in our own generation. It was in the dark days of Moderatism that paraphrases were added to the psalms in the Bible, and it was in the dark days of our own time that uninspired hymns were added to the word of God by men who were not satisfied with the word of inspiration, for which God visited them with the plague of spiritual blindness. Nothing should be added to the Bible, besides what has been given by the inspiration of the Spirit—that is, nothing that purports to be of equal authority with the word of the Lord.

The awful manifestations that attended the giving of the law as spoken by the Lord showed, on the one hand, the holiness, the justice, and the majesty of the Lawgiver, and, on the other hand, the sinfulness of the people who had broken this law, and had made them-

B

selves liable to eternal punishment as transgressors of it.
It was given in the midst of thunderings and lightnings,
and the noise of the trumpet, and the mountain smok-
ing; so that not only the mountain shook, but the
people also were struck with terror, and fear; and even
Moses himself, though a holy man, said, '' I exceed-
ingly fear and quake '' (Heb. xii. 21, cf. Deut. ix. 19).
The people feared so much that they could not endure
God speaking to them immediately, and they said to
Moses, '' Speak thou with us, and we will hear: but let
not God speak with us, lest we die '' (Ex. xx. 19).
Moses spoke to pacify them, and said, '' Fear not: for
God is come to prove you, and that His fear may be
before your faces, that ye sin not '' (Ex. xx. 20). It is
remarkable that amidst the terrible convulsions which
surrounded the people none of them was killed.   For
He spoke, not to kill them, but to prove them.

When the Lord convinces the sinner by the law, the
sinner cannot endure God speaking to him, without a
mediator.   When he is dealt with by the law only, he is
apt to conclude that he is to perish forever, but when God
speaks to him in the Gospel through the one Mediator,
Jesus Christ, he begins to hope that, notwithstanding
his ill-desert as a transgressor of the law, he may be
saved.

III. *The ends for which the law was given*:

The law was not given as a covenant of works, on
the terms of which sinners might be saved, as it was
given to the first Adam.   It was, at his creation,
engraven upon the heart of Adam, and also it was
given formally or in express terms.   As a condition the

law required perfect and perpetual obedience, and, failing that, death was the penalty. All who seek salvation by their obedience to the law think that the law was given, the second time, as a covenant of works. The Apostle Paul was for a long period of his life of this opinion, but, when his eyes were opened by the Holy Spirit, he saw the spirituality of the law, taking cognizance not only of his outward actions, but also of the thoughts and intents of his heart. He saw the impossibility of his being saved in that way, and he began to preach to others, that " by the deeds of the law no flesh could be justified in the sight of God." He was taught " a more excellent way " of salvation by Jesus Christ, who magnified the law, and made it honourable, by His obedience unto death. Some may say, if the law was not given as a covenant of works, why was it then given at all? It was given for more than one reason : (1) It was given as a means to convince of sin, as a looking-glass in which the sinner might see his real portraiture, as a sinful and ugly creature, as one that had lost the image in which he was originally created. Thus the Apostle James speaks of the law, and says, that the sinner by nature " is like unto a man beholding his natural face in a glass. For he beholdeth himself "—in other words, he sees how ugly he is as a sinner, and, because he does not like to see himself as he really is, he quickly turns away from the law, and soon forgets what manner of man he is (James i. 23, 24). Sinners do not like the law of God, because it shows them their sinful and depraved condition. Many, in a state of nature, are like a man that never saw his face in a looking-glass, and, although he was a very ugly man, thought himself the prettiest man in the country, when one day he happened to come before a looking-glass, and, behold, he saw that he was one of the ugliest men in the whole world. If the sight of ourselves as thus seen in the looking-glass of God's law were blessed to us, we would change the opinion we naturally have of our own goodness, and begin to cry to God to change us by His grace so that we might be created anew in Christ, and restored to the image of God, which consists in knowledge, righteousness, and holiness.

(2) It was given as a rule of life, according to which we are to regulate our conduct going through the world. Christ is the way of redemption, but the law is the King's highway on the way to heaven ; and, although believers are no longer under the curse of the law, they are the only persons who do their best endeavours to obey the law as a rule of life.

3. It was given as a means of restraining sinners from transgressing it for fear of punishment. Many have been kept from gross sins from fear of punishment, and not from any love to the law. The law is useful in all these respects.

Although the law was not given as a covenant of works, yet it is spoken of in Scripture as a covenant, but in this latter sense law is taken in a wider sense than the exclusively moral law. Thus, at the giving of the law at Mount Sinai, God entered into a covenant with the people of Israel, as the Apostle Paul tells us in the eighth chapter of his epistle to the Hebrews. He there speaks of a new covenant, and states that this new covenant was not according to the covenant God made with their fathers in the day in which He took them by the hand to lead them out of the land of Egypt. In a covenant there are two parties. It is different from a vow in which there is but one individual. God was one party to that covenant, and the people of Israel were the other party, and when God proposed the covenant the people agreed to it, saying, " All the words which the Lord hath said will we do " (verse 3). They were too hasty in saying this. They should have added, " If God will give us grace, to do what we promised, we will obey His word." They were too self-confident, and soon, very soon, they broke the covenant, for during the absence of Moses in the mount they turned to idolatry.

The law was given to Moses to teach it to the people. The law is to be preached as well as the gospel. By the law is the knowledge of sin, and by the gospel is the knowledge of the Saviour, and of salvation. The law prepares the sinner for the reception of the gospel. A godly woman, who is now in glory, gave an excellent illustration of this in the course of a conversation, the last time she was at a communion at Dingwall. That woman was well known throughout the Highlands. We mean Isabella Murchison, who lived at Plockton, Lochalsh. The illustration was this :—If a dressmaker begins to make a dress, she requires to use a needle, but, if she uses only a needle, she can never make the dress. She requires, along with the needle, thread in the needle. If indeed she uses thread without the needle, she will not succeed in her work. But if she uses both the needle and the thread in the needle, she can easily manage to sew the dress. She meant by the needle the law, and by the thread the gospel. As the needle makes a hole for the thread, so the law pierces and wounds the sinner, and the gospel heals that wound. " By His stripes we are healed."

There was once a deputation sent from a vacant congregation to a Presbytery within the bounds, craving the Court to get a minister for them. They were asked what kind of a minister they desired to have. They said that they desired to get a pastor that was wounded by the law and healed by the gospel.

There was a godly man in Lewis who got a good deal of law work before he was brought to gospel liberty. This man, when speaking to the question on the Friday of a communion, made use of his experience at sea, for he was a fisherman. On a certain day, when at sea along with his companions in the boat, the wind arose and developed into an awful gale, so that they were afraid of being drowned. They turned back to get into the harbour, but there was between them and that place of safety a long promontory of land stretching forth into the sea, and he was wishing that that promontory never existed because of the difficulty of getting to the other side of it; but somehow they got round the point—he could scarcely say how—and when they got to the other side they were sheltered by that point of which he was so much afraid, and he was now thankful to God that that point existed. The application he made of this was, that when under law work he wished that the law which revealed the justice of God by which he was condemned as a sinner never existed; but when he was relieved by the gospel, he thanked the Lord with all his heart that the law which once condemned him was now on his side, no longer an enemy, but a friend, demanding his salvation by Him who satisfied justice.

In conclusion : It becomes us to examine ourselves as to our relation to the law. Are we still under its curse, or are we delivered from the curse of the law by Christ, who was made a curse that His people might be redeemed from that awful curse? Although there is no salvation by the deeds of the law, are we careful to obey the law from the principle of love to God? There are many avowed Antinomians, and there are many more practical Antinomians. If we are ministers, do we preach law and gospel, yea, the whole counsel of God, whatever we may suffer from opponents in the discharge of our duty? And, if we are only hearers of the word of God, are we opposed to the preaching of the law? If so, it is a bad sign. It is a sign that we are still under the curse of the law, which pronounces a curse upon every one that continueth not in all things which are written in the book of the law to do them (Gal. iii. 10).

Many live as if they had nothing to do with the law of God, but these shall in mercy or in judgment find out that the law has to do with them. All by nature are under the law as a covenant of works, and, as the Apostle says, " those who are under the law are under the curse," and the law binds them under that curse, so that none can deliver them from it but Christ. Let them, then, in a day of mercy, cry to Him to deliver them from the curse of the law, or the law shall continue to curse them throughout eternity without a remedy.

May the Lord bless our remarks on the subject to poor perishing sinners. AMEN.

IV.

The Fourth Commandment

" Remember the Sabbath Day to keep it holy. Six days shalt thou labour and do all thy work. But the seventh day is the Sabbath of the Lord thy God; in it thou shalt not do any work, thou, nor thy son, nor thy daughter, thy man-servant, nor thy maid-servant, nor thy cattle, nor thy stranger that is within thy gates. For in six days the Lord made heaven and earth, the sea and all that in them is, and rested the seventh day, wherefore the Lord blessed the Sabbath Day and hallowed it."—Exodus xx. 8-11.

In this chapter we have an account of the giving of the law by God at Mount Sinai. The thunderings and the lightnings, and the noise of the trumpet, and the mountain on fire, which attended the giving of the law, indicated the holiness of God and the dreadful judgments that would befall the transgressors of the law. Although the ceremonial law was abolished at the death of Christ, the moral law is of perpetual obligation, binding on men to the end of time. The moral law was not given as a covenant of works, but as a rule of life.

The Fourth Commandment is in the very heart of the moral law, and is as binding as the other commandments. God knew that men would be apt to forget to keep the Sabbath Day holy, and therefore He says, " Remember the Sabbath Day to keep it holy." There were two ordinances instituted by God at the creation of man—the Sabbath and marriage, to be continued to the end of time. It would be as unreasonable to abolish the ordinance of the Sabbath as to abolish the ordinance of marriage. The question concerning observing the sanctity of the Sabbath is not to be decided by the opinions of men, but by the word of God. When the **people of** Israel were in Egypt it is not likely that the Sabbath was generally observed by them, but we think that the Lord's people among them observed it as much as they could ; but when they were brought out of Egypt the Sabbath was revived, and the keeping of it holy was inculcated by the Lord of the Sabbath. This was done when the manna was given to the people in the wilderness. God forbade the people to go out to gather the manna on the Sabbath Day ; but there were rebels then as now who went out to gather it, but they found none, and God expressed His displeasure at them for their disobedience to His command. There was no excuse for their going out on Sabbath to gather the manna, for the Giver of it gave them a double supply on Saturday.

The Sabbath is the day of rest from our worldly employments and recreations that are lawful on other days. By recreations is meant not sinful recreations, but such as are necessary for the body. How is the Sabbath to be sanctified ? The Shorter Catechism, which is founded upon the word of God, supplies the answer :—'' The Sabbath is to be sanctified by a holy resting all that day, even from such worldly employments and recreations as are lawful on other days ; and spending the whole time in the public and private exercises of God's worship, except so much as is to be taken up in the works of necessity and mercy.'' The whole of the Sabbath Day, from beginning to end, is to be spent in the exercise of public and private worship of God.

The only works allowable on that day are works of
necessity and mercy.   If your house were on fire, it
would be a work of necessity and a duty to do your
utmost to extinguish the fire; and as for works of mercy,
Christ healed the sick on the Sabbath Day, and it is a
work of mercy for doctors to attend to the sick on that
day.   But many make a work of necessity of many
things they do on the Lord's Day which are not works
of necessity at all.   There was a young girl from the
West Highlands on service in a family in the South.
Her work was to nurse the children.   On a Sabbath,
when putting on the boots on one of the children, a
button on the boot came off.   Her mistress asked her to
sew on the button, and she asked her mistress—" Have
you the Fourth Commandment?" and refused to sew
the button on the Lord's Day.   The master of the house
heard the conversation, and clapped the girl on the
shoulder for the stand she had made for the Sabbath.
It would be a good thing if there were in our day many
servant girls like that.   With the exception of works
of necessity and mercy, the only work that is lawful on
the Sabbath is the worshipping of God in public and
private.   If you were to examine the conduct of those
who advocate ploughing on Sabbath, it is very likely
that you would find that they do not worship God in
their families daily.   It is to be borne in mind that
there are two classes of people in every age—God's
friends and His enemies—and while the former obey
His commandments, the latter manifest their enmity by
trampling upon His commandments, and are excusing
themselves in their rebellion against divine authority.
In the Fourth Commandment there are reasons given
for keeping the Sabbath Day holy.

(1) God gives us six days for our work, but the seventh is not ours but His ; and to do our own work on that day, which is not ours but His, is a stealing—a sacrilege. So that it may be said that Sabbath-breakers are spiritual thieves. There was a godly catechist in Skye, named Donald Macqueen, who on his way to church on a certain Sabbath met boys playing. The catechist was a wise man, and took a wise way of rebuking the Sabbath-breakers. When he came where they were he sat down, and said to the boys that he would tell them a story. The boys, as all boys are, were delighted to listen to the story. The catechist said that there was once a man on a journey who had £7 in his pocket. Robbers met him on the way and demanded his purse. He said to them—" I have seven pounds in my purse, and I will give you six, but I need the seventh myself." But the robbers would not be satisfied with the six pounds, and demanded the seventh also, or they would have his life. The catechist asked the boys— " What do you think of the robbers ?" They answered that " they were most cruel and wicked." The catechist said to them—" You are the robbers. God gave you six days for your worldly work, and you may play on these days, but you rob God of the seventh." The boys went home, and henceforth gave up playing on the Lord's Day.

(2) The second reason is that God rested on the seventh day and hallowed it, or set it apart for His own worship. The seventh day was to be kept holy in commemoration of His finishing the work of creation, as the Christian Sabbath is to be kept holy in commemoration of the finishing of a greater work—that of

redemption by Christ; so that we have a greater reason
for keeping the Christian Sabbath holy than there was
for keeping holy the seventh-day Sabbath. Those who
desecrate the Christian Sabbath despise and hate Christ
our Redeemer. The keeping of His commandments is
a mark given by Himself of those who love Him. He
said, " If ye love Me, keep My commandments."

There are many forms of Sabbath-breaking in our
day, such as the running of trains on the Lord's Day;
but railway companies who are guilty of this sin lose
by accidents and disasters what they gain on the day
that is not theirs, and it is clear to any unbiassed
observer that God manifests His displeasure at them in
this way. It has been observed by some that Sabbath-
breakers do not prosper in their business in the world
as those who observe the sanctity of that day. Another
form of Sabbath-breaking which is very common in this
age is the taking of long walks on the Sabbath after
having been at church, and in this way bidding defiance
to God. Members, and even office-bearers, in some
churches are guilty of this sin, and in this way show
that their profession of religion is a mere sham.

There is a new form of Sabbath-breaking threatening
to appear in our midst which was not heard of in the
past, at least in Scotland, and especially in the Highlands. I mean the proposal to begin ploughing on the
Lord's Day; but this proposal is made by the enemies
of God, His people, and cause in the world. This is
lamentable when we are in the midst of a terrible war,
which is evidently a judgment by the Most High on our
nation and other nations for our sins, and, among other
sins, that of Sabbath-breaking. It would be expected
that when God's judgments are abroad in the earth the

inhabitants of the world would learn righteousness; but instead of that, we as a nation are getting more hardened and more wicked. It is not by sinning against God that we can expect victory over our enemies, for so long as we continue in that evil course it is not only the Germans and their Allies that fight against us, but God Himself is fighting against us, and will continue to do so till we are brought to repentance and reformation. It is not by sinning against God that we are to get plenty of the fruits of the earth, but by obeying Him. God brought famine upon people in the past for their iniquities, and especially for their Sabbath-breaking. He punished the Israelites for Sabbath desecration by giving them over to the hands of their enemies, who brought them into captivity, and during their long absence from their own land the land enjoyed her Sabbaths. God is the same holy God still, and as He punished the Israelites for their sins, He is now punishing us as a nation. Some quote Scripture in support of Sabbath-breaking—'' The Sabbath was made for man, and not man for the Sabbath.'' It was not to break the Sabbath, but to keep it holy, that the Sabbath was made for man. The Eighth Commandment, which forbids stealing, was made for man, not to give him license to steal, but to prevent him from that sin. The law of our country was made for its subjects, but any one that transgresses that law shall be punished according to the degree of his offence.

Who are addressed in the Fourth Commandment?

(1) The individual—'' Thou.'' The individual is bound to keep the Sabbath Day holy, and shall be

3

responsible at the Day of Judgment for his conduct on that holy day.

(2) The family—" Thou and thy son and thy daughter." The head of the family is bound by this commandment to see to it, not only that he himself keeps the Sabbath Day holy, but also that all the members of his family keep it holy too.

(3) The master who has servants in his employment is also addressed—" Thy man-servant and thy maid-servant." There are many masters who do not keep the Sabbath Day holy, and who never command their servants to keep it holy. Not only are servants not to be employed in doing their own worldly work, but their cattle are not to work on that day. Horses are not to be used in ploughing on the Sabbath, nor is an instrument propelled by motor power to be used either.

(4) The magistrate of a town or city is addressed. This we infer from the mention of " gates." The Town Council are bound to see to it, so far as they can, that those whom they represent should keep the Sabbath Day holy. It is deplorable that there are Provosts in Scotland who advocate ploughing on the Lord's Day, but we are thankful that the Provost of the town of Dingwall is strongly opposed to this innovation.

(5) The King is addressed. He is bound by this commandment not only to keep the Sabbath Day holy himself, but to do his utmost, by precept and example, to see that his subjects keep it holy too. This was done by godly kings in the past, and if there were godly kings now it would be done in our day. As we mentioned

magistrates, we may refer to the godly Nehemiah, who was a magistrate, and who put a stop to Sabbath-breaking within his gates, as we have it recorded, in his book at the 13th chapter, 19-21—'' And it came to pass that when the gates of Jerusalem began to be dark before the Sabbath, I commanded that the gates should be shut, and charged that they should not be opened till after the Sabbath ; and some of my servants set I at the gates, that there should no burden be brought in on the Sabbath day. So the merchants and sellers of all kinds of ware lodged without Jerusalem once or twice. Then I testified against them, and said unto them, Why lodge ye about the wall ? If ye do so again I will lay hands on you. From that time forth came they no more on the Sabbath.''

In the 56th chapter of Isaiah there are promises of blessings given to those who keep the Sabbath Day holy —'' Blessed is the man that doeth this, and the son of man that layeth hold on it ; that keepeth the Sabbath from polluting it, and keepeth his hand from doing any evil.''

.   .   .   .

Let us take to heart what has been said on this important subject, as individuals, families, communities, and nation, and act up to the command given in our text. This is the way to prosper spiritually and temporally. Then we shall be like the blessed man spoken of in the First Psalm—'' He shall be like a tree planted by the rivers of water, that bringeth forth his fruit in his season ; his leaf also shall not wither, and whatsoever he doeth shall prosper. But the ungodly are not so, but are like the chaff which the wind driveth away '' (verses 3, 4). Sabbath-breakers are like the chaff, and shall be burnt in the fire of God's wrath unless they repent of their evil ways.

It is the duty of ministers who profess to seek the welfare of immortal souls to keep the Sabbath holy themselves, and to warn their congregations to do this also. Christ's ministers do this, but Satan's ministers neglect to do their duty in this respect.

Some are asking when will this war in which we are involved come to an end. I am not a prophet, but I can tell from God's word that it shall not come to an end till we begin to hearken to and obey the word of the Lord. '' Oh, that My people had hearkened unto Me, and Israel had walked in My ways. I should soon have subdued their enemies and turned My hand against their adversaries. The haters of the Lord should have submitted themselves unto Him, but their time should have endured for ever. He should have fed them also with the finest of the wheat, and with honey out of the rock should I have satisfied thee '' (Psalm lxxxi. 13-16). If we were brought to obedience to the word of the Lord, not only would the war come to an end, but He would give us the victory over our enemies, and supply us with all good things, spiritually and temporally.

Those who advocate ploughing on Sabbath think that it is by disobeying the word of the Lord they shall have plenty of the fruits of the earth, but they shall be sorely disappointed, as they deserve. There were some men who were hanged for murder, and they confessed before their death that their wicked career began by Sabbath-breaking. This should be a warning to others who are transgressing God's commandments. Every sin you commit without repentance hardens your heart and blunts your conscience, so that at last it is seared, so that you can sin more easily. But your conscience will awaken at death and assert its power as a witness for God within you, and without repentance you will find it as a worm that dieth not in condemning you for ever and ever. Ah, Sabbath-breaker, take warning, turn from your evil ways in a day of mercy, and all your sins shall be forgiven. "Let the wicked forsake his ways, and the unrighteous man his thoughts, and let him return unto the Lord, and he will have mercy upon him, and to our God, for He will abundantly pardon" (Isaiah lv. 7). AMEN.

V.

Grace Abounding

" Moreover the law entered, that the offence might abound. But where sin abounded, grace did much more abound."— Rom. v. 20.

IN the 13th verse the Apostle says : " Until the law, sin was in the world, but sin is not imputed where there is no law." In the 14th verse he adds : " Nevertheless death reigned from Adam to Moses, even over those that had not sinned after the similitude of Adam's transgression." That is, before the law was given on Mount Sinai—two thousand and five hundred years after Adam had sinned—sin was in the world, and the effects of sin were seen in the fact that infants, who did not commit actual transgression like Adam, died as an effect of sin, proving that sin was imputed to them. They sinned in Adam. There was a law which they in their covenant head had transgressed. That law was God's command not to eat of the forbidden fruit. Adam's first sin, by which he broke the covenant, is imputed to his posterity, so that children are guilty born into the world, before they are capable of committing actual transgression in their own persons. But the law entered that the offence might abound.

We have two things to notice in our text :—

I. That the law entered that the offence might abound.

II. That where sin abounded, grace did much more abound.

I. *The law entered that the offence might abound.*

The law spoken of here is the moral law. That law was given by God on Mount Sinai. It was given, not that man might be saved by his endeavours to obey it, but that he might see, as in a glass, his sinfulness and his need of God's provision of salvation. The end for which it was given is told in our text—" that the offence might abound," or be made greater. The law did not make sin greater than it was before in the sight of God, but greater in the sight of the sinner. " For by the law is the knowledge of sin." The sinner thinks that sin is a small thing, till the law comes to show him that it is great. Saul of Tarsus, in his time of ignorance, thought that he was innocent, according to the righteousness of the law ; but when the law entered his soul in the hand of the Spirit, sin revived, and was seen greater in his sight, and he died as to his hope of being saved by it. " By the works of the law no flesh shall be justified in the sight of God." Sin is always a great evil, as it is against God, but it is the law that throws light on its greatness. Hence it is to be preached to sinners that they may see their need of Christ to save them. All men, being possessed of a moral nature, feel, and are constrained by the force of conscience to confess, that they are sinners. But conscience needs the word of the law to enlighten it in the true knowledge of sin. The Apostle tells us that it was for this end that the law entered.

II. *Where sin abounded, grace did much more abound.*

What is meant by the word grace here ? Grace is sometimes used in Scripture to mean grace as wrought

in the soul by the Spirit.   In that sense we speak of
faith, love, and *hope* as graces.   At other times the term
is used to mean grace in God, which is the efficient
cause of salvation—grace by which sinners are saved.
This is the meaning of it here.   For although great
sinners received a greater measure of grace than others
who were not so great sinners in practice, yet the more
we are conscious of our sinfulness, by means of the law,
the more the grace of God that brings salvation appears,
and grows in our estimation.   It is not, then, in our
opinion, grace in the stream, but grace in the fountain
—yea, in the great ocean—that is meant by grace here.
It is in this sense the Apostle speaks of grace in
Ephesians ii. 8, when he says, " By grace are ye saved."
Grace communicated by the Holy Spirit to believers is
but a stream out of grace in God.   How then, it may be
asked, can it be said that grace in God can abound, or
grow greater, seeing that it cannot in itself grow greater
than it is, as God is unchangeable ?   It abounds or grows
greater relatively to us.   The more we know ourselves
as lost and ruined sinners, and the more our eyes are
enlightened to see God's way of salvation by grace, the
more God's grace grows and increases in our view, and
the more we are shut up to it as the only but all-sufficient ground of hope for eternity.   If you are a
believer, the longer you are in the world, and the more
you learn by sad experience the evil that is in your
heart, the more the grace of God grows in your view,
and the more you acquiesce in God's way of salvation.
It is this that keeps you from sinking in despair, and
you thank God that it is by grace you are saved.   Let
others seek salvation by the works of the law, but as
for you, you are shut up entirely to salvation by grace,

which excludes boasting, and gives all the glory to the God of all grace.

The phrase, " Grace did much more abound," is very significant. It signifies that the remedy exceeds the disease in efficacy. This must be true even in nature. The doctor's medicine, if it heals, must be more powerful to heal than the disease is to kill, otherwise it cannot heal, and the patient must die. Man's way of salvation is impotent to deliver us from sin and its fatal effects. But God's way of salvation is more powerful to save us than sin was to destroy us. There is a " much more " in it, and Paul, who calls himself the chief of sinners, discovered this for himself, and you and I must find out this for ourselves if we are saved. There was grace in the stream in Paul, but that did not deliver him from his affliction ; but Christ came to rescue him, and said, " My grace is sufficient for thee." Ah, it is grace in God that will save us from first to last. The Apostle, when speaking of salvation by grace, repeats in this chapter, again and again, "much more " to encourage God's people and penitent sinners who might be afraid that they might, on account of their sins, be lost. He says in effect, Do not despair ; look up to the infinite ocean of grace that is in God.

In conclusion: The grace of God, of which we have been speaking, has come to us in the word of the Gospel. But has it come to us " in power, in the Holy Ghost, and in much assurance," as it came to the Thessalonians? If so, we know in some measure the meaning of the words of our text: " Where sin abounded, grace did much more abound." The law as an instrument in the hands of the Spirit entered into our souls, not to

make our sins appear greater than what they really
were, but to reveal to us how great they were, as committed against the great God, and as a transgression of
His law, which is " holy, just, and good," and deserving eternal punishment. It was not the sin of Adam,
in which we were involved, that troubled us then, but
our own personal actual transgressions. Nor did we
excuse ourselves because these transgressions flowed
from the depraved nature we derived from Adam, as
many sinners do. But as knowledge of sin is by the
law, knowledge of the Saviour and of salvation is by the
Gospel. We, by grace imparted by the Spirit by means
of the word of the Gospel, cordially closed with salvation by grace, and we began to ascribe the glory of our
salvation to God, and we will continue to do so during
our time on earth and throughout eternity in heaven.

VI.

God's Name Proclaimed

" And he hewed two tables of stone, like unto the first; and Moses rose up early in the morning, and went up unto Mount Sinai, as the LORD had commanded him, and took in his hand the two tables of stone.

" And the LORD descended in the cloud, and stood with him there, and proclaimed the name of the LORD.

" And the LORD passed by before him, and proclaimed, The LORD, The LORD God, merciful and gracious, longsuffering, and abundant in goodness and truth,

" Keeping mercy for thousands, forgiving iniquity and transgression and sin, and that will by no means clear the guilty; visiting the iniquity of the fathers upon the children, and upon the children's children, unto the third and fourth generation."—Exodus xxxiv. 4-7.

WE have here Moses, in obedience to God's command, coming to the mount with the two tables of stone for the re-writing on them of the law—the ten commandments—and the Lord, as an introduction to that solemn work, proclaiming His name. His name here is the revelation He has given of Himself as the God f Salvation. This name is most encouraging to poor guilty sinners. Let us examine it, and seek to know it by the teaching of the Holy Spirit. For it is they that know His name that will put their trust in Him (Ps. ix. 10). It is the Lord Himself that proclaims His name. We would remain ignorant of Him as the God of Salvation were it not that He made His name known, viz. : —

(1) "*The Lord, The Lord God.*"—In this point of
the proclamation of His name He revealed Himself as
the Triune God, Father, Son, and Holy Ghost.   The
doctrine of the Trinity was indicated at the creation of
man : " Let *us* make man in *our* image, after *our* like-
ness " (Gen. i. 26).   And here, in the writing of the
law, the second time, on the two tables of stone, He
repeats His name as the Three in One.   It intimates
also that He is the only Lord, and God, the Self-
existent God, who gives being to all creatures, and on
whom they depend.   Jehovah means this, and the fact
that it is repeated excludes all rivals.   He is the only
Jehovah.   In giving the law, which forbids any other
god before Him, it was becoming that the proclamation
of His name would begin with this, " Jehovah,
Jehovah."   The name Jehovah also intimates His un-
changeableness as the covenant God of His people.
Though they broke His law, He did not break His
covenant of peace.   He is still Jehovah.   He changes
not.   This is very encouraging ; and for this end we
believe He tells them that He is Jehovah.   He is also
God—" Jehovah, Jehovah God."   This name, God,
means strength.   He who proclaims His name as God
reveals Himself as the Almighty Saviour of His people.
He is strong in power, and will strengthen them.   He
is also able to subdue their enemies.   They shall all be
made His footstool.

The proclamation of His name as Jehovah, Jehovah
God, bespeaks His majesty and glory, and the awful
reverence due to Him by His worshippers.   He is to be
feared in the assembly of his saints.   " Let us
have grace whereby we may serve God with reverence
and godly fear " (Heb. xii. 29).

(2) *He is merciful.*—Although He is transcendently high above His erring creatures as Jehovah, Jehovah God, yet we may approach Him at the throne of grace, that we may obtain mercy, and find grace to help us in time of need. For He is merciful. Mercy is an essential attribute of His nature, and therefore He is naturally disposed to show mercy to sinners in this world, who are in misery, if they cry to Him for mercy. But His mercy can only be extended to us through the atonement—the atonement made by Christ when He offered up Himself—once for all—a sacrifice to satisfy divine justice, and to reconcile us to God. When God proclaims His name, as He does here, He preaches the gospel to sinners. He says, " I, Jehovah, Jehovah God, am merciful.'' He is in Christ reconciling the world unto Himself, not imputing their trespasses unto them (2 Cor. v. 9). When the publican cried for mercy, he was not only conscious of his guilt and misery, but he had an apprehension of the mercy of God in Christ. He knew that it was on the ground of Christ's atonement he could obtain mercy. The word mercy, then, implies this. All taught by the Spirit of God are taught to know that God's mercy (although He is naturally inclined to show mercy) comes to them on that ground alone. For God is just as well as merciful.

(3) *He is gracious.*—When God shows mercy to the miserable sinner, He does it without respect to any merit in him. He does it freely, " without money, and without price.'' It is a pure act of grace on the part of God. " By grace ye are saved.'' If He were to deal with us according to our own desert, we would never be saved. But we are saved because He is

gracious. The doctrine of salvation by grace was early taught. God Himself was the revealer of it, and was the first preacher of it, and He commanded His prophets, apostles, and ministering servants to the end of time to preach it. It is the only doctrine that can meet our case as sinful, unworthy, and lost in ourselves, the only doctrine that can give hope to the poor sinner struggling under a sense of sin and misery, and needing to be saved. God is graciously disposed to save sinners, and He made a provision of grace in the eternal covenant to save such as we are.

(4) *He is longsuffering.*—The people of Israel were impatient, murmuring at the least difficulty that crossed their path, but their God was longsuffering. This is part of His name as now proclaimed by Himself; and as His name is, so He is. We are monuments of His longsuffering. How often we provoked Him by our sins—how long He has borne with us! It is of His merciful longsuffering we are not consumed.

(5) *He is abundant in goodness.*—Paul says, " God is rich in mercy." Here He Himself, in proclaiming His name, says, He is abundant in goodness. God is love, and goodness is the outflow of His love to sinners in doing them good. " Thou art good, and Thou doest good." It was out of abundant love He gave His only-begotten Son to suffer and die for His sinful people. There is none absolutely good but God. As He is good, He communicates His goodness to the sinful and un-deserving. He does good to all men in this world. His goodness in providence extends to all. His goodness in grace He freely bestows upon His redeemed people.

Our God is a good, yea the only good God. This is the God of Salvation. He is the God that can and will meet our case. We are abundant in evil. "In our flesh no good thing dwelleth," but our God is abundant in goodness. Let us, then, come to Him that we may receive of His fulness. All uncreated goodness originally and essentially centres in God, dwells in Him, and all goodness in grace and providence flows from Him.

(6) *He is abundant in truth.*—He is the only true God. His word is truth, and He is faithful in all His promises to His people and His threatenings to His enemies. "To Him it is impossble to lie."

(7) *Keeping mercy to thousands.*—From the former parts of the proclamation of His name, showing what a God He is, He now proceeds to tell what He does; and first, "He keeps mercy for thousands." In proclaiming His name, He told us that He is merciful. Here He tells us that He keeps mercy. He not only shows mercy, but He keeps it. He keeps it as in a store. It is mercy we sinners need. He showed mercy to many, but the store is not exhausted. If it were, what would become of those who have not yet obtained mercy? There would be no hope for them. But the God of Salvation keeps mercy. He is rich in mercy. There is enough in the covenant of grace. There it is kept. For whom is it kept? For thousands. Not for a few, but for many. Not for Jews only, but for Gentiles also. "Is He the God of the Jews only? is He not the God of the Gentiles also? Yea, of the Gentiles also" (Rom. iii. 29). All to whom the Gospel comes are invited to come to God through Christ, that

they may obtain mercy. This is enough warrant for
any sinner to cry to God for mercy.

(8) *Forgiving iniquity and transgression and sin.*—
This is one of the mercies of the covenant in which
mercy is kept. But it is kept there that it may be
bestowed on or ministered forth in time of need to poor
convinced sinners, and to His now believing people, who
need daily forgiveness, and who need this blessing,
more particularly after a course of backsliding, as in
the case of the people of Israel, when the Lord proclaimed His name to them. We may observe here: (*a*)
That it is God, and He only, whose prerogative it is to
forgive sin. " Who can forgive sin but God only." Low
as the Jews had fallen in ignorance in the time of the
Saviour on earth, they retained this much of truth, that
no mere man could forgive sin, that none could do this
but God. The doctrine that a mere man can forgive
sin is an invention of a later date. But it is a delusion.
It is He only, who proclaims His name as forgiving
iniquity, that can pardon the poor guilty sinner. To
Him, then, poor sinners should come for that blessing.
(*b*) That He forgives all sins to those who come to Him.
Iniquity, transgression, and sin include all sins of omis-
sion and commission, original and actual. (*c*) That He
forgives all sins for His own name's sake, as He proclaims His name here as, " Jehovah, Jehovah God,
merciful and gracious, longsuffering, and abundant in
goodness and truth." That is, in other words, that He
forgives on the ground of the ransom He found in
Christ. " Being justified freely by His grace, through
the redemption that is in Christ." We are justified by
the blood of Christ as the only but all-sufficient ground

on which God forgives sins. The New Testament account of the ground of forgiveness accords with the proclamation God made of His name to Moses, as the God of Salvation.

(9) *And that will by no means clear the guilty.*— This is not contrary to His being a forgiving God. All whom He forgives were guilty, and in forgiveness He cleared them—acquitted them from all the guilt of their sins. The guilty, whom He will by no means clear, are, we think, those who refuse to accept of the only way of forgiveness proposed to us in the Gospel. Whatever other way or ways sinners may take to have their guilt removed from them, they must remain under the awful burden of their guilt, and under the sentence of condemnation. " He that believeth not the Son shall not see life, but the wrath of God abideth on him " (John iii. 36). It is God who forgives sins, and He does so on the ground of the satisfaction rendered to His justice by Christ, and the sinner who does not accept of His way of clearing the guilty, must remain under his guilt for ever. God, who alone can forgive sins, will by no means clear him. This is what appears to me to be the meaning of this part of the proclamation of God's name, and it is confirmed by the passages of Scripture adduced, and many other passages to the same effect might be brought forward if it were necessary. He is just as well as merciful.

In conclusion, then, God is to be known by His name. True, He revealed Himself by His works of creation, to which revelation the Scriptures also bear

4

witness. There He reveals Himself as the Creator and
upholder of all things.   When we look at the world,
and ask the question, Who made or created it? the
work of creation furnishes the answer.   In that work
there are signs of intelligence—design, infinite power,
goodness, and personality—which argue the existence
of a first personal cause separate from the creation,
which is only an effect produced by Him who is the
Creator of all things.   Apart from the revelation of
Scripture, men who make a right use of their reasonable
and rational powers come to the necessary conclusion,
from their study of the work of creation, of the existence of God, whereas men who deny His existence
trample under their feet the rational powers of mind
God gave them.   They may boast of their intelligence,
but in fact they make themselves lower in intelligence
than irrational brute creatures, which have no mental
faculties like man to exercise.   The work of creation,
we say, answers the question, " Who made it?"   But
when the sinner comes to the question, " What must I
do to be saved?" creation is silent, it cannot tell.   The
work of creation is only a revelation of God's name as
the Creator, Preserver, and Governor of all things.   It
cannot tell—it was not meant to tell—how the sinner
can be saved.   Therefore, if God is to be known as the
God of Salvation, there must needs have been a further
revelation of His name.   This revelation He has graciously been pleased to give.   We have it in the Scriptures of the Old and New Testaments.   We have it in
the portion of Scripture we have now considered.   He
proclaimed, preached it to Moses as an encouraging
preface to the law.   It would be in vain to give the
law to sinners without the preface.   There would be no

hope set before them. But with the preface, sinners may draw nigh to God with the confident hope of obtaining mercy and of finding grace to help in time of need. It is full of encouragement to poor sinners. Here the Gospel is preached, not by many, but by God Himself, and that in its richness, fulness, and freeness, to those who deserved nothing at His hand but eternal wrath. '' Who is a God like unto Thee!'' '' Blessed is the people that know the joyful sound.''

In the plan of salvation the three Persons of the Godhead are concerned, and each Person has His own peculiar part in it. The contrivance of the scheme of salvation is ascribed to the Father. The working out of redemption is ascribed to the Son, and the application of redemption is the work of the Holy Spirit—in all that are saved. If sinners desire to be saved, let them earnestly pray for the outpouring of the Holy Spirit upon them, that they might be made partakers of Christ's redemption, and let them ascribe the glory of their salvation to Father, Son, and Holy Spirit. AMEN.

VII.

The New Covenant

" For this is the covenant that I will make with the house of Israel after those days, saith the Lord; I will put My laws into their mind, and write them in their hearts; and I will be to them a God, and they shall be to Me a people : And they shall not teach every man his neighbour, and every man his brother, saying, Know the Lord : for all shall know Me, from the least to the greatest. For I will be merciful to their unrighteousness, and their sins and their iniquities will I remember no more."—Heb. viii. 10-12.

IN this epistle the Apostle shows that the Old Testament dispensation, so far as the ritual of it is concerned, came to an end, and that the New Testament dispensation was set up in its stead. He quotes a passage of Scripture from Jeremiah (xxxi. 33-34) which foretold this change.

In speaking from our text, we shall notice :

    I. The covenant spoken of.
    II. The parties with whom it was to be made.
    III. The manner in which it was to be made with them.

    I. *The covenant spoken of:* What is this covenant ? The Lord made several covenants, such as, the covenant of works ; the covenant of grace ; and the covenant He made with the children of Israel at Mount Sinai. The covenant spoken of here is not the covenant of works, for that covenant was made at the creation of man, whereas this covenant was yet to be made. It is not the covenant of grace, for that covenant was made from all eternity. Neither is it the covenant made at Mount Sinai. What, then, is this covenant? It is the New Testament revelation of the covenant of grace. In the original the word rendered covenant here means a Testament. The Bible is divided into two parts, the Old Testament and the New Testament, and it is the New Testament revelation of the way of salvation that is **meant** by the new covenant. It is called a *new* covenant. It was not according to the covenant made with their fathers at Mount Sinai, in which they had not continued. In that covenant Christ was set forth in types and shadows, **whereas** in this covenant He is set forth in the preaching of the Gospel in a clearer manner. In Hebrews x. 1 the Ceremonial Law is called a shadow. Although it foreshadowed good things to come, it was the shadow of Christ Himself. The shadow of a man may be seen before he appears himself. You cannot see your shadow in the dark; there must be light in order to there being a shadow. Thus there was in the old economy teaching explaining the meaning of the Ceremonial Law. If you walk having your back to the east when the sun rises, your shadow is very long, as seen before you; but, as the sun rises higher in the sky, the shadow gets shorter and shorter, and when the sun rises to its meridian height, it disappears under your feet. In like manner there were a great many things to be seen in the Ceremonial Law, which were but a shadow of good things to come, such as, bloody sacrifices, meat offerings, and drink offerings, and diverse washings with water. But whereas there were then many priests and many bloody sacrifices, we have now one priest, Christ,

C

and one sacrifice, which He offered up once for all, a sacrifice not to be repeated. We have also, now that the shadows have passed away, a simplicity in the means of grace, which are but three in number, viz., the word, sacraments, and prayer. Some, like others before them, may ask, "What are these among so many?" and so they make an addition to them of their own invention. But the word, sacraments, and prayer were means appointed by the Head of the Church, and are made effective unto salvation to the elect. Christ, by His death, abolished the Ceremonial Law, and it has no place in the Christian Church. He nailed it to His cross, and it was buried in His grave, and, although Christ rose again, that law never had a resurrection, and never shall have. It was by Moses that that law was given, and as no creature knows the place of his burial, so no more can the typical law be raised from the dead. Besides this, if men knew the grave of Moses they would be worshipping it, and that would be idolatry, just as the people of Israel worshipped the brazen serpent, which was a type of Christ, and it was idolatry on their part. Many in our day try to revive the Ceremonial Law, but they have not succeeded in raising it from the dead. They light candles in church in daylight. They sprinkle the people with what they call holy water; but those that would be still under the Ceremonial Law are bound to observe the whole law, and not a part only. They make themselves bound to offer up bloody sacrifices and to observe many other things in that law, but this would be too expensive, and therefore they omit them.

II. *The parties with whom the covenant was to be made*—the house of Israel and the house of Judah.

The people of Israel were a type of the people of God, and in this sense it is written that " all Israel shall be saved," so that we may say that the covenant is made with all that have been given to Christ in the covenant of grace. He made this covenant with many of these in the past, who are now in glory, and He is still making it with them in the present generation, and shall continue to make it with them till the end of time, when all spiritual Israel shall be saved. It is not necessary to dwell longer on this head, and therefore we proceed to consider the third head.

III. *The manner in which it is to be made with these.* There are several things in the manner in which it is made with them.

(1) " I will put my laws into their mind, and write them in their hearts." Law here means the word of God, as it often does, say in the 119th Psalm, where the word of God is spoken of as law, statutes, judgments. The fact that they are put in the mind, implies that those with whom God makes the covenant understand the Scriptures. It is by the mind we know anything. Many have the word of God in the Bible who have it not in their mind, and are ignorant of its meaning, but those who are taught by the Spirit understand the Scriptures. Christ not only expounded the Scriptures to his disciples, but he opened their understanding to understand them (Luke xxiv. 27). They are taught to know and understand the word of God as it testifies of our state by nature as sinful and lost. They are taught to know and understand the word of God as it testifies of the way of salvation by Christ;

and they understand, in some measure, all the doctrines of God's word. They have an unction from the Holy One, and know all things (1 John ii. 20). A little boy, taught by the Spirit, understands the word of God better than the most learned man without grace.

(2) He writes His law in their heart. As the mind is the seat of knowledge, the heart is the seat of affection. Those with whom the covenant is made not only know and understand the word of God, but they love it. " O how love I Thy law: it is my study all the day" (Psalm cxix. 97). The moral law was engraven on tables of stone so that it could not be erased without breaking or destroying these tables. In like manner the word of God is engraven in the hearts of the Lord's people in such a manner that it cannot be taken away without destroying the new heart, a thing impossible. The Lord's people shall not carry the Bible with them to heaven, in the letter, but they shall carry with them its doctrines, put in their mind and written in their heart. Although they shall then be perfect, so far as the image of God on them is concerned, we believe that they shall be increasing in knowledge. It is written that " the Lamb who is in the midst of the throne shall feed them and lead to fountains of living water." He shall lead them more thoroughly into the mystery of redemption, and explain to them His dealings with them in the world, some of which they did not understand while on earth. Jacob said, " All these things are against me," but he shall know that all these things were for him, and know that " all things work together for good to them that love God." Christ said to Peter, " What I do thou knowest not now : but thou shalt

know hereafter '' (John xiii. 7). Dr Love, who met
with manifold temptations, said that he could not
understand the Lord's dealings with him in this manner
till he got to heaven. In all His dealings with His
people in the wilderness, they found and testified that
the Lord did all things well.

(3) The third thing in the manner is, '' I will be to
them a God, and they shall be to Me a people.'' It is
a great privilege to put His laws in their mind, and to
write them in their heart; but it is infinitely greater
that He should be their God. Theirs, in all He is,
and in all He has, but this is what He promises to do.
He will be their covenant God, and as He will be their
God, they shall be His people. They shall enter into
covenant with Him. He shall make them willing in
the day of His power to be His people. The people of
Israel entered into a covenant with Him at Sinai, but
many of them broke the covenant and forsook Him;
but neither party shall break this new covenant. God
will continue to keep His own part of it, and His people
shall continue to keep their own part of it. Neither
sin nor Satan can make them break the covenant. It
is written that when God would do good to His people,
notwithstanding their sinfulness, '' that He remembered His covenant ''; and as sure as He remembers
His covenant, they shall remember it also. O this is
a covenant worth entering into!

(4) The fourth thing in the manner is, '' And they
shall not teach every man his neighbour, and every man
his brother, saying, Know the Lord, for all shall know
Me, from the least to the greatest.'' Some understand
this of the time of the millennium, and say that the

knowledge of God shall be so general among men that there shall be no necessity for the preaching of the Gospel and observing the means of grace; but this is a mistake, for the preaching of the Gospel was never before so universal as it shall be then. Even at that glorious period the Lord's people are not perfect in their knowledge, and they shall need to be taught, and they shall be hungering and thirsting to hear the Gospel preached. What we understand by "not teaching every man his neighbour, and his brother, saying, Know the Lord," is, that it will not be necessary to say to those who are taught of God, Know the Lord, as if they were ignorant of Him as the heathen now are, and the great majority in Christian lands are, for it is said that "they shall all know Him, from the least to the greatest."

(5) The fifth thing in the manner is, "I will be merciful to their unrighteousness, and their sins and their iniquities will I remember no more." Their sins are put in three classes—unrighteousness, sins, and iniquities. As God dealt with His Son Jesus Christ, in strict justice till He endured the penalty of their sins and made an end of them, He will now deal with them in mercy by freely forgiving them all. As He forgives their sins, He shall never remember them against them; but although He remembers them no more against them to condemn them, they shall remember them themselves. Although God forgave them their sins, they shall not forgive themselves during their time in this world, and the Lord permits this to humble them and to keep them from boasting. Their sins are thus as a ballast in a ship, to keep from capsizing in a

storm. The remembrance of their sins, though forgiven, causes them pain and the wound to bleed anew.
In heaven the remembrance of their sins causes no such
pain, but, on the contrary, it excites their gratitude to
their Saviour, that they sing His praise in the language
of Scripture: " Unto Him that loved us, and washed
us from our sins in His own blood, and hath made us
kings and priests unto God and His Father ; to Him be
glory and dominion for ever and ever. Amen " (Rev.
i. 5, 6). But while they are in this world their sins,
which were put as far away from them as east is from
the west, come back to them again and again. On the
great day of atonement the scape-goat carried on its
back all the sins of the people (in type) into a distant
wilderness. The people were very happy, and could
sleep well that night ; but if we suppose that one of
these happy people, who felt so happy and who slept
so well, should, on rising and opening the door, find
that the first object to meet his eyes were the goat,
having the burden of his sins on its back, would he
not cry out—Are you here again ? He would feel
miserable. Well, this is not true in fact in the case
of the scape-goat, but it is often true of the experience
of those whose sins are forgiven.

In conclusion: What a great privilege we have in
the New Testament dispensation, as compared with
those enjoyed under the Old! Under the Old, the
Gospel was confined to one nation—the Jews—but now
the Gospel is for all the nations of the world. But we
ought to bear in mind " that to whom much is given,
of them much shall be required." Although the new
covenant, in the sense of our text, is not made with

every individual of the human race, the Gospel is to be preached to all who come to hear the joyful sound, and, although faith is the gift of God, the duty of believing in Christ is binding on every individual to whom Christ is preached. Happy are those with whom God makes the new covenant. These shall be in heaven after they finish their course in the world. They shall see many wonders there. Among these wonders is that they are in heaven themselves. They shall not wonder so much that others are there as that they are there themselves. They do not wonder so much that Manasseh and Mary Magdalene are in heaven as that they are there themselves. Like the Apostle Paul, they consider themselves less than the least of all saints, as it is written, " In lowliness of heart, let each esteem others better than themselves." The more they are ripening for heaven, the less they grow in their own estimation. It was to His own disciples Christ said, " Except ye be converted and become as little children, ye cannot enter the kingdom of heaven." The believer considers any person who is the subject of saving grace, however little his gifts may be, greater than himself. It is not a mark of growing in grace to think of one-self greater than the rest of the Lord's people. It was observed of some who thought much of themselves in their youth that, as they were ripening for glory, they cast off that conceit as a filthy rag, and became as little children in their own estimation.

Let us all examine ourselves as to whether God made this new covenant with us. We shall soon be in eternity, but it is in this world that the covenant must be made with us if we are saved. The thought to enter eternity without Christ is overwhelming to those who take to heart the things which belong to their ever-lasting peace. May the Lord in mercy awaken careless sinners to think of these things ere it be too late, and may He encourage every poor sinner who seeks to be saved, and uphold His own people under the pressure of the temptations of the devil, and other tribulations to which they are liable in their wilderness journey. Amen.

VIII.

Jacob's Dream

" And he dreamed, and, and, behold, a ladder set upon the earth, and the top of it reached to heaven : and, behold, the angels of God ascending and descending on it. And, behold, the LORD stood above it, and said, I am the LORD God of Abraham thy father, and the God of Isaac : the land whereon thou liest, to thee will I give it, and to thy seed."—Gen. xxviii. 12, 13.

WE have in this chapter an account of Jacob leaving his home and going to Padan-aram. What made him leave his home? He left for fear of his life. Esau, his brother, threatened to kill him after their father's death. His mother was informed of Esau's intention, and she advised Jacob to flee to her brother Laban at Padan-aram. Another reason was that he might not take a Canaanite for his wife, but one of his own kindred.

Before he left, his father called him to bless him, and to pray for him. This was a good parting. Dutiful children leave home with the blessing of their parents. Isaac sent away his son with his blessing, good advices, and prayers. Jacob started on his journey to Padan-aram, and, as the journey was long, he could not arrive at his destination in one day. When the sun set, when he came to a certain place, he tarried there all night, and made a bed to himself where he tarried—the earth for his bed and a stone for his pillow. He had no bed-clothes but the garment which he wore. Although he was not converted then, we think that, from the good example he received at home, he conducted worship before retiring to sleep. After a day's journey he would feel tired, and he slept well, and never found a pillow so soft and comfortable as the stone on which he lay his head that night. During his sleep he saw a dream. In that dream he saw a wonderful sight, and heard wonderful words spoken to him by the Lord. In Old Testament times the Lord spoke to the fathers by the prophets in divers manners, or ways, and dreams were one of these ways. Though this is not His ordinary way now, He sometimes reveals Himself to His people in dreams, and makes them truly happy, as Jacob was. Although the body is sleeping, the mind is awake, and it is wonderful how correctly one speaks when one is asleep. God has access to the spirit of man when the body is asleep, but we are not to depend upon dreams, apart from the word of God, for Satan sends dreams to the careless, to deceive them. He may make them dream that they are in heaven, in order that they might not be concerned about the salvation of their souls. Satan is very cunning, so that you need to come to the test of Scripture with your dreams.

In speaking on this subject, we shall notice:—

I. The ladder that Jacob saw, the like of which was never seen in the world, the one end on earth, and the other end reaching up to heaven. The ladder meant Christ as the way, the only way to heaven. It represented Him in His two natures as God and man, who, while on earth, was at the same time in heaven. While on earth He spoke of Himself as " the Son of man, who is in heaven." Christ is the only way to heaven. The ladder of man's own righteousness is too short to bring the sinner to heaven, for, by the works of the law no flesh is justified. The angels of God were ascending and descending on this ladder. There is no communication between heaven and earth but by Christ. Without Him as the ladder, no message of mercy could come to us from heaven, and no prayer could ascend up to heaven from sinful creatures such as we are. As the ladder, He is the only Mediator between God and men. There is no doubt but Jacob understood that it was Christ as the way to heaven that was meant by the ladder he saw, for, as God-man, Christ was in heaven even while He was on this earth. We, mere creatures, cannot be in two places at the same time, but Christ was more than a mere man, and could be in both places at the same time. In order that we who have fallen from the state in which God created us can ascend up to heaven, there are necessary steps which we must **take in ascending** by Christ as the way. The first step, without which we can never ascend, is to believe in Christ. We cannot take this step without being born again. As Christ said to Nicodemus, "Verily, verily, I say unto thee, except a man be born again he cannot see the kingdom of heaven" (John iii. 3). The second necessary step is to be justified on the ground of Christ's death. The third step necessary for ascending to heaven is to be sanctified or conformed to the image of Christ; and as this is a progressive work, it includes all the other steps upward to heaven. It is a growing up unto Him who is the Head, so as to come up to the full stature of a perfect man in Christ. The last step is to enter heaven to be glorified with him. This is their own desire, and it is Christ's desire also, as He says, "Father, I will that they also, whom Thou hast given

Me, be with Me where I am ; that they may behold My
glory, which Thou has given Me, for Thou lovedst Me
before the foundation of the world '' (John xvii. 24).
This much at present on the ladder.

II. We shall consider the great and wonderful
things that God spoke to Jacob. It is to be observed
that it was through Christ that God spoke to Jacob.
He saw the Lord standing above the ladder, and from
that place He spoke to him, saying, '' I am the Lord
God of Abraham thy father, and the God of Isaac,''
and now He was to be the God of Jacob. He is the
covenant God of His people in all ages, and in all places
of the earth. This was the time of Jacob's conversion.
He left home in a state of nature, which is a state of
sin and misery, and now in a wilderness, alone, God
met him, and changed him from a state of nature to a
state of grace. His father and mother had a purpose
in sending him away from home, and God had a purpose
also, and that was to save him in that solitary spot of
the earth. When the Lord purposes to have a personal
dealing with a sinner, He brings him aside from his
fellow-creatures for that purpose. Some are converted
hearing the Gospel in the company of assemblies
gathered together in the public means of grace, but
others, like Jacob, are converted when they are alone,
far away from their fellow-sinners. We might mention
several cases of this kind if it were necessary to do so,
but we forbear. Some are converted through the
instrumentality of godly ministers, but there are others
who are converted without the instrumentality of men,
but by means of the word of God spoken to them by
God Himself. This was the case with Jacob, and it

5

may be said Providence worked together with the word
of God in the change he underwent that night in the
solitary part of the earth in which he was. The Lord
gave promises to him of temporal and spiritual blessings. With regard to temporal blessings, He promised
to give the land whereon he lay to him, and to his seed.
He promised him also that his seed would be numerous
as the dust of the earth, and that they would spread
abroad to west, east, north, and south. He promised
him, moreover, that Christ would descend, according to
the flesh, from him, and that in his seed—Christ—all
the families of the earth should be blessed. This great
promise that was given to his grandfather—Abraham—
was now renewed to Jacob. He promised to keep and
protect him in all places whither he went. This
promise was much needed by Jacob, who fled for fear
of his life, and must have been a great comfort to him
as coming from the Most High, who preserves man and
beast. It was a word in season to him, which encouraged him greatly to proceed next day to Padan-aram,
and in the midst of all the troubles and dangers which
met him there, this promise sustained him in them all,
notwithstanding the power of unbelief. He promised
also that He would bring him back to his native land in
peace and safety, and that He would not leave him
until He had done that which He had spoken to him of.
There is nothing that supports and comforts the believer
like the word of the Lord.

After a sweet sleep, Jacob awoke and began to
ponder upon his dream, and he had no need of a Daniel
or a Joseph to interpret the dream to him. The Holy
Spirit was his interpreter, and Jacob understood that
the Lord met him in that place, and he had no hesita-

tion in saying, " Surely the Lord is in this place." If
he was so sure, why did he add, " I knew it not " ? It
was not because he doubted that He was there that he
said this, but because he did not expect when he left
home that the Lord would meet him in that place.

III. We shall now notice the effect the dream had
on Jacob. (1) The first effect was that he was filled with
reverential awe before the Most High who revealed
Himself to him. This made him exclaim, " How
dreadful is this place." This must be the experience
of all to whom the Lord reveals Himself in a saving
manner. This was the experience of Isaiah when the
Lord, in His glorious majesty and transcendent holiness, revealed Himself to him, so that he exclaimed,
" Woe is me; for I am a man of unclean lips, and I
dwell in the midst of a people of unclean lips, for mine
eyes have seen the King, the Lord of hosts " (Isaiah
vi. 5).

(2) The second effect was that he was made truly
happy. He found himself in that wilderness in the
house of God and at the gate of heaven. " This is none
other than the house of God, and this is the gate of
heaven." Wherever God reveals Himself to you as the
God of salvation, you may call that spot the house of
God and the gate of heaven. The church is the gate of
heaven, but not the door, as Christ is. Outside the
Church of Christ you cannot enter heaven. As it is
the gate of heaven, you must enter through the gate in
order to enter heaven. When Jacob said this is the
house of God and the gate of heaven, he felt heaven
and earth very near each other. There was a godly
woman in the Highlands hearing the late Mr McBain,

Fort-Augustus, preaching the Gospel with great liberty, and she used to say afterwards that she never felt heaven and earth so near each other as she felt during the sermon. Jacob gave a new name to the place where the Lord revealed Himself graciously to him. He called it Bethel, though its original name was Luz.

(3) He vowed a vow, saying, "If God be with me, and will keep me in this way that I go, and will give me bread to eat, and raiment to put on, so that I come again to my father's house in peace, then shall the Lord be my God. And this stone, which I have set up for a pillar, shall be God's house; and of all that Thou shalt give me, I will surely give the tenth to Thee." The vow runs in the line of God's promise to keep him and bring him back in safety, and he on his part promises to do the following things:—To adhere to God as his God; and to worship him in this place, which he called Bethel, or, the house of God, and as a memorial he set up the stone on which he laid his head as a pillar to mark the place. Jacob was very modest in his desire for food and clothing. He did not ask luxury—he was content with bread to eat; and he did not ask clothes of the best quality, but any ordinary clothes to put on. He promised also that of all that the Lord would give him to give the tenth part for the maintenance of His cause.

In conclusion—(1) How mysterious God's providence is towards those whom He purposed to save, as in the case of Jacob. In order to fulfil His purpose concerning him, He permitted his circumstances at home to be so disagreeable and dangerous to him that he was compelled to leave his father's house and go to a distant country.

(2) Not only the time but the place of their conversion has been purposed from all eternity. Jacob, in order to be converted, must go to that solitary place in the wilderness where the Lord met him, and communed with him. The woman of Samaria, in order to her conversion, must go to Jacob's well, not only on that day, but at the very hour when the Saviour met her, of whom it is said that " He must needs go through Samaria that day." Not only the day but the very hour in which Saul of Tarsus was converted was fixed in God's purpose before the world was. Some of the Lord's people regret that they had not been converted earlier ; but God fixed the time of their conversion in His eternal purpose, and when that time came the change took place, and not earlier or later. It was the set time to favour Zion.

(3) God meets those whom He purposes to save when they least expect it, as in the case of Jacob, who said that he did not know that the Lord would meet him on his journey when he left home.

(4) The time and place of conversion is a memorable time and a memorable place. If you have been converted, you put up a stone as a memorial of that great event, and in your Christian course afterwards you often look back to it as the place of the turning point in your spiritual history—like David, " you remember the days of old."

(5) You daily afterwards see your need that God would keep your feet from sliding, and your eyes from

shedding bitter tears for your folly. " His people are kept by the power of God through faith unto salvation," and not by their own power.

(6) In soul distresses, in doubts and fears, you vow that if God will relieve you that you will cleave to Him with full purpose of heart, and give as much as you can to support His cause in the world. You will not be covetous for worldly riches; you will be content with bread to eat and raiment to put on, as Jacob and the Apostle Paul were. " Having food and raiment, let us be therewith content " (1 Tim. vi. 8).

(7) The Lord sometimes gives to His people of the good things of this life, " exceeding abundantly above all that they ask or think " (Eph. iii. 20). Jacob was modest in his desire for these things, but the Lord gave him much riches, in cattle and other things, so that, although he left home comparatively poor, he returned with much riches.

(8) If you vow a vow to the Lord, forget not to perform it. Jacob delayed beyond the proper limit to perform his vow; he had to be reminded of it by the Lord, who said, " I am the God of Bethel," and this brought to Jacob's mind his vow in that place, and then he and his family went up to Bethel and performed his vow.

(9) People never lose by giving to the Lord's cause or doing any kind act to His people. At the time of the Disruption, in 1843, many proprietors refused sites to the Free Church for building churches and manses. Among other places where sites were refused we may

mention the parish of Moy and Dalarossie. But there
was a young proprietor who gave sites for church and
manse. We mean the late Mr Mackintosh, Balnespick.
He was at that time a young man, and went to India.
Before he went, a godly man in the parish went to see
him, and said to him, " You are going to India, Mr
Mackintosh, and because you gave sites for church and
manse, I assure you, for I have it from the Lord, that
for your kindness to us, you will come back safely and
wealthier than you went." And so it came to pass.
Mr Mackintosh returned, and worshipped in the Free
Church.

Lastly.—Seek to know Christ as the ladder, the way
to heaven, and to have God as your covenant God, and
then you shall have all that you need for time and
eternity. Amen.

IX.

The Fulness of the Time

"But when the fulness of the time was come, God sent forth His Son, made of a woman, made under the law. To redeem them that were under the law, that we might receive the adoption of sons."—Gal. iv. 4, 5.

THE Apostle Paul preached the Gospel in Galatia, and it was blessed to many there. He preached in other places, and in his absence false teachers came to Galatia who taught the people that they were still under the ceremonial law, and could not be saved without observing it. The Apostle having heard of this, wrote this Epistle to warn the people against this error, and to show that Christ, by His death, abolished that law, which was indeed a schoolmaster leading them to Christ, but when Christ Himself came in the fulness of the time, He delivered them from that yoke of bondage. It was in this connection Paul spoke the words of our text, which may be divided into the following heads:—

I. The fulness of the time.
II. That which God did, when the fulness of the time was come.
III. His purpose in sending forth His Son.

I. *The fulness of the time.*

In the original, the same root-word, meaning fulness, is used by the Apostle in his Epistle to the Philippians, iv. 19, as here. The word means the filling up abundantly of needs and wants, without leaving any want unsupplied. In our text it means the filling up of a period of time. Say that a pole was set up in the garden of Eden when Christ was promised, and another pole set up at the time when Christ came. That was a very long stretch of time to be filled up, amounting to 4000 years. There was a great space between the two poles I have mentioned, but it had to be filled completely before God sent forth His Son. Many things and events were to take place between the promise and the fulfilment of it. In the first promise Christ was spoken of as the seed of the woman, and it is supposed by some that when Eve said at the birth of Cain, " I have gotten a man from the Lord" (Gen. iv. 1), she thought he was the promised Messiah, but the fulness of the time was not yet come. Abraham, to whom the promise was renewed, had to be born. God said to him, " In thee (that is, in thy seed) shall all the families of the earth be blessed" (Gen. xii. 3). But Christ did not come in Abraham's time, and the promise was renewed to Isaac and Jacob, but Christ did not come in their time either. After the patriarchs, we may mention the kings who were appointed to fill up the space. Christ, according to the flesh, descended from King David, who was of the tribe of Judah. He is thus called in Scripture the Son of David. " He was the root and offspring of David" (Rev. xxii. 16). His root as God, and His offspring as man. As time goes on, the woman, whose seed Christ was to be, is mentioned : The Virgin Mary. She was a descendant of the royal family in the line of David. In her time the royal family was in a low condition, so that it is spoken of in Isaiah xi. 1 as a tree cut off with the stem left in the ground. It was when it was in that condition that He who came to humble Himself was born in human nature into the world.

Another thing that was to go to fill up the space was the typical dispensation set up in the Church through the instrumentality of Moses, which dispensation continued to be observed till the Antitype came. Then it was abolished so far as the ritual of it was concerned. In that dispensation Christ was set forth in the bloody sacrifices as He who was in due time to give His blood to be shed to make atonement for sin.

The heathen monarchies were another item that had to go to fill up the space. There were four such monarchies especially that had to appear before God should send forth His Son, namely, the Babylonian, the Persian, the Grecian, and the Roman. Nebuchadnezzar saw an image of these monarchies in a dream. He saw also a stone cut out of the mountain without hands breaking in pieces the four monarchies and filling the whole earth, and that stone represented the Kingdom of Christ. It was under the fourth monarchy (the Roman) that Christ came. He was crucified by the Romans as a malefactor. Crucifixion was not practised by the Jews as a way of punishing evil doers, but it was practised by the Romans.

There were many other events intended to fill up the space, such as the destruction of Sodom and Gomorrah, the deluge, Pharaoh, and many other things.

II. *That which God made when the fulness of the time was come.*

He did the greatest thing that could be done for the salvation of perishing sinners. He sent forth His Son into the world in human nature. It was the greatest on God's part, and the greatest on the Son's part. It may be said that although God sent forth His Son into the world, the Son remained with Him in heaven, for Christ speaks of Himself while on earth as the " Son of Man who is in heaven."

Now as to the manner in which God sent forth His Son note:

(1) He sent Him forth in human nature, made of a woman. Why not of man? Christ had no father according to his humanity, and no human father or mother with regard to His divine nature. He was promised as the seed of the woman. He was conceived in the womb of the Virgin Mary by the Holy Spirit and born of her without sin, although there was sin in her.

(2) He was made under the law. What law? (a) The moral law: not as Adam was made under the law when he was created, but under the law as broken, a law which breathed out curses on its transgressors. He was made under the precept of the law and under its penalty, as the surety and substitute of His people. By sin they ceased to obey its precept, and by transgression they became liable to its penalty. He perfectly obeyed its precept, and endured its penalty to the fullest extent, and His obedience unto death not only paid the debt incurred by His people but also merited eternal life for them. His divine nature not only supported His human nature in His sufferings, but added infinite merit to the sacrifice which He offered up to satisfy justice, and to reconcile us to God.

(b) The ceremonial law: He was circumcised, which was a rite of the ceremonial law, and a seal of the covenant. He observed the passover, and acknowledged the priesthood till that order was superseded by Himself, who is now the only Priest of the New Testament Church. When He healed the leper He said to Him, "Go and show thyself to the priest, and offer the gift that Moses commanded for a testimony unto them" (Matt. viii. 4). Instead of circumcision we have now baptism, and instead of the passover we have the Lord's Supper. Christ our passover is sacrificed for us (1 Cor. v. 7). Baptists deny that baptism is now instead of circumcision, and in support of their view say that it was only males that were circumcised, whereas females are baptised as well as males. But they forget that under the New Testament dispensation there is neither male nor female ; all are alike as to their privileges. Besides, their argument against us cannot be valid, because it would prove too much. It would prove that females had no right to attend the public means of grace, for under the Old Testament dispensation it was men only that went up to Jerusalem to attend the public feasts. It would prove also that women had no right to partake of the Lord's Supper, for it was only men that partook of the last passover which Christ attended, or, which means the same thing, sat with Him at the first Communion. By His obedience unto death Christ magnified the moral law and made it honourable, and both fulfilled and abolished the ceremonial law, so that it is not now to be observed in whole or in part.

III. *The purpose for which God set forth His Son :*
There are two things in the purpose : (1) To redeem them that were under the law. You and I, and all the fallen race, are under the law as a broken covenant, not only by the sin of Adam but also by our own transgression of the law. The word redeem means to buy. Christ is the only Redeemer, and He bought His people at a great price. " Ye are not your own, ye are bought with a price." In Israel when a man lost his inheritance and sold himself as a slave, it was the next of kin that had the right, if he had the means, to redeem his poor brother by paying the redemption price. Christ, in order to become our next of kin, assumed our nature, and in that nature paid the price of our redemption by His humiliation unto death. The Apostle Paul, in the Epistle to the Hebrews (ii. 1) shows the necessity, for this

end, of His assuming our nature, and says "that both He that sanctifieth and they who are sanctified are all of one, for which cause He is not ashamed to call them brethren." Christ redeemed His people by His blood, as Peter declares: "Forasmuch as ye know that ye were not redeemed with corruptible things as silver and gold . . . . but with the precious blood of Christ as of a lamb without blemish and without spot" (1 Peter ii. 18, 19).

(2) The second thing in the purpose is that we might receive the adoption of sons. To adopt children is to receive them from another family, and to bring them up as one's own children. All God's children are taken out of Satan's family, and received into God's family, and have a right to the privileges of the sons of God. God's adoption of sinners is different from that of men. Men cannot change the nature of those whom they adopt, but God changes the nature of all whom He adopts. They are born again in His house. There are three kinds of adoption mentioned in Scripture—(1) The adoption that is common to all believers both under the Old Testament and under the new; (2) The adoption that is peculiar to believers under the New Testament; and (3) The adoption of the body at the resurrection. It is the second of these three kinds of adoption that is meant in our text. None of God's children under the Old Testament dispensation attained to this adoption. Not even Abraham, great as he was, attained to it. The patriarchs and the godly kings and the prophets did not attain to it. The Apostle speaks of Old Testament believers as heirs who have not yet come of age, who as such were under tutors and governors until the time appointed of the Father. Under the tuition of the ceremonial law as a schoolmaster and under its yoke of bondage they were more like servants than sons. He

thus rebukes the Galatians, who, having been once
delivered from the ceremonial law, were going back to
it again, calling them " Foolish Galatians." If you
saw an heir that came of age going next day to an
elementary school, you would say to him, " O foolish
man, you have soon forgotten that you have come of age,
and that you got beyond going to school along with boys
in their teens." The Church under the New Testament
are regarded as persons that had finished their education
under the ceremonial law, so long their schoolmaster.
That law was a schoolmaster leading them to Christ as
the great teacher come from God, but when Christ Himself came they ought to sit under His teaching and not
to return like other foolish Galatians to their old teacher.

Application.

Consider : (1) How soon professing Christians, who
were taught from their youth in the doctrines of Christi-
anity turn to error. This is caused chiefly by false
teachers, as was the case with the Galatians. But ministers who are taught of God ought by teaching to point
out their error, and warn them, and do their utmost to
lead them back to the truth and the doctrines of God's
Word ; and this teachers of the right sort do, and those
who will not obey their teaching must suffer for their
disobedience.

(2) What a gracious provision God made for perishing sinners and at what cost it was secured. It cost His
Son His humiliation unto death, but it is offered freely
to sinners without money and without price.

(3) How sure it is that God will fulfil all His promises
to His people. Although the promise of sending His
Son to the world to work out everlasting redemption took
a long time in being fulfilled, yet He fulfilled His
promise in due time. So also, Christ shall come again

the second time to judge the world in righteousness, but, before His coming again, Scripture foretold many events that were to take place in the interval, that is, between His first and His second coming. These events are mentioned in a sermon from 2 Thess. i. 7 : " And to you who are troubled rest with us, when the Lord Jesus shall be revealed from heaven with His mighty angels," etc. It is therefore not necessary to repeat them here. It should be our great concern to seek preparation for death, and as death leaves us, the last judgment shall find us, for as the tree falleth so it shall lie. May the Lord add His blessing to His own Word. AMEN.

X.

Ihis Name Jesus

"And thou shalt call His name Jesus; for He shall save His people from their sins."—Matthew i. 21.

WE read in this chapter that the Lord sent an angel from heaven to Joseph to relieve him of his perplexity concerning Mary, who was with child before they were married. There was an engagement between them, but as yet they were not actually married. After explaining to him that she had conceived by the Holy Ghost, the angel told him that Mary would bring forth a Son, and he commanded him to call His name Jesus, because He would save His people from their sins.

From these words we shall notice two things—

I. The Person whose name is Jesus.

II. His work: "He shall save His people from their sins.

I. *Jesus:*

This name signifies a Saviour. Under the Old Testament there were two eminent men called by the same name—Joshua, who succeeded Moses in leading the children of Israel to the land of Caanan, and Joshua, the high priest who officiated in the office of the priesthood at the time of the building of the second temple, after the return from the captivity. Joshua means the same in Hebrew as Jesus in Greek. Both these men may be taken, as they really were, as types of the Saviour of the world. The one was a leader, a captain or king, the other a priest—a high priest. Christ is Priest and King, but in order that He might be Jesus He is—

(1) God—without his being God He could not be the Saviour. A creature cannot save sinners. But Christ is God equal with the Father in nature, power, and glory. The Jews denied this, Socinians deny it; and there are many in our own day who call themselves Christians that deny that Jesus is God. But their denial does not change the fact. Not only did Jesus claim to be God equal with the Father, but he did miracles which no other but God could do.

(2) Emmanuel. Jesus is "God with us"—God in our nature. It was necessary that He should assume human nature in order that, not only He might suitably represent those He came to save, but also that He might be susceptible of enduring the penalty of their sins. Therefore "The word was made flesh." The eternal Son of God took to Himself a true body and a reasonable soul. His human nature did not of itself constitute a person; but He took it into union with His divine Person. Although it did not of itself constitute a person, it belonged to Christ's Person as Mediator between God and man. He is the God-man.

(3) As Prophet the Mediator was appointed to His office to reveal the Father, to "declare the decree," and to restore the knowledge of God, which was lost by sin. None knows the Father as He does, nor can restore the knowledge of God to men who have become darkness by their apostacy.

(4). He is Priest. We are by nature guilty as well as ignorant. Sin is not only an evil, which deprives us of the knowledge of God, it is also guilt. Hence our need of Christ as Priest to atone for our sins by the sacrifice of Himself and to intercede for us.

6

(5) He is King. We are rebellious; we are enemies to God, to ourselves, and to our fellow-men. Who can subdue our rebellion? We cannot do it ourselves; our fellow-men—even God's people—cannot do it; holy angels cannot do it; no creature can do it. Christ alone can do this work. He makes His people willing in the day of His power. He has been appointed King to subdue us to Himself, to rule and defend us, and to restrain and conquer all His and our enemies.

Now, in order that the Mediator might be Jesus— the Saviour—He is God from all eternity, and becomes Emmanuel in time, so that as Prophet, Priest, and King—a complete Saviour—He might be able to save to the uttermost all that come to God by Him.

II. *His work: He shall save His people from their sins.*

Mark (1)—Those whom He shall save. Who are these? "His people." As the people of Israel were given to Moses to deliver them from the bondage of Egypt, and to Joshua after him to lead to the land of promise, so those people were given to Christ to save them. They were given to Him by the Father in the everlasting covenant, which is ordered in all things and sure. They are God's elect people. Many in our day, as in former days, deny the doctrine of election. They object to the Confession of Faith because among other things it contains the doctrine of election. But supposing they would take that doctrine out of the Confession, they would still meet with it in the Bible. They cannot get rid of it unless they, as many do, deny that the Bible is the Word of God. But there is an election of grace, and a people that no man can number were given to Jesus, and all those He shall save.

(2) That from which he saves them—" Their sins."
" He shall save His people from their sins." Sin is the
great evil that separated us from God; that made us
liable to all the miseries of this life, to death itself, and
to the pains of hell for ever. It is a transgression of the
law of God, or in the words of the Shorter Catechism : —
" Sin is any want of conformity unto or transgression of
the law of God." In our souls there is a want—a complete want—of conformity to God's holy law, and from
this fountain, which is original sin, flow all actual transgressions. The law of God—the ten commandments—
is the glass in which we can see—if our eyes are opened
by the Spirit—our sinfulness. That law was written by
the finger of God on two tables of stone. The first table
contains our duty to God; the second, our duty to our
fellow-men. The first begins with the command : —
" Thou shalt have no other gods before Me"; the
second with—" Thou shalt honour thy father and thy
mother"; and the sum of the whole is—" Thou shalt
love the Lord thy God with all thine heart, with all thy
might, and thy neighbour as thyself." Now in our
natural state we do not do what God commands us to
do—on the contrary we do the very reverse of what He
commands. We set up other gods before Him. We
hate, instead of loving, the only true God, and we hate
our fellow-men. The world is full of evidences of this.
What forgetfulness of God there is even among people
in Christian lands; what enmity to one another among
men! Surely we have fallen from the state in which
God created us; we have sinned, and we are guilty in
the sight of God. We need Jesus to save us from our
sins.

(3) How Jesus saves His people from their sins. This
He does : (a) By satisfying the requirements of God's law

for them. This He did when He offered Himself a
sacrifice to satisfy divine justice and to reconcile us to
God. His people could never be saved from their sins
without this. But Jesus bore all their sins—that is, the
guilt and punishment of them—in His own body on the
tree, and put them forever away by the sacrifice of Himself. Christ's atonement is the only ground on which
salvation from sin is possible. (b) By the effectual work
of His Spirit in applying His redemption to them
through the word. He makes them new creatures. He
gives them a new nature, they are made the children of
God. (c) He saves them from the guilt of their sins in
their justification. It is on the ground of His atonement God justifies them. (d) He saves them by sanctifying them. This work goes on till their death, when
they are made perfect in holiness. Their bodies shall
be raised up perfect at the resurrection. They shall be
raised up in glory. (e) He saves them from the punishment of their sins. He endured that punishment Himself—there is therefore nothing of it left for them. He
is " Jesus, who hath delivered us from the wrath to
come."

In conclusion: We have been considering this great
subject in a doctrinal way. In preaching, doctrine
should have the first place, and in our day when the
doctrines of salvation are so much neglected by many
ministers, there is the more call for our preaching them.
Some content themselves with an occasional mention of
sin, the Saviour, etc., in order to give their sermons an
appearance of the Gospel ; but they do not explain what
sin is, what the Saviour is, and the consequence is that
hearers are left in a mist of ignorance regarding the
fundamental doctrines of salvation. Let us now come to
the practical application of the subject.

(1) A word to the unconverted sinner. You have heard what sin is. Have you found out that you are a sinner? or are you still ignorant of your state in the sight of God? Do you live without prayer? Do you seek your happiness in the world and follow the course of the world; its sins, its vanity, its pleasures? Remember that this world shall pass away with its lusts, and that you must pass away from time to eternity in order to give an account of the deeds done in the body, and that you shall perish eternally if you die in your sins. Oh turn now to God ere it be too late, forsake your sinful course, for it leads to everlasting destruction. You heard of Jesus, who He is: the eternal God—God manifest in the flesh—in our nature—the Prophet, Priest, and King of His Church, able to save to the uttermost all that come to God by Him. We preach the Saviour to you, invite you to Him. If you come to Him and receive Him as your Saviour you shall be saved, all your sins shall be forgiven—though they be red as scarlet and as crimson. The blood of Jesus Christ the Son of God cleanseth us from all sin. I delivered to you God's message. I am clear of your blood if you perish. I leave the matter between you and the God before whose august tribunal you must soon appear!

(2) A word to the anxious enquirer. You have been awakened out of your spiritual slumbers. You have seen to some extent the evil of sin. You forsake it. You ask, "What must I do to be saved?" To you we say, "Believe in the Lord Jesus Christ and you shall be saved." You may be perplexed as to whether you are one of those people given to Christ to save. You have nothing to do in the meantime with the secret purpose of God. Knowledge of your election is not your warrant in coming to Christ, but the invitation of the

Gospel. That invitation is addressed to you as a sinner
—a lost sinner. The mark of the elect is that Jesus
saves them from their sins. If you seek to be saved not
merely from wrath—the wages of sin—but from your
sins, you are welcome to the Saviour. He will in no
wise cast you out, but receive and save you. Come then
to Him, cast yourself upon Him. Rest not in your own
duties—your repentance—your own righteousness—but
in Christ's finished work. His righteousness is the only
but all-sufficient ground of the sinner's salvation from
first to last. May the Holy Spirit lead you by faith to
Jesus and enable you to receive Him as He is freely
offered in the Gospel.

(3) A word to the believer. Unto you that believe
Jesus is precious. The Spirit convinced you of your need
of Him, enlightened your mind in a saving knowledge
of Him, worked faith in you, and made you willing to
embrace Him as your Saviour, your Lord and portion
for ever. He saved you from your sins, and yet you feel
that you need to be saved from them still. All the guilt
of your sins has been taken away, but your nature is but
partly renewed. You are perfect in your justification
but not in your sanctification. You have still need of
Jesus to save you from your sins. Look to Him, cry to
Him, be diligent in the use of the means of sanctification
He will make you perfect in your sanctification.

You need Jesus also to save you from the tribulations
of the wilderness, from the enemies that seek the life of
your soul and the life of your body. The devil is as a
roaring lion after you, wicked men are after you. But
Jesus is your protector. All thine enemies are conquered and chained by Him. He can say to them,
" Hitherto ye shall come and no further." Many are
the deliverances He has in the past given you from them ;

and this is an encouragement to trust Him in what remains of your pilgrimage on earth. He knows their plots, their evil devices against you, but He is your shield. He keeps you as the apple of His eye. Till you reach heaven you shall not know how He watched over you with tender care to save you from your spiritual and temporal enemies. It shall be revealed to you then, and it will add a new note to your song of praise.

Endeavour to serve Him, to glorify Him with your body and spirit, which are His by creation and redemption. Seek more and more to know the meaning of the text, " And thou shalt call His name Jesus, for He shall save His peope from their sins."

May the Lord bless His own word, and to His name be all the praise. AMEN.

XI.

The Sword Smiting the Shepherd

" Awake, O sword, against my Shepherd, and against the man that is my fellow, saith the Lord of hosts; smite the Shepherd, and the sheep shall be scattered; and I will turn my hand upon the little ones."—Zechariah xiii. 7.

WE are drawing near the time when the Sacrament of the Lord's Supper is to be dispensed in our congregation, and it is proper to think beforehand of His death, and we have His death in this text.   It is beyond doubt that it is Christ that is meant by the person against whom the sword is to awake; for He Himself, as we read in Matthew xxvi. 31, quotes this text, and applies it to Himself.   Shortly before His crucifixion, He said to His disciples, " All ye shall be offended because of Me this night; for it is written, I will smite the Shepherd, and the sheep of the flock shall be scattered abroad" (Matt. xxvi. 31) ; but, further, He says: " After I am risen again, I will go before you into Galilee" (32nd ver.).   In the beginning of the chapter in which we have our text, it is mentioned that a fountain was to be opened to the house of David and to the inhabitants of Jerusalem for sin and for uncleanness— that is, for the removal of the guilt of sin and its defilement.   It was not water but blood that was to fill the fountain.   The ground in which the fountain was to be opened was not created in the time of Zechariah, nor for centuries thereafter.   The ground was the human nature of Christ, and the instrument which was to

open the fountain was a sword—hence the call,
"Awake, O sword." In speaking from these solemn
words, we shall call your attention to the following
particulars : —

I. The Person against whom the sword is to
awake.
II. The call to the sword to awake and smite this
Person.
III. That which was to follow the smiting of the
Shepherd.

I. The Person against whom the sword is to awake
was already mentioned. The fact that Christ quotes
the words of the text, as fulfilled in Himself, puts it
beyond doubt that He is the Person against whom the
sword did awake. He is spoken of with regard to His
Godhead, His humanity, and His office. As to His
Godhead, He is the Father's fellow ; as to His humanity,
He is man ; and as to His office, He is the Shepherd.
He is the Father's fellow in a sense in which no
creature is, whether man or angel. His people have
fellowship with the Father, but He is of the same
nature or essence as the Father, and equal with Him
in power and glory. He is the second Person of the
Godhead. As God, He was incapable of suffering,
therefore He took to Himself human nature, which
consists of two parts—a true body and a reasonable soul. The Westminster Divines, in order to keep
people sound in the faith, teach that Christ took to
Himself "a true body and a reasonable soul," and
they say this in order to refute a certain error regarding Christ's human nature. Some held that it was not

a true body that Christ took, but a phantom, and others
held that He had not a soul, but that His Divine nature
supplied the place of the soul; but the truth is that He
took to Himself a true body and a reasonable soul, as
we have, but free from sin.   He took to Himself the
whole nature of man in close union with His Divine
Person, so that His human nature is not of itself a
person, for it did not exist for one moment separate
from His Divine Person.   Herein is a wonder full of
teaching.   When we see human nature united to God,
we learn that man, who by sin was separated from God,
was to be united to Him again, and as the union
between Christ's human nature and His Godhead was
everlasting, it teaches us that believers' union with Him
is so also, and that as He brought His human nature
to heaven, He shall bring His people there too.   As to
His office, He is called the Shepherd.   The name
Shepherd is an official name.   Ordinarily a shepherd
has a personal name, but Christ is called Shepherd
because of His office.   Christ holds a threefold office,
as Prophet, Priest, and King, in order to meet our
threefold need.   By sin we lost the knowledge of God
which man had at His creation, and, in order to restore
that knowledge, Christ was appointed Prophet.   We
were also guilty, and could not atone for our guilt by
anything we could do or suffer, but Christ was appointed
Priest, in which office He made full atonement by His
obedience unto death.   We were by nature not only
ignorant of God and guilty, but also rebellious, and no
creature could subdue our rebellion, so Christ was
appointed King to subdue our rebellion.   When Christ
met Saul of Tarsus on His persecuting tour, Paul
thought he would never submit to Christ; but when

Christ spoke to him as King, this rebellious man fell down helpless at His feet, and said, " Lord, what wilt Thou have me to do?"   As King, He subdues His people to Himself, rules and defends them, restrains and conquers all His and their enemies. This is the Person against whom the sword was to awake.

II. *The call to the sword to awake, and smite the Shepherd.*

It was not the flock but the Shepherd that was to be smitten. The flock were guilty, but " He suffered, the just for the unjust, that He might bring us to God." Who gives the call to the sword? It is God the Father. In the scheme of redemption the three Persons of the Godhead have their peculiar share. The first Person, representing the Godhead, takes up the position of one demanding satisfaction to the broken law, before any sinner can be saved. The second Person, representing His people, takes up the position of one rendering the satisfaction required. The third Person undertakes to apply Christ's redemption to all that are saved. The call to the sword is not a mere permission, but a command—" Awake, O sword."

A sword is a weapon of war, and is of a twofold use, defensive and offensive. Every nation has a sword, even in times of peace, in order to defend itself in the event of its being attacked by enemies. What was to be defended in the present case? There were two things to be defended—(1) The glory of God. If sinners are saved, it is in a way that is consistent with the glory of God. (2) The second thing that was to be defended was the flock. There was no safety for them except by the sword awaking against the Shepherd, and smiting Him.

The sword is also used to punish offenders. The sword awoke against Christ to punish Him, as He took upon Himself the sins of His people. Although He was innocent in Himself, He became guilty, by imputation, as He put Himself in the room of His people under the broken law. It was He and not they that endured the penalty due to sin, and although He was God's dear Son, He was not spared on that account—" He that spared not His own Son, but delivered Him up for us all, how shall He not with Him also freely give us all things ?" (Rom. viii. 32). See how the Lord cares for His people—" God laid on Him the iniquities of us all"— and also the punishment due to them. There is no more punishment for them. Christ made an end of their sins and of their punishment. He secured their deliverance. "If ye seek Me, let these go away."

We now enquire, What is the sword which awoke against the Shepherd, and smote Him ? If we ascertain the instruments which inflicted sufferings on Christ, we shall then know what the sword was. We know from Scripture that He suffered from men, devils, and the wrath of His Father. These were the sword. He suffered from men when they were at their worst. When are men at their worst?—When God withdraws His restraining grace from them, and allows them to work according to their sinful nature. Without restraining grace, God's people could not live in the world. Restraining grace is given to those who have not saving grace. Restraining grace was withdrawn from those who had a hand in putting Christ to death. One would think that they were just come out of hell.

Those near Him spat in His face, and struck Him by the palm of their hands, and those who could not get near Him cried loudly, " Away with Him, away with Him, crucify Him," and when Pilate asked for His release, they cried, " Not this man, but Barabbas"— who was a murderer. They are spoken of by Christ Himself, in the 22nd Psalm, as wild beasts. He suffered also from devils. He was led by the Holy Spirit into the wilderness, to be tempted by the devil. Is it not remarkable that He was led by the Holy Spirit to suffer from the evil one ; but He had to endure that temptation as the Substitute of His people, who by sins made themselves liable to such an awful temptation. Near the end of His sufferings, when His Father put the cup of wrath in His hand to drink, it would appear that a large host of devils surrounded Him to intimidate His human nature, so that He said, " Father, if Thou be willing, remove this cup from Me ; nevertheless, not My will but Thine be done" ; but He recovered strength and courage, and said, " The cup which My Father hath given Me, shall I not drink it ?" When men and devils did their utmost, the Father said in effect, Have you done all that you could in smiting the Shepherd ? They answered, Yes. Then He said, Stand aside, and I will smite Him Myself. He suffered immediately from His Father. When He was in the garden of Gethsemane, He suffered from His Father in such a manner that the agony of His soul caused a bloody sweat to issue freely through His holy body, and brought the bitter cry from His utmost soul, " My God, My God, why hast Thou forsaken Me ?" The sword, which included wicked men and devils, was all along in the Father's hand. A sword lying on the field of battle can do no harm, but when used in the hand of a mighty man it will do mighty work. Men and devils could not do any hurt to Christ, except as they were used in the hand of Almighty God. Pilate said, " I have power to crucify Thee, and I have power to release Thee," but Christ answered, " Thou couldst have no power at all against Me except it were given thee from above." The smiting of the Shepherd began as soon as He appeared in human nature in the world. When He was born, Herod sought to kill Him, but, as He was not to be put to death till the due time came, He was carried into Egypt for protection, and remained there till His persecutor died. The smiting continued during His state of humiliation on earth, till the last stroke was given on the cross, when He cried triumphantly, " It is finished." There was no more suffering ; He was brought to the dust of death, but He rose again, to die no more.

III. *That which followed in consequence.*

The first thing that followed the smiting of the Shepherd was the scattering of the sheep. The disciples forsook Him.   Peter denied Him.   Christ was left alone, but the Father was with Him.   The scattering of the disciples on that occasion was not a willing one on their part. It was like the scattering of a flock who loved their shepherd when a wolf pounced upon them, and they fled away from the shepherd for fear of their life.   It was slavish fear that made Peter deny his Saviour, and caused the other disciples to forsake Him. It was a time of danger to all who professed to be followers of the Saviour. If the enemies put Christ,

their Master, to death, what could they expect but to
be killed also? We may find fault with the disciples,
but if we had been in their position we would do as
they did, unless we had more grace than we have.
When Christ is smitten in His word and cause, there
is a scattering of His followers. This may be seen in
history. At such times, not only do nominal Christians
forsake Christ, but even some of His true disciples may
do so also through slavish fear. We need more grace
when a time of trial comes. There is a great forsaking
of Christ and His truth in this evil age. Many follow
Christ when they have nothing to suffer for doing so,
but when persecution arises, or when they are to part
with worldly goods, they turn their back on Him.
Many in this age forsook Christ because they could not
carry with them churches and manses and salaries.
They were not called upon to suffer death in following
Him, but to suffer the loss of stone and lime. The
forsaking of Christ on the part of these was not a mere
backsliding, but it is to be feared, in the case of some,
an apostasy, as He said of some, " that they walked no
more with Jesus." There are, however, some true
disciples of Christ who had no difficulty in leaving
behind them ecclesiastical property, in preference to
turning their back upon the Saviour and the doctrines
of His word. The Apostle Paul tells us that he
suffered the loss of all things for Christ's sake, and that
he considered these things as dung in comparison with
Him. He suffered the loss of these things that he
might win Christ, and therefore his loss was great gain
to him, and so it is with all those who follow His example
—for having Christ they have all other blessings with
Him, and as for worldly matters which they need on

earth, they lack nothing; and however they may be reproached by graceless professors, they esteem Christ's reproach greater riches than the treasures of this world.

The second thing that followed the smiting of the Shepherd was, the gathering again of the scattered flock. Christ told beforehand not only of the scattering of His disciples, but also of their gathering. They were scattered at His death, but gathered together after His resurrection. The first thing He did after He rose from the dead was to go as the Good Shepherd to gather His sheep. No sooner He rose from the grave than He began this good work. He found two of them on their way to Emmaus, disappointed and sad because they did not find Him in Jerusalem. He gathered all of them, and they appeared with Him in Galilee. They were not only gathered by Christ Himself, but also by the Father. It is the Father that speaks in our text and says, " I will turn My hand upon the little ones." It is the very hand that held the sword by which the Shepherd was smitten that He used in gathering them. He is so satisfied with the finished work of His Son that He takes the greatest pleasure in gathering the little ones. When He calls them little ones, He shows how dear they are to Him. The term little in Scripture is one of endearment, as the loving John in his epistles calls believers, " My little children." They may be called little in numbers as compared with those who are not His true people. Christ calls them a small flock. They are small or little in families—many families without any of them at all. They are small or little in congregations. They are small or little in kingdoms, and, indeed, in the whole world. They are little in the eyes of the world, and they are little in their own estimation, like Paul, " less than the least of all saints," but before the end of their gathering they shall be a great multitude which no man can number. This first gathering takes place at their conversion. Their second gathering is after backsliding, and their last gathering shall be to heaven, where they shall be forever with the Lord.

In conclusion: We have been discoursing on a very solemn subject—the smiting of the Shepherd, or, the death of Christ. As already mentioned, we are drawing near a Communion season to commemorate the death of Christ. On such an occasion there is a gathering of many of the Lord's people to the mount of ordinances. In the past, Dingwall was a central place to which many of the Lord's people resorted to remember the Lord's death at His table, and notwithstanding that many of these have been removed to their everlasting rest in heaven, there are still many coming from north, south, east, and west to this town, and we feel the better of their presence with us.

What a gracious, wonderful, and all-sufficient provision God made for the salvation of such as we are! He smote the innocent for the guilty who deserved to be smitten for ever and ever. This was taught by types and shadows under the Old Testament dispensation. The innocent lamb was slain for the guilty, but now it is not in type that the way of salvation is set before us in the Gospel. Christ, the Antitype, came, and in due time, when we were without strength, Christ died for the ungodly (Rom v. 6). O sinner, come to Christ. If you do so, God will not smite you with the sword, but if you continue as you are till

7

death, He shall smite you for ever in eternity. It is His prerogative to save all that believe in Christ, and to punish the impenitent, and although hand join in hand, the wicked shall not go unpunished. He must have the glory of His grace in your salvation, or the glory of His justice in punishing you. Which shall He have in relation to you? What answer are you to give? The answer must be given in your lifetime. Death will decide your state unalterably in eternity. So long as you live, you are invited to Christ. Make good use of this privilege. Seek grace to make you willing to come to Him. If you perish in your sins, we are clear of your blood. You alone must bear the burden of your rejection of the Saviour.

May God make you wise unto salvation. AMEN.

XII.

Christ seeing of His Travail

" He shall see of the travail of His soul, and shall be satisfied : by His knowledge shall my righteous servant justify many ; for He shall bear their iniquities."—Is. liii. 11.

THERE is an intimate connection between the 53rd, 54th, and 55th chapters of this prophecy. The 53rd speaks of the sufferings of Christ; the 54th, of the fruit of His sufferings ; and the 55th, of the call of the Gospel to gather sinners to Him. Our text speaks of His sufferings, and also of the fruit of His suffering.

In speaking on this subject, we shall notice—

I. The soul travail of Christ.
II. The fruit of it.
III. That He shall be satisfied with the fruit of
His soul travail.

I. *The soul travail of Christ, wherein His incarnation and sufferings are included:*

Christ assumed the whole of man's nature—soul and body, and suffered in both, though here it is only His soul that is mentioned. Though the sufferings of His body were great, His soul sufferings were much greater and most severe to endure. It is well known by experience among men in all generations that mental or soul trouble is more difficult to endure than bodily trouble. The soul of Christ is mentioned in the text to indicate the magnitude of His sufferings. He lays emphasis on this Himself when He says, " My soul is exceeding sorrowful unto death." By His sufferings in soul and body, which He finished by His death on the cross, He obtained everlasting redemption for His people.

II. *The fruit of His sufferings: " He shall see of the travail of His soul."*

Christ's soul travail shall not be in vain ; it shall yield abundant fruit, which shall be to the glory of God, and the good of men. This is made certain in Scripture. " Verily, verily, I say unto you, except a corn of wheat fall into the ground and die, it abideth alone ; but if it die, it bringeth forth much fruit " (John xii. 24). Many other passages of Scripture speak to the same effect. The time of Christ's sufferings was the time in which He sowed, and afterwards came the time of His reaping. He sowed in tears, He reaps with joy. Let us notice some of the most important fruits that spring from His sufferings :

(1) The satisfying of God's law, which was violated by man. Christ rendered full satisfaction to the law in its precept and penalty by His obedience unto death. The typical sacrifices could never do this, hence they had to be offered up from year to year for the space of 4000 years, till Christ came. But He, by the one offering of Himself satisfied all the requirements of the law. It does not need more; yea, it does not accept more. The typical sacrifices were repeated because of their imperfection and their inability to take away sin ; the sacrifice of Christ is not to be repeated because of its perfection. " He offered Himself once "—once for all. To offer up Christ again, as some pretend to do, would be an insult to heaven, an insult to the

justice of God, and an insult to Christ, who cried, triumphantly, '' It is finished.''

(2) The glory of God is another great fruit. '' I have glorified Thee on the earth.'' He did so by His finished work. '' I have finished the work which Thou gavest Me to do.'' Man by sin dishonoured God. How can he make amends for this ? He can never do it in his own person. But here is his remedy—Christ, as the glorious Substitute of the sinner, glorified the' Father by His sufferings. He rendered glory to God with large interest, so that God has now more glory in the salvation of the sinner—the chief of sinners—than He could have if man had never sinned or fallen. What an encouragement this is to poor sinners who are afraid that God will not save them because of the dishonour they have cast upon Him. Poor soul, God shall have no loss of glory in your salvation if you come to Him by Christ who glorified Him ; yea, He will have more glory, as we have said, than if you had never offended Him by your sins !

(3) Another fruit is eternal life. Christ did two things by His sufferings—(1) He satisfied the law, for the breach of it by sin. (2) He merited eternal life. He paid the debt, and at the same time purchased the blessings of salvation. The value of His work arises from the dignity of His Person as the God-man. God is surely more satisfied with Christ's atonement than He could be with the sinner though he were able to make atonement in his own person. This is the greatest encouragement to convinced sinners to come as they are to God by Christ, pleading His merits. Let not, then, your sins, however great, keep you back from coming. The devil would drive you to despair, for he

has no gospel, but God bids you come to Him, and assures you that though your sins be as scarlet, and red like crimson, they shall be as white as wool, "For the blood of Jesus Christ, His Son, cleanseth from all sin." —(1 John i. 7).

(4) Another fruit is the ingathering of sinners to Christ, and their conversion to God. "He shall see His seed." "And I, if I be lifted up from the earth, will draw all men unto Me." This is to be accomplished by the preaching of the Gospel, and the outpouring of the Holy Spirit, and His saving work in the souls of sinners. For this end God set up the Gospel ministry in His Church on earth. It shall answer, without fail, God's purpose as a means of grace and salvation. Let us notice this fruit and effect on the travail of Christ's soul:

(1) Christ saw of the fruit of His redemption before He suffered. For the space of 4000 years He was gathering in from generation to generation this kind of fruit. God gave a long credit to His Son on the ground of His promise before He actually paid the price of the redemption of His people. Christ's promise of working out redemption was accepted of the Father, knowing that He who promised was faithful to fulfil it. All the Old Testament believers received salvation on the ground of that promise. They received grace and glory.

The first of this kind of fruit was Abel, and probably his parents—Adam and Eve. Abel was the first of the human race that entered heaven. For his entering that glorious place he must have been a sight to the holy angels, who desire with delight to look into this redemption, and who rejoice at the repentance of even one sinner. And his own wonder and joy could be no less than that of the happy company he joined. Though the only solitary creature of a different race there, he felt himself at home in his Father's house. He could sing a song which the angels that never sinned could not sing. He was the first martyr, and the first to receive the crown. He received the crown, not on the ground of his own blood, which was shed for his faith in Christ, but on the ground of the blood of Christ, that was shadowed forth in the bloody sacrifice he offered up to God. This was the first ripe fruit Christ gathered in as the fruit of his soul travail. More fruit shall follow. It is only the beginning of the great harvest. "Ye shall see greater things than these."

From Abel to the time of the Flood the true religion ran in the line of the posterity of Seth, while the posterity of Cain, the persecutor and murderer, were left without the fear of God, and were practical atheists, if not professedly so. At the time when Enos was born, and for a considerable time thereafter, it appears that there was a large outpouring of the Spirit of grace and supplication, and a great revival of religion took place, for it is said, "Then began men to call on the name of the Lord" (Gen. iv. 26). There were praying people before then, but it would appear that now the number was largely increased. The true worship of God, of which prayer is an important part, was general, and it is supposed that at this time many families assembled together to worship publicly as a congregation. This is highly probable, as there is such notice taken of this time in Scripture. " *Then* men began to call upon the name of the Lord." Though it

is only the principal men of that age whose names are
given as possessed of true piety, yet we may well believe
that Christ gathered in a large harvest in that generation as the fruit of the travail of His soul.   Many shall
be seen in heaven whose names are not mentioned either
in the Bible or in Church History.

At the time of the Flood, Christ's flock was very
small, but there was a remnant.   Noah alone is mentioned as having found favour or grace in the sight of
the Lord.   As the effect of that favour he was righteous,
and as the effect of his being righteous " he walked with
God."   While God was provoked to sweep away from
the face of the earth that wicked generation of men, He
took good care to preserve a seed from which Christ
should see in after ages to the end of the world more
abundantly of the travail of His soul than He had
hitherto seen.   There were in the ark representatives
of all future nations.   Shem, Ham, and Japheth were
the seed that was to take root, spring up, and fill the
world with human beings.   Christ shall see of the
travail of His soul among all the peoples and nations of
the earth.   Though Ham was wicked, yet the command
was, " Destroy him not," for some, yea, many of his
posterity were to be saved.   He was spared because
Christ would see of the travail of His soul in his
posterity, however remote.   Wicked people are spared
for the same reason.   From the Flood, to the time of
the giving of the law through Moses, the true religion
still ran in the line of Shem, one of Noah's sons, and a
direct descendant of Seth.   During that period Christ
saw much of the travail of His soul.   Among the rich
harvest He reaped of saved persons, we find some who
were head and shoulders above others in eminent piety

and usefulness, such as Abraham, Isaac, and Jacob, and from Jacob sprang the twelve tribes of Israel. The promise of the coming Messiah was renewed to these patriarchs successively in their respective generations ; and as the Gospel was thus preached to them, it may on good grounds be believed that many were gathered into the fold of Christ as the fruit of the travail of His soul.

During the sojourn of Israel in Egypt they had many tokens of the Lord's lovingkindness, and the true religion was kept alive and shone in the midst of the darkness by which it was surrounded. They were brought into that heathen country in a very mysterious manner, and their deliverance out of it was marvellous. " It was the doing of the Lord, and wondrous in our eyes," and so it is in ours. Notwithstanding the decay that true piety had undergone in this idolatrous kingdom, Christ saw of the travail of His soul to some extent among them. When the Lord delivered the people out of their bondage in Egypt, the true religion was revived and firmly established in a manner which it had not hitherto attained. The people were formed into a nation, and organised into one congregation to worship the Lord at one place of worship—the Tabernacle. A written law was given them to guide and regulate them in their duties to God and man. The moral law, which was of binding obligation, was designed to remind them of their sinfulness, to deter them from sin, and to show that by the deeds of the law no flesh could be justified in the sight of God. The ceremonial law, which was only temporary, showed them the way of salvation by the blood of Christ, of

which the bloody sacrifices were a type, and the civil
law was meant to guide them in their civil transactions
with one another and with their heathen neighbours.
So far as these laws were concerned, everything was
now complete. At this time God entered into a
covenant with them, and they by profession complied
with the covenant. Though many of them broke the
covenant, yet Christ saw of the travail of his soul in a
considerable number of them, especially among the
young that came out of Egypt, and others that were
born in the wilderness. All that came out of Egypt,
except two—Caleb and Joshua—died in the wilderness.
Their children entered the promised land. The exclusion of the great bulk of the rest was because of their
unbelief (Heb. iii. 9). Some, however, who died there,
died in the faith and entered heaven. Among these
were Aaron and Moses and others. Christ had a
gleaning among them.

When the Lord brought the people of Israel into
the land of Canaan according to His promise, with
Caleb and Joshua of the old generation at their head,
and settled them in their inheritances, the true religion
advanced and made more progress than it had hitherto
done. It is probable that Christ had reaped a large
harvest from among the young generation that were
brought across the Jordan in such a miraculous manner.
In the time of the Judges, religion had its ups and
downs; but even then we find among the people some
who were stars of the first magnitude. The tribe of
Judah appears to be prominent in this respect. And
in the time of the Kings, up to the revolt of the ten
tribes under " Jeroboam, who made Israel to sin," the

true religion prospered considerably, and Christ saw of the travail of His soul very largely. It got an impetus when David began to reign, and went on prospering during his lifetime, and afterwards it was he that brought the ark that wandered, for a short time in the land of the Philistines, and for a much longer time in the land of Israel, to its resting place in Jerusalem.

During the greater part of Solomon's reign the Lord's cause was advancing more and more, but towards the end of his reign it was marred by the countenance he gave to idolatry. Though he was brought to repentance, the evil he did in this respect was visited with the Lord's displeasure and judgment, by rending the kingdom in the beginning of the reign of his son, Rehoboam, which resulted in the revolt of the ten tribes. This division continued till the captivity. Sin is the cause of division in the visible church. If all adhered to God and the rule of His word there would be no division. Jeroboam was given as king, like Saul, in God's anger, and the kings of Israel that succeeded him bore the same stigma. The kings of Judah, though not perfect, were, as a rule, godly and good kings. It was in their line that true religion was kept pure, till towards the end they fell into the mire of idolatry as deep as Israel, or deeper, and they followed Israel into captivity in Babylon, where for seventy long years they saw and bitterly felt the error of their ways, and learnt to say, " What have I to do any more with idols ?" They were sent into captivity that they might see that it was an evil and a bitter thing to have forsaken the Lord. The Lord did not utterly forsake them there, though they forsook Him. It was a token for good that He had some of His prophets with them in their banishment.

When they were, in God's good providence, brought back from captivity, the Lord's *cause* was revived. The division between Judah and Israel came to an end. All that came back went by the name *Jews*. The two parties—Israel and Judah—were melted in the furnace, and they were now blended into one party. Some will be for contriving methods for healing the divisions that are in the visible church. Many methods are proposed, but *true repentance* is that which succeeds in bringing the different sections of the Church together. There must be first a return to God and His word, and then a union between themselves will easily follow as the result.

A great revival of religion followed the deliverance from the captivity. The temple, which was so long in ashes, was rebuilt, the walls of Jerusalem were repaired, the worship of God was set up, and many sinners were converted and built up in the faith, and thus Christ saw much of His soul travail. It was the glory of the second temple that the Messiah Himself came to it, not in type as in the first temple, but personally in human nature. '' God was manifested in the flesh.'' The Church, which shone with such glorious lustre at and for some time after the rebuilding of the temple, was so benighted with unbelief and error that the Jews did not know their long looked for Messiah when He came. But there was a remnant among them that knew Him, and hailed His coming with delight. These were a seed from which Christ was in due time to reap a rich harvest. '' He shall see of the travail of His soul.''

This is a faithful promise, and is sure to be fulfilled. This fact is a strong evidence of the truth of Scripture. The promise of Christ's first coming took 4000 years in its accomplishment, but it was fulfilled, and so will all the other promises in the Bible be fulfilled.

Christ was seeing of the travail of His soul during His state of humiliation. He was sowing and reaping at the same time. It was then He called and gathered around Him those whom He afterwards, after His resurrection, sent forth as His apostles to preach the Gospel to all nations and to add to the canon of Scripture. It is a good sign in any age when Christ raises up Gospel ministers in His Church, though the number of other converts be small. It is a sign that He has a work for them to do, and that He will bless their labours.

Christ saw of the travail of His soul after He finished the work of redemption. He got the salvation of the Old Testament believers on the credit of His promise to finish the work. He gets the salvation of the New Testament believers, not on credit, but on the actual payment of the debt and the meriting of their salvation. The day of Pentecost was the beginning of the great harvest in this respect. Three thousand were gathered into His fold by means of one sermon preached by Peter. The Apostles went forth and preached everywhere, and there were numbers converted and added to the Church, even as many as should be saved. It would appear that every sermon was blessed to some. The word of the Lord was used in the conversion of each and all. We have no record of any being converted without God's word, which is a strong argument against

those who maintain that the heathen may be converted
to God without the Gospel. " How shall they believe
in Him of whom they have not heard?" The Apostle's
question implies an impossibility, and he spoke by the
inspiration of the Holy Spirit. " To the law and to
the testimony, if they speak not according to it, it is
because there is no light in them." " The Gospel is
the power of God unto salvation to every one that
believeth, to the Jew first, and to the Gentile also."
During the Apostles' lifetime Christ reaped an
abundant harvest of souls by the means of their
preaching. They preached the Gospel throughout the
most at least of the Roman dominions, which then
included the known world, and gathered as instruments
many sinners—Jews and Gentiles—to the fold of
Christ.

In the first century after the death of the Apostle
John—the last of the Apostles—errors began to creep
into the Church. The first of the apostolic fathers,
who saw and heard the Apostles, kept in the main
sound in the faith, but the fathers that succeeded these
brought errors into the Church, which were added to
from time to time thereafter, till the predicted great
apostasy came to a height in the 7th century. The
light of the Gospel was then put under a bushel, and
darkness covered the earth, and gross darkness the
people. The light of the Gospel was not, however,
extinguished in the world. It shone brightly in some
corners of the earth. It shone in some parts of France,
Switzerland, and even in some parts of the Highlands
of Scotland. When thick darkness covered the
Egyptians in Egypt, the people of Israel had light in

Goshen, where they dwelt.   So it was during the
" Dark Ages."   The Gospel is like the sun that always
shines somewhere in the world, and like the fire that
came down from heaven to burn the sacrifice: it never
went out till Christ came.   The Gospel shall continue
to shine in the world till Christ comes again.   It shall
answer the end for which it was sent to us.   By means
of it Christ shall see of the travail of His soul.   " It
shall not return unto Me void, but it shall accomplish
that which I please, and it shall prosper in the thing
whereto I sent it " (Is. lv. 11).

At the time of the Reformation in the 16th century
the Gospel began to shine more brightly, and to diffuse
its light more widely throughout the kingdoms of
Europe, dispelling the darkness that so long covered
these countries.   " He shall see of the travail of His
soul."

III. *That He shall be satisfied with the fruit of
His soul travail.*

He shall be so satisfied that He shall not receive any
addition to the number of the saved.   The door of
mercy shall be shut forever, and although some would
knock at that door, it shall never be opened.   All the
members of the mystical body of Christ are gathered in
and united to Him.   The Church which is His body is
said to be the fulness of Christ (Eph. iv. 13).

It will take to the end of the world till all shall be
taken in.   Then the world itself, which some compare
to a scaffolding set up to a house when building, and
taken down when the house is finished—the world itself
shall be reduced to nothing when the spiritual building

is completed. This is the day of our opportunity, and the Gospel calls upon sinners to come to Christ to be saved; but the call stops at death, it will not follow sinners into eternity. As it was in this world that Christ finished the work of redemption, it is in this world that the redemption is applied to those that believe in Christ. Seek, then, the Holy Spirit to apply the redemption to you, and seek the Lord while He is to be found, and call upon Him while He is near. **AMEN**.

XIII.

A Free Salvation

" I counsel thee to buy of Me gold tried in the fire, that thou mayest be rich; and white raiment, that thou mayest be clothed, and that the shame of thy nakedness do not appear; and anoint thine eyes with eye-salve, that thou mayest see."— Rev. iii. 18.

THIS is a part of Christ's address to the Laodicean Church, in which He gives the best counsel, offers the choicest blessings, which sinners of mankind may have, on the cheapest and most gracious terms.

In considering the text, I propose to notice a few particulars—

    I. The party that Christ addresses.

    II. The manner of His address.

    III. The blessings He proposes, and offers.

    IV. The terms on which these blessings may be
        had.

According to this arrangement, let us notice—

I. *The party that Christ addresses here.*

He addresses (1) the Laodicean Church. It was to that church the words contained in the passage were originally addressed, and therefore it is necessary that we should notice her first as the party addressed. Let us then take a brief survey of her condition and character as described by Him who is the Searcher of

8

all hearts, and who knows the real condition and character of all men infinitely better than they do themselves.

Christ describes the Laodicean Church as (1) luke-warm. She was not professedly against Christ, nor was she, on the other hand, practically for Him. Whatever was her position once, she now takes up a neutral ground, a position which the Saviour tells in another portion of Scripture is inconsistent with a state of grace. '' He that is not with Me is against Me '' (Matt. xii. 30). Nor does He own her in her lukewarm state. He threatens to spue her out of His mouth, as lukewarm water, which is nauseous and unpleasant to the stomach of man ; and if He really do that, woe unto her, for He will never again return to her in mercy ! (2) He describes her as to her own thoughts of herself. She has good thoughts of herself, but she is nothing the better of that, but a great deal the worse. Let us hear what she thinks and says of herself : '' I am rich, and increased with goods, and have need of nothing '' ! If true, thou oughtest to be in heaven, and not on earth ; but if false, what a mercy that thou art still on earth, where thou mayest obtain mercy from the Lord ! But this is thy own testimony concerning thyself. Let us see if it agree with that of Him who is the true and faithful witness. What does He say regarding thee ? (ver. 3) '' and knowest not that thou art wretched, and miserable, and poor, and blind, and naked.'' How different are Christ's thoughts of her from her own. Which must be true ? Assuredly Christ's. Let God be true, and every man who gainsays what He says a liar. Her real condition and character, as described by Christ, she must abide by. Her good thoughts of her-

self through self-conceit was the cause of her lukewarm-
ness, and she had these good thoughts of herself because
she was blind, and consequently could not see her sad
condition. Christ in the first place addresses the
Laodicean Church.

2. Christ addresses here all who profess His name,
whose real state and character, in a spiritual point of
view, are identical with the state and character of the
Laodicean Church. And how many such are there in
the visible church! How many profess to be Christ's,
and to be on His side, who are yet as lukewarm in their
profession as that church was! And their spiritual
indifference evinces their real spiritual condition. It
clearly evinces that they are strangers to the saving
grace of God, and that, whatever they may think of
themselves, they are in the sight of God as "wretched,
miserable, poor, blind, and naked," as she was. Oh,
that all such would in a day of mercy take this to heart,
and seek grace ere it be too late—ere Christ spue them
out of His mouth, and reject them for ever!

3. Christ addresses here all sinners within the
boundaries of the visible church who make no open
profession of His name at all; yea, all such in all places
and ages to whom the Gospel of salvation comes. The
character of the Laodicean Church, as "wretched,
miserable, poor, blind, and naked," is that of all
sinners by nature. It is the character of us all. Our
state by nature is a state of sin and misery. We are
poor, as we are without Christ, without hope, and without God in the world. We are poor, having nothing to
pay the great debt which we owe to God's justice. We
are wretched, as devoid of the holy image of God, which
we lost by the Fall. We are naked, having lost our

first righteousness, and having none now in our natural
state to defend us from the wrath which is to come, and
which even now abides upon us, or to make us accept-
able to God. We are blind, for Satan, the god of this
world, has blinded our spiritual eyes. This blindness
has not been effected since we entered this world
(though confirmed). We were born blind. We
are thus spiritually blind, and cannot see our
ruined condition. Christ would have us believe
all this and more; and He for that end addresses all
sinners of mankind to whom this Gospel of salvation
comes.

II. *The manner of His address: " I counsel thee."*

In which we may notice (1) Christ's great condescension. Oh, is it not a great condescension on the
part of Him who is King of kings, and Lord of lords,
to stoop down from His high and glorious throne in
order to speak in love and mercy to such great sinners—
enemies and loathsome creatures as we are! But this
He does in the manner in which He here addresses us.
(2) His great compassion in remembering us in our low
condition. He says (though not expressly) here, as He
said on another occasion: " I have great compassion
on the multitude." Yes, Christ has great compassion
on us in our misery, or He would never say to us, " I
counsel thee." (3) His friendliness. An enemy would
not advise us for our good. Christ counsels us for our
good—eternal good; and herein He shows that He is
our best Friend, and, though we are His enemies, yet
He shows Himself most friendly to us. He offers to be
our Friend—the Friend that sticketh closer than a
brother. He speaks to us in a most friendly manner.

He gives us a friendly counsel, and thereby manifests that He is indeed, what others in a taunting manner said He was, "A friend of publicans and sinners." Oh, how amply He proved to be in reality such! And here is one great proof of the fact. (4) His suitableness to counsel us. We are not sufficient to advise ourselves in the important matter of salvation. Our heart is deceitful above all things. If we go by the counsels and guidance of such a heart, it is sure to lead us in the wrong direction. We shall go further and further away from God, and from our own happiness, and vain is the help of all fallen men unless Christ undertake for us. But, blessed be His great name, He does undertake for us, and He is perfectly fitted to give us counsel. He is so (1) because He is the omniscient Jehovah. As such He knows all things. He knows our real state—all our needs and wants, and He knows what is good for us—the best method we should adopt in order to get that which would be for our true happiness in time and in eternity. This makes Him most fitted to counsel us, poor, blind sinners, who are but of yesterday, and know nothing. (2) He is most fitted to counsel us because He is the All-wise God. In Him dwell all the treasures of wisdom, as well as those of knowledge. He is called Wisdom itself, as He is the great author of all true wisdom, and the infinite Fountain whence His intelligent creatures, who possess any true wisdom, derived it. Then as the All-wise God He is perfectly fitted to counsel us—foolish sinners, who, if left to ourselves, will choose, not that which is good, but that which is evil. Oh, our need of Christ to make us wise unto salvation! I shall mention only one other qualification which makes the Saviour most fitted to counsel us, poor, frail sinners, and that is His great sympathy. He can sympathise with us. Our great and glorious Counsellor is God in our nature. He assumed flesh of our flesh, and bone of our bone, yea, the whole nature of man—a true body, and a reasonable soul. One of the reasons for which He took to Himself our nature was, that He might be able to sympathise with sinful men. That was not, of course, the great reason, but it was one reason. Though in Him there was no sin, yet He took the guilt of sinners upon Him—that of His own people, and He had bitter experience of the ill-desert of sin—the wrath of God—which did beat upon Him in most awful fury. And seeing that we are by nature exposed to that wrath, He sympathises with us, and He is able to do so from the fact that He felt in an awful manner the wrath under which we are. Christ is perfectly fitted in every point of view to counsel sinners for their eternal welfare. He was set apart and appointed by His Father to be our great Counsellor, and among the various names He has is that of Counsellor. As such the Father says: " This is My well-beloved Son, in whom I am well pleased : hear ye Him.''

III. *The blessings that Christ proposes and offers to sinners:*

These, as brought before us in the text, are three in number—(1) Gold tried in the fire ; (2) white raiment : and (3) eye-salve. We shall consider each in their order :

1. " Gold tried in the fire." This is the first blessing spoken of, and it is not put first perchance, but of deliberate purpose. What are we to understand

by the gold? I think it means, in the first place, Christ Himself. Gold is the most precious metal, so it is well fitted, so far, to represent Christ as the most precious Person. " Unto you that believe, He is precious." Gold is most enriching. One who possesses abundance of gold may be said, in a worldly point of view, to be rich. Infinitely richer is the man that has the heavenly gold—Christ—for his treasure and portion ; and that Christ may be meant by gold here may be confirmed by Scripture, our only authority. Besides the many allusions to this effect to be seen in this book of Revelation and Song of Solomon, we read of the unsearchable riches of Christ (Eph. iii. 8), as also the treasure hid in the earth (Matt. xiii. 44), the pearl of great price (Matt. xiii. 46), and many other passages to the same effect. Let us then understand in the first intention by gold Christ Himself. But the gold spoken of is a gold " tried in the fire." So was the gold, Christ. Never was any other gold tried in the fire as He was. He was tried in the fire of men's hatred, malice, wrath, and persecution, even unto death. He was tried in the fire of Satan's temptations, and He was tried in the fire of His Father's wrath. " Awake, O sword, against My Shepherd, and against the man (Christ) who is My fellow . . . I will smite the Shepherd." " It pleased the Father to bruise Him " ; and who can describe the awful manner in which Christ was " tried " as the heavenly gold ! None can except Himself. He felt the trial : His strong cries, tears, agony, bloody sweat, and death on the accursed tree, bespeak how He was " tried." And all this He underwent that sinners who are spiritually poor might be made rich (2 Cor. viii. 9). Christ was tried, and He stood the trial. He proved to the last that He was pure gold. He was not put in the fire of trial (as His people are) in order to purify Him. No, for He ever was, is, and shall be '' the Holy One of God,'' '' harmless, undefiled, and separate from sinners.'' '' In Him there was no sin,'' but He was smitten for the iniquity of His guilty people!

But by gold may be understood the graces of the Spirit, whereby Christ adorns and beautifies His Church. Thus we read in Ps. xlv. 13, '' The King's daughter is all glorious within: her clothing is of wrought gold.'' And this is a far richer ornament than can be had by the daughters and sons of any earthly king without an interest in Christ, how much soever they may adorn themselves with the gold that shall perish. But it may be asked how can the gold, taken in that sense, be said to be '' tried in the fire''? (1) Inasmuch as Christ, who secured it for sinners, was tried. It was tried in Him. (2) To show its superlative excellency above any natural endowment, or anything whereby Christless souls try to enrich or adorn their immortal spirits. The blessings of grace are to be understood thus as spoken of under another similitude. We read in Is. xxv. 6, of these as '' wines well refined,'' indicating the best wines. So on the same principle may gold, in the sense in which we now take it, be said to be '' tried in the fire,'' declaring it to be the best gold. And it may be added that as sure as this grace was tried in Christ, it will be tried in His people—tried in all who are made partakers thereof. We read of the trial of faith—a grace more precious than any earthly gold; and as faith is tried, all other graces are tried also, and that according to their measure.

2. " White raiment." This is the second blessing that Christ offers to sinners, and counsels them to get. We need raiment to clothe us, as well as gold to enrich us. This the Saviour tells us. He says that we are naked as well as poor. We have nothing to cover our naked, guilty and sinful souls—nothing to defend us from the wrath of God. And if we think, as it is natural for us to think, that we have any such garment, it is but " filthy rags." And how can we appear before the just and holy God in such rags ? We dare not do it, at least with a view to our acceptance. It is true that we must appear before His judgment seat whether in these filthy rags or clothed with a better garment. We cannot do with our own. But we are left without an excuse, for there is a better provided for such as we are. Here it is displayed, and offered by the Saviour of sinners. It is a " white raiment "—the righteousness of Jesus Christ—not, indeed, His personal righteousness, but that which He wrought out by His obedience—active and passive—for naked sinners of mankind. Our raiment is black—as black as sin could make it : His is " white." There is no stain on it. It stands the justice of God, His holiness, and purity. It is the best robe, better than that worn by our first parents in their state of innocency, better than that wherewith the holy angels appear around the throne in the highest glory. It is better than these, being wrought out by Christ, who is the brightness of the Father's glory, and the express image of His person. It is in an eminent sense the " white " and the best raiment. In it the chief of sinners may stand justified in the sight of God, who is a consuming fire against sin and against sinners.

3. " Eye-salve." This is the third blessing, and we need it as much as the other two ; for we are, as Christ says, " blind," as well as poor and naked. Here is an antidote for our blindness—the only one that can restore our spiritual vision. Then, how important and desirable to have it ! Without it we must continue in our blindness for ever ! There is no other remedy for us. And what is it ? It is the Holy Spirit, the third Person of the glorious Trinity (1 John ii. 20). It is the Spirit that applies Christ's salvation to sinners, and in doing so, He first opens their eyes to see, on the one hand, their own ruined condition, and, on the other, the gracious provision which God made in Christ for them. It was for want of this blessed " eye-salve " that the Laodicean Church was so very blind that she imagined herself to be in such a good and independent state as she said she was, while in truth she was in the sad condition which Christ described, and it is for want thereof that many in her condition think equally well of themselves. Now it is not enough that we hear about this eye-salve which Christ commends to us. We must, in order to receive our spiritual sight, anoint our eyes therewith. This is what He commands us to do : " Anoint thine eyes with eye-salve, that thou mayest see." In a secondary sense it may mean also the word of God—contained in the blessed Bible—in connection with which the Spirit opens the eyes of the spiritually blind. The Spirit uses the word of the law to open our eyes to behold our lost condition, to see our sinfulness. " By the law is the knowledge of sin." But the Spirit uses the word of the Gospel to reveal Christ to us, to unite us to Him by faith. The word as a means, through the agency of the Spirit,

may thus be meant, and we have Scripture authority for it: " The commandment of the Lord is pure, enlightening the eyes" (Ps. xix. 8). The word of itself cannot, it is true, effect this great work. It cannot of itself open the eyes of the spiritually blind. This requires the almighty power of Jehovah. The Spirit is equal with the Father and with the Son in nature, power, and glory ; and He it is that has been appointed, and that has undertaken, from all eternity, to perform this work —to open the eyes of sinners to see their lost condition, to enlighten their minds in a saving knowledge of Christ, and to apply to them His redemption. Oh, our great need of this all-essential " eye-salve "—our need of the Holy Spirit, without whom we cannot be saved !

IV. *The terms on which we may have the blessings of salvation:*

" Buy of Me," Christ says, in which words we may observe—(1) Of whom we are to buy them. We are to buy them of Christ. " Buy of *Me*." Many would buy the blessings of salvation of the law. This was the way with others (Rom. x. 3), and it is the way that is natural to us all. For we are by nature under the covenant of works, and not till we are by grace—and it is grace alone that will do it—shut in to Christ will we cease to buy salvation of the law. The terms of the law are more than we can comply with in our fallen state. It requires perfect obedience, and satisfaction, which is as difficult for us to render as to create a world, which we never think we are able to do. Others would buy salvation of God's people (Matt. xxv. 8). These err as much. God's people have nothing to spare. They are in their own experience but poor and needy— spiritual beggars—much needing daily, yea, constantly, to crawl up to the market of free grace to buy of Christ, who makes them welcome, and sells to them according to their need.

It is of Christ we are to buy. He alone is the great storehouse, and Disposer of these blessings. It pleased the Father that all the fulness of grace which we as sinners need should dwell in Him. Neither is there salvation in any other; for there is no other name given under heaven among men whereby we *must* be saved. All His people have received of His fulness; and of Him we also are counselled to buy. '' Buy of Me.''

(2) But observe the terms on which we are to buy. What are these? '' Without money, and without price '' (Is. lv. 1). Most wonderful buying, and most gracious terms! But so it is: '' The free gift of God is life eternal through Jesus Christ our Lord'' (Rom. vi. 23). '' By grace are ye saved, through faith, and that not of yourselves; it is the gift of God'' (Eph. ii. 8). The terms are, '' Without money, and without price,'' according to these and many other passages of God's word, and according to the arrangement of the covenant of grace. And, Oh, if it were otherwise, who could have the least ground of hope to be saved? None of our fallen race. Here is our only ground of hope. This is the Gospel, the glad tidings of great joy. Come forward to this market of free grace, and sinners, even the very chief, buy of Christ on His own most gracious terms, '' without money, and without price.'' Be not shy in your approach, if you feel your great need of salvation, though you have no money. He bids you come with an empty purse and empty hand. '' Ye that have no money, come.''

XIV.

The Gospel the Power of God

"For the preaching of the cross is to them that perish foolishness; but unto us which are saved it is the power of God." —1 Cor. i. 18.

IT appears from this chapter that there were divisions in the church at Corinth, and there are several parties mentioned. Some said, "I am of Paul": others, "I am of Apollos": a third party said, "I am of Cephas": while a fourth affirmed, "I am of Christ." The Apostle beseeches them by the name of the Lord Jesus Christ that there should be no such divisions among them, but that they should "be perfectly joined together in the same mind and in the same judgment."

Now, these divisions were caused by a departure from the doctrines of the Gospel—of that Gospel which Paul and those other apostles preached to them, and this has been the cause of divisions in the church in every age. There were no divisions in the church originally, but when men forsook the faith, or as Paul says the doctrines of the cross of Christ, then the divisions arose. In our text the Apostle tells why some forsook those doctrines, and the reason he gives is that they were foolishness to them, and then he proceeds to tell a more awful thing. He says that those to whom the preaching of the cross was foolishness were to be lost for ever in eternity. A truly awful thing! and a thing as true of our own age as it was at the time of the Apostle. Many in this age bear the mark of those that shall be lost for ever, and that mark is a departure from the fundamental doctrines of the Gospel. No one need envy those that forsake the truth. Even in this world they bear the mark of the eternally lost, and a very black mark it is. The Apostle Paul, in one of his epistles to Timothy, foretold that such would happen, especially after he left this world to receive the crown of righteousness which the Lord was to give him. He said the time was drawing near when people would not endure sound doctrine, but after their own lusts they would heap to themselves teachers, having itching ears, and these teachers, instead of preaching the Gospel, would preach fables— setting forth opinions that had no foundation in the Word of God. In endeavouring to direct your attention to this portion of God's Word, I shall consider : —

    I. The preaching of the cross.
    II. That the preaching of the cross is foolishness to
        those that are lost.
    III. That the preaching of the cross is the power of
        God to them that are saved : that which is a
        savour of death unto death to some is a
        savour of life unto life to others.

I. *What is meant by " the cross" here?*

It does not mean the material cross upon which Christ died, for it would be but a poor Gospel to preach the instrument by which Christ was put to death. As well might one take Judas Iscariot, who betrayed Christ, as a subject for preaching ; or it would be as reasonable to extol and praise the crown of thorns as a subject for preaching : but that would be a despising of Him who endured in order that we might be saved. It is clear that the Apostle does not here mean the material cross upon which Christ laid down His life. In the Church of Rome a great deal is made of the material cross. It has a great place in their public worship, and on their death-beds a cross is set up before the eyes of their people .that they may look to it in their last moments. They are directed to look upon that cross as their saviour, instead of to Him who suffered and died on that instrument of death. The apostles never used material crosses in preaching the Gospel. You may examine the whole of the Acts of the Apostles, and you will find no mention of a material cross connected with their work as ambassadors of Christ. In searching for the origin of the material cross in the Church of Christ, we find that it was brought in, after the apostles left the earth, by the enemies of Christ and not by His friends: and not only so, but it is kept in by His enemies to this day! It is a most serious matter for people to maintain in a Christian church anything brought in by the enemies of Christ. The cross was introduced first by placing it on the top of the church, then at door, and at last it was taken inside. The devil is very cunning. First he stands on the top of a church or sits at the door, and says, " I am an ornament," but when he gets inside he shows that he is more than an ornament. The cross should never have existed in this world except as it was permitted in the providence of God to be the instrument of Christ's death, for it was not at all by chance that the cross was so used. It had been foreordained from all eternity that Christ should die the cursed death of the tree, and this He Himself foretold shortly before His death : that He would fall into the hands of wicked men who would deliver Him up to be crucified. Now, a word or two more ere I leave this question of the material cross having no place in the worship of God. Some say that it is a symbol. A symbol of what? Oh, a symbol of Christ's death. No. To say such a thing is to confess ignorance. Even little children going to school can tell you from the Shorter Catechism that the symbol of Christ's death is the Lord's Supper, which He Himself instituted. "As often as ye do this, ye show forth the Lord's death till He comes." What a pity it is that people who have had the Bible in their hands and in their homes so long should be under the delusion that the instrument upon which the Saviour laid down His life should be the symbol of His death. I tell such people that they are ignorant of the Word of God, and I tell them that, not from any ill-feeling, but from sincere pity and from a desire that they should learn.

What, then, is meant by "the cross" here? It means the doctrines of the Gospel of Christ. The Apostle speaks of the preaching of the cross. "Christ sent me not to baptise but to preach the Gospel : not with wisdom of words, lest the cross of Christ should be made of none effect," that is, lest the sufferings of Christ revealed in the Gospel should be made of none effect. The Gospel is Christ Himself, for the Gospel is not preached unless Christ is preached. The Apostle says in another place, "Whom we preach, warning every man, and teaching every man." Christ is the sum and substance of the Gospel, and, from what is left to us of the teaching of the apostles during their time on earth, we know that Christ was the central point of their preaching, that He was the all and in all of their preaching. "Whom we preach." Christ in His Divine Person, in His two natures, in His threefold office, in His finished work, in His death, in His resurrection, and in His ascension to heaven. Not only that, but they preached Him also in His work of atonement. "For He made Him Who knew no sin, to be sin for us : that we might be made the righteousness of God in Him." In the preaching of the

Gospel, Christ is preached; not a picture of Him, not a representation of Him. No: but Christ Himself. His atonement is preached in the Gospel as that which satisfied Divine justice and as the only ground of reconciling sinners to God. There is no other foundation upon which a sinner can be saved but the atoning sacrifice of the Son of God in human nature, and that ought to satisfy the guiltiest sinner, because it satisfied Him against Whom we sinned. It ought to satisfy the guiltiest sinner on earth, because it satisfied the Divine law in all its demands: and so Paul, who wrote this epistle, says, "This is a faithful saying and worthy of all acceptation, that Jesus Christ came into the world to save sinners, of whom I am chief." Ah, my friends, where could our hope be if there were no atonement made to satisfy God's law. There would be no hope at all. In my endeavour to preach the Gospel I would try to urge myself and my hearers to think more of the atonement of Christ—to come oftener to the atonement. It was made to be used, and not to be despised. There is in the preaching of the Gospel a free and full forgiveness of sins offered to all who come to Christ and receive Him as their Saviour. If you come to Christ you will hear God through His Word saying to your soul, "Thy sins are forgiven thee," and what a blessing that is! The Psalmist speaks of the man whose sins are forgiven as the only blessed man in this world. Christ Himself, in His last discourse to His disciples before He ascended to heaven, commanded that repentance and remission of sins should be preached in His name unto all nations. What a privilege we have in the land of the Gospel! May God arouse the careless to think of their great privileges. Forgiveness of sins is offered to every guilty

9

sinner. Yea, all the blessings of Christ's purchase are set forth in the Gospel, and offered to sinners, to whom nothing belongs by nature but sin and misery. Instead of this the Gospel offers forgiveness and happiness, grace and peace. The apostles often in their prayers for the churches desired for them "grace and peace": not only grace in this world, but also glory in the world to come, and they did so because in preaching they were to set forth all the blessings that God offers in the Gospel to sinners. But notwithstanding all this, sinners refuse to accept these great and glorious privileges. If left to themselves they are unwilling to part with their sins and misery for happiness and forgiveness. Some people ascribe great power to the will of man as he is by nature, but that is a heresy that was refuted and confuted centuries ago by great men of God. Yet it is revived in this age, and as in centuries gone by you find many to believe it. Ah! it is a great pity that people will not make use of their boasted free-will in accepting of Christ; but, no: they will have none of Him. What, then, is the use of their free-will? What is the use of a giant that sleeps all his days? The free-willers are at variance with the Word of God, for the carnal mind is enmity against God. As there is darkness in the mind there is rebellion in the will, and till that rebellion is removed by the effectual work of the Holy Spirit the sinner is not willing to accept of the Saviour.

II. The Apostle here tells us that the Gospel in the estimation of some is foolishness, and if people do not declare this with their tongue they proclaim it by their practice. Tell them there is no salvation by the works of the law, and they will not believe you. Tell them they have only to receive Christ in the Gospel, and it is foolishness to them. Especially was this true in the time of the apostles. So-called philosophers and others who considered themselves wise men scoffed at the Christians for trusting to a crucified Saviour, to a Saviour who could not save Himself. It was foolishness to them, and it is foolishness to those who, while giving their assent to the truth of the Gospel, go about like the Jews of old, seeking to establish their own righteousness. But who are they to whom the preaching of the cross is foolishness? Ah! Paul tells us. It is to them that perish : not only to them that are in a lost state now, but who are sure to perish eternally. The Gospel in its freeness and fulness is regarded by them as foolishness. That is their mark, a black mark, and a mark borne by many in this generation. It is a fearful thing to be lost for ever. But perish eternally you must, unless Christ becomes precious to you. There is no escape. Ah! how people allow the bustle and noise of this world to blind their eyes and close their ears from seeing, and hearing, and thinking of being eternally lost. Take care, then, that you will not allow the world to come between you and the salvation of your immortal soul. How many there are in this age to whom the cross of Christ is foolishness! How many in this country. It is with grief of heart we think and speak of it, and we are regarded as enemies because we endeavour to warn sinners who are on the brink of hell, but better far to try to arouse them to a sense of their danger than to cry, Peace, peace, when there is no peace. It is an awful thing for a congregation to pay a salary to a minister to keep them on the road to hell. It is madness, terrible madness, and yet it is done by many congregations in Scotland to-day, though not intentionally. The language of the congregation to their minister is, Keep us at ease, do not tell us the truth.

Ah! they do not require a shepherd to keep them from Christ and to drive them to hell: they will go there sure enough. People don't like to hear about hell. It is better to hear of it now than to experience its torments throughout eternity. It is said of Angus of the Hills that the portion of God's Word that was first blessed to him by bringing him under concern and driving him to Christ was, " Behold, the day cometh that shall burn like an oven." That man heard about hell in a day of mercy and escaped its torments, while those who do not wish to hear of it in this world will have an eternity to experience it.

III. The preaching of the Gospel has another effect on another class of hearers. They form a better estimate of it, for the preaching of the Gospel is to them that are saved the power of God. It is not the same view those that perish and those that are saved take of the Gospel at all. They are of quite opposite opinions about it. What is life to God's people is death to them that perish. The Apostle Paul says in another place, " For I am not ashamed of the Gospel of Christ, for it is the power of God unto salvation to every one that believeth, to the Jew first and also to the Gentile," that is, it is the only powerful means that God appointed for the salvation of sinners, and every other way of human invention is of no power at all to save sinners. Have you ever felt the power of the Gospel affecting your heart or influencing your mind? Well, God's people have felt it to be the power of God unto salvation. One word of the Gospel coming in the hand of the Spirit is full of power. It puts life where there is but death, and it revives life where life seems to be extinct. Ah! my friends, the Gospel has power. You hear people say sometimes that the power of the pulpit is gone, and indeed in this age it has gone to a very large extent; but it has not gone from the pulpit where Christ's true messengers are. We maintain that while the pulpit may have to a great extent lost its power, yet the Gospel has not lost its power. People ought to make a distinction between the Gospel and the pulpit. The pulpit may be filled with men who do not know the Gospel at all. The Gospel is and shall be the power of God unto salvation. You will notice how the Apostle draws a distinction between the two classes, between those to whom the Gospel is foolishness and those to whom it is the power of God. He speaks of the former class as "them that perish," that is in the future; but in speaking of the latter class he says "them that are saved," that is, them that are even now saved. This distinction clearly shows that there are two classes of people under the Gospel even in this world, viz., those to whom it is foolishness or those that shall perish, and those to whom it is the power of God or those that are even already saved.

I leave these things with you. What do you think upon during the day? What do you think yourself of these things? For myself I have to say that there is not a Sabbath I live but I have to think upon the importance of eternity with regard to myself and others. What do you think of it?

May He bless His Word!

XV.

Natural Unwillingness

"And ye will not come to Me, that ye might have life."—
John v. 40.

THIS is a charge that Christ brings against the Jews
to whom He declares His message. They professed
great respect for the Scriptures, and, as Christ tells
them here, they thought that in the Scriptures they
had eternal life. Now, in endeavouring to address
you briefly from these words of the Saviour, I shall
notice :—

I. That there is an unwillingness in men by
   nature to come to Christ for eternal life.

II. The cause of this unwillingness.

III. That before any sinner will come to Christ
   this unwillingness must be removed.

I. *There is an unwillingness in all sinners by nature.*

Not only was this true of the Jews, who, when He
came to His own, received Him not, but it is true of
all sinners wherever they are throughout the world.
They are unwilling to come to Christ to be saved. This
is the teaching of Scripture, although some who are
wise above what is written ascribe great power to the
will of man as he is by nature to believe in Christ.
Now you will observe Christ traces their unbelief to
the will, and whatever men may say, in ascribing power
to the will of man as he is in his natural state to believe
in Christ, this is what Christ, who knows what is in

man, says of the will of man. This point has been in
past ages a matter of controversy between those who
advocated what is called the doctrine of free-will, and
those who held Scriptural views regarding the will of
man in his fallen state. This point was very much
discussed at the time of the Reformation. The
Romanists held that the will of man by nature had
some power to believe and repent, and they held this
view, as it was held long before them by the " School-
men." It was very natural for them to ascribe some
power to the will of man, as he was by nature, to
believe in Christ ; and this was what was taught
regarding the will in what are known as the dark ages.
Shortly after the Reformation, again, the power of the
will was advocated by those who held Arminian views,
and Arminians to this day hold the same view concerning the will of man by nature. Of course they admit
that he needs the help of God's grace, but that he is
able to believe and repent himself. This is not the
teaching of the Reformed Churches, as you will find
in our Standards—the Confession of Faith, and the
Larger and Shorter Catechisms. You will find that
the Reformers set down in those subordinate standards
Scriptural views regarding the will of man, and until
a few years ago this view, which is founded upon
Scripture, and which is contained in the Standards
of the Presbyterian Church of Scotland, was
held in the early Free Church, but there was
a change made, as you all know, in 1892, when
those who had imbibed and adopted Arminian views
were in the majority. The Creed of the Free Church
was then changed by the introduction of the Declaratory Act, and that Act was made purposely that

ministers might teach the power of free-will, and deny
predestination and other important doctrines of the
word of God. If you read for yourselves the preamble
to the Act, you will find that it was made to remove
difficulties and scruples in the case of some who would
not take office in the Church under the Creed of the
Church. No one can deny that the Act was made for
the very purpose that Arminianism, and even
Pelagianism, which is worse, might be preached in the
pulpits of Scotland ; so that the creed of one of the
largest Presbyterian churches in Scotland is Arminian
to the core, and even Pelagian : for the difference
between Pelagianism and Arminianism is that Pelagians
deny that sin and the fall of Adam affected his
posterity and that children are born into this world in
a state of sin, whereas Arminians admit that sin and
the fall of Adam affected to some extent his posterity,
and that they come into this world with a nature
somewhat tainted by sin.

It is very lamentable, my friends, that one of the
largest Presbyterian churches in Scotland should have
committed herself to such a creed as this. We do not
assert that every minister in that Church will teach the
errors her creed allows ; but it is to be feared that the
coming generation will be taught all the errors that the
Act allows. We are bound to point this out, and to
warn the people of that which is not according to
Scripture. This much, then, on the first head, viz.,
that there is an unwillingness in all sinners by nature
to come to Christ, and that the will is the very obstacle
and cause that keeps them from coming to Him. This
is what Christ tells here.

II. *There is a cause for this unwillingness, which we are now to enquire into.*

How is it that they are unwilling to come to Christ and be saved? As far as we can learn from God's word, the cause is the depravity of man's nature, and in the portion of Scripture we have read—that is, in the third chapter of the Epistle of Paul to the Romans —there is a description given which shows that all men are depraved in their nature. Not only are we sinful in our practice, but even by nature we are all sinful. Now this depravity of nature is total—that is, it affects not merely some faculties of our souls, but it affects all the faculties and powers of our souls. Arminians seem to think that the will at least escaped, but this is not the teaching of Scripture, and the teaching of Christ here shows that no faculty of the soul escaped the ruin that was brought upon our nature by sin. This also is the experience of those taught of God, for you find the Apostle Paul making this confession: " In me, that is in my flesh, no good thing dwelleth"; and he means by flesh there his sinful nature as he came into the world, even apart from the actual transgression of God's law. He says in the Epistle to the Ephesians, " We were by nature the children of wrath, even as others." Now this is the teaching of Scripture, and how terrible is it of man to gainsay what God declares in His word! The nature of man is wholly sinful. You will find that the West-minster Divines taught this in the Standards of the Church, in the Confession of Faith, and in the Larger and Shorter Catechisms. In that precious little book, the Shorter Catechism, the question is asked, " What is the sinfulness of that estate whereinto man fell ?" And the answer is: " The sinfulness of that estate

whereinto man fell consists in the guilt of Adam's first
sin, the want of original righteousness, and the corruption of the whole nature, which is commonly called
original sin, together with all actual transgressions
which proceed from it." The statements of the
Confession of Faith and Catechisms of our
Church were not only designed to declare the
truth, but also to refute error, and the answer
to this question had two errors in particular to
oppose. The first was the error of Pelagius, who taught
that Adam's posterity had no federal connection with
him, and were not affected by Adam's sin, and to meet
that error the Westminster Divines placed as the first
thing " the guilt of Adam's first transgression." And
this is in accordance with what the Apostle Paul says :
" We were by nature the children of wrath, even as
others." And to say " by nature " is the same as to
say, " as we came into this world," and in that state
we are not only depraved but guilty, and without a change
of state and nature we are exposed to the wrath of God.
The next thing mentioned is " the want of original
righteousness," and what is meant by that is, that man
in his original state had conformity to the law of God :
bore His image : but that, through sin and the fall, he
had lost, not only for himself, but also for his posterity,
that conformity or original righteousness that we had
in the first creation. The Roman Catholic Church
denies that the original righteousness here spoken of
was a part of the image of God in man. Their view of
the subject is that it was after God had created man
in His own image that He super-added this original
righteousness, and on that account their view leads to
this, that after baptism children are holy, and that the

righteousness they have got is no doubt the righteousness which God super-added along with His own image. But the teaching of Scripture is that " there is none righteous ; no, not one " ; and the Apostle had in view the righteousness spoken of here—the original righteousness in which God created us—for the image of Christ consisted in knowledge, righteousness, and holiness.

The third thing that is true of our state by nature (we are speaking of the cause of our unwillingness to believe in Christ) is the corruption of our whole nature, and the word " whole " was put in here to meet and confute the doctrines of Arminians, who, while admitting that man was sinful, held that the depravity was not total, not universal. As I have already stated, you will find that the Westminster Divines were careful not only to declare sound doctrines, but at the same time to refute error, and you will find that those who have adopted Arminian and Pelagian views care very little for the Confession of Faith or for the Shorter Catechism. The Declaratory Act was framed so as to relieve ministers of preaching sound doctrine, and to give them liberty to preach error ; and when we consider that every statement of the Confession of Faith and of the Larger and Shorter Catechisms is founded upon the word of God, is it not a sad thing that people should throw away these doctrines ? But this is no new thing. If you read history, you will find that in every age of declension, when personal piety is decreasing, changes have been made in the creed of the Church. And I may refer you to this fact as proof that there is a sad decline in personal religion in the churches in our day, when those who go to the Lord's Table are to be found at the dance and at the theatre the next day. But those that profess religion, and at the same time claim to have liberty to live carelessly, will surely require to make their creed just as wide as their practice. We, however, who keep to the creed of the Church of Scotland since the Reformation, will not allow any that profane the Sabbath, or go to theatres, dances, and concerts, to sit at the Lord's Table. We would bring such to task, and suspend them from church privileges.

You will observe that the corruption is not of part of our nature, but of our whole nature. If the whole nature be not corrupted, then man does not require salvation. You are to notice that if the whole nature be not corrupted, as Arminians say, and as may be preached from the pulpits of the United Free Church. then you need only a partial salvation, and if you rest on this, then you must assuredly perish, because you may search the Scriptures from end to end and you will not find a partial salvation. This corruption of the whole nature is the fountain, as the Divines say, from which proceeds all actual transgressions, and Christ teaches the very same truth. '' For out of the heart proceed evil thoughts, murders, adulteries, fornications,'' &c. (Matt. xv. 19). Every outward evil, every actual transgression, proceeds from the sinful heart ; but if the Arminian view be the correct one, then they do not need to be renewed in their whole nature, for you find that sanctification is a renewal, not of part of the man, but a renewal of the whole man. It is a very serious error to hold that the depravity of man's nature is not total, because, if not total, then you do not need the renewal of the whole nature. And if it were possible that you could go to heaven, you would be a creature to be looked at there with wonder, as one whose whole nature was not perfect, because you held while in the world that your whole nature was not corrupted. There is great need in our day that people should be taught this, because it is in the measure in which we come to see, and believe, and experience the truth of this that we appreciate God's way of salvation. Those who do not go to the root of the evil cannot appreciate the remedy which God provided to remove the evil. This is very prevalent in many congregations now; instead of going to the root of the evil, ministers simply plaster up their people by telling them that it is an easy matter to believe, and to be saved, and that they are sure of going to heaven. Ah, my friends, the remedy will be despised by those who hold such views. Christ teaches, " They that be whole need not a physician, but they that are sick " (Matt. ix. 12)—not only sick in fact, but sick in their own experience, and realizing their condition.

III. Before the sinner can or will come to Christ, this unwillingness must be removed, for, as long as the unwillingness remains, it is impossible for the sinner to come to Christ. Not only that he *cannot* come, but he *will not*, for Christ says, " Ye *will not* come unto Me, that ye might have life." A change must take place. The unwillingness must be removed, and those that are unwilling must be made willing to come to Christ, and to believe in Him to the saving of their souls. Now, who is to remove the unwillingness? For it must be removed, or the sinner must be lost for ever. Though I and ministers of the Gospel should be pressing acceptance of Christ upon you during your lifetime, you would just say, " No, I will not come to Christ," and the cause of your unwillingness is the depravity of your whole nature. For as there is ignorance in the mind, there is rebellion in the will, and that rebellion must be subdued before any can come to Christ. Who, then, is to accomplish this? Well, some say that God and the sinner himself will remove it; that there must be a co-operation between God and the sinner who is unwilling. This was a great point of controversy at the time of the Reformation between the Reformers and the Papists. The latter held that in the application of salvation there was a co-operation between God and the sinner. Now, to show the absurdity of this view, not to speak of the falsity of it, we ask, What co-operation could be expected of a dead man in bringing himself to life? What co-operation could be expected of Lazarus when Christ raised him from the dead? None whatever. Lazarus was absolutely passive in the change that was effected upon him from death to life. He gave no helping hand to Christ; and the sinner being dead in trespasses and sins, it is a great error to say that there is a co-operation between him and God in effecting the change from death to life. The Reformers held that man was spiritually dead, and that he was passive until he was brought to life, whatever he might be enabled afterwards to do through the grace of God. Then this error regarding the removal of man's unwillingness led to another one, viz.: Seeing that man could co-operate at least a little with God before he was regenerated and converted, there was therefore something praiseworthy to be found in man in his natural state, and the Papists said that this praiseworthy thing was the merit of congruity—that is, that it was congruous to the cause of his conversion that he co-operated with God. And after his conversion, they said, there was a still higher merit in man, viz., what they term the merit of condignity. This view of man's state by nature, and of what is required in order to change that nature, leads Protestants into the same error of thinking that man merits something by his own works, for Popery is in the heart, though not in the creed, of every human being. The ignorant Protestant says " Ah, I will do my best, and God will work in me ; I will try to be good and to merit salvation." But the sinner himself cannot remove this unwillingness, however much he may try to do it. His fellow-creatures cannot do it ; no man, or angel, no created being whatsoever can remove your natural unwillingness to come to Christ. If I were to tell you that by walking to Wick all night on your bare feet you would merit heaven, I believe you would try to do that ; but if I ask you to come to Christ, you say, " No, I will not come to Christ ; I prefer to walk on my bare feet to Wick, though the night be ever so dark, if my sins will be forgiven, and if I shall be saved, but I will not come to Christ." Though I press acceptance of Christ upon you from Sabbath to Sabbath, you will not accept Him. What a sad proof of the truth of His own words : " Ye will not come unto Me, that ye might have life," and what an error it is, yea, making God a liar, for any man to say that sinners are able to come to Christ. Well, no creature can accomplish the task of removing the unwillingness, but God alone can do it. What is impossible with men is possible with God. He does this in the case of all who are saved, and He does it by the agency of the Holy Spirit, and by the means of His word of truth. You will find this work of God clearly stated in the Shorter Catechism, in answer to the question, "What is effectual calling?" Is effectual calling there referred to as the work of man? The Westminster Divines, who were guided by the Spirit, say that effectual calling is the work of God's Spirit. And what does He do? He convinces us of sin and misery, and enlightens our minds in the knowledge of Christ. What more? (and this is more to the point in hand). He renews *our wills*. Arminians hold that the will escaped the effects of the Fall, and requires no renewal, but the Westminster Divines, taking the word of God as their rule, show that the will must be renewed before the sinner can come to Christ. "We will not have this man to rule over us." But now, by the work of the Spirit, the will is renewed, as it is written in another place. "Thy people shall be willing in the day of Thy power" (Ps. cx. 3). It is the same power that raised Christ from the dead that quickens the dead soul. Now the rebellion of the will is removed, and the sinner is made willing to come to Christ to receive and rest upon Him alone for salvation, as He is freely offered in the Gospel. This is in accordance with the teaching of Scripture, and in accordance with the experience of God's people whom He saves. He renews their will, so that there is no barrier in the way of coming to Christ. At the Council of Trent the Romanists tried to condemn and anathematise all the doctrines of the Reformers, who taught that the saving grace of God was irresistible. They meant by that, that when the sinner was changed by the grace of God, his will was renewed, and the call of the Gospel was effectual, as we speak of the effectual calling in contra-distinction to the universal call of the Gospel. The Romanists charged the Reformers with what they were not guilty of, viz., with teaching that violence was done to the will of man; that he was forced to believe. The Reformers did not teach that: the Romanists tried to misrepresent all their doctrines. We have the Reformers' views in our Confession of Faith and the Catechisms.

The unwillingness, then, must be removed in the case of all that believe in Christ, and of all that shall be saved. This is the teaching of God's own word, and although you cannot change yourself, give you the work to God: for although you are dead in trespasses and sins, you are a reasonable being, and in saving sinners God deals with men as with reasonable beings, and not as with blocks of wood or stone, as the Papists charged the Reformers with teaching. They taught nothing of the kind. They taught and showed that man, though fallen, was still a reasonable being: that though his rational faculties were wholly corrupted, as far as soul and mind were concerned, they were still in existence. Give the work to God. If you go to eternity without this work being accomplished in you, it were better, as Christ said, "that you had never been born." I beseech you, though you cannot do the work yourself, give the work to God.

May He add His blessing. AMEN.

10

XVI.

The Gospel Invitation

" Come unto Me, all ye that labour and are heavy laden, and I will give you rest.

" Take My yoke upon you, and learn of Me; for I am meek and lowly in heart : and ye shall find rest unto your souls.

" For My yoke is easy, and My burden is light."—Matt. xi. **28-30**.

IN this chapter Jesus Christ asks His hearers what they thought of John the Baptist. Then He tells them what He thought of him Himself: that he was greater than any of the Old Testament prophets—not greater in grace, but greater in his office, as he was the forerunner 'of Christ. The Old Testament prophets could only say that Christ, the Messiah, was coming, but John could say—and did say—that He came, and he pointed Him out to his disciples as the Lamb of God that taketh away the sin of the world (John 1. 29). But, great as John the Baptist was, the least in the kingdom of God, under the New Testament dispensation, is in a sense greater than he. John was a link between the two dispensations, the Old and the New. But the least in the kingdom of God can say—and did say—that Christ died for our sins. This was more than it was given to John to say. For although John saw Christ come, and pointed Him out to others, he was brought to heaven by a violent death before Christ died. After Christ's death not the apostles only could and did say that Christ died, but the least in the kingdom of God, that is, under the New Testament dispensation, could say and did say so also. It was in this sense that the least in the kingdom of God was greater than John.

After this Jesus Christ began to upbraid the cities in which He preached and performed mighty works, or miracles, and He upbraided them because they repented not, and He tells them that the punishment of the people of Sodom and Gomorrah would be more tolerable at the day of judgment than their punishment. If you die without repentance in the land of the Gospel, your punishment in eternity shall be greater than that of the heathen who never heard the word of the Gospel. Then He proceeds to speak of the sovereignty of God in salvation, saying, "I thank Thee, O Father, Lord of heaven and earth, because Thou hast hid these things from the wise and prudent, and hast revealed them unto babes. Even so, Father, for so it seemed good in Thy sight." The Gospel was preached to them, but the things revealed in the Gospel were hid from those who were in their own estimation wise and prudent. But He revealed them to those who had an humble estimation of themselves, and who reckoned themselves like babes. It seemed good in His sight, and it was His will to hide these things from the former and to reveal them to the latter. This was His sovereign will. Then, after thus speaking of the sovereignty of God in salvation, He sends forth the universal call of the Gospel to sinners—which call we have in our text. There are some who hold the opinion that ministers who preach the sovereignty of God in salvation cannot preach the universal call of the Gospel, but that is not true, for it is those ministers who believe and preach the sovereignty of God in salvation who can preach the universal call of the Gospel according to Scripture. Christ Himself, the greatest preacher, did so, not only in our text but in other parts of Scripture, and even in the Old Testament Scriptures, as when He says: "Look unto Me, and be ye saved, all the ends of the earth, for I am God and there is none else'' (Isaiah xlv. 22).

In speaking from our text we shall notice :

I. Those called or invited.
II. The invitation itself.
III. The promise given to those who will comply with the invitation.

I. *Those invited—all ye that labour and are heavy laden.*

Here (a) we have the universal call of the Gospel. All who come to hear are invited to come to Christ. Young and old, rich and poor, white and black. Sinners of every grade of iniquity, even the chief of sinners are called. The reason for sending forth the universal call of the Gospel is twofold : (1) That sinners might be brought to Christ, and added to the church, and (2) for encouragement to the Lord's people who may be doubting that they were effectually called. These latter are not left to despair, for there is an open door set before them in the universal call of the Gospel. There is a description given by Christ of those who are invited, they labour and they are heavy laden. We shall (1) speak of the load, the heavy load, under which they are. There are several things in this load.

(1) The guilt of Adam's first transgression, which is imputed to all his posterity that descend from him by ordinary generation. The child that is born into the world is a sinner, bearing, as to his state, the guilt of Adam's first transgression.

(2) The want of original righteousness. By sin we lost our original righteousness in which man was originally created, so that in a state of nature " there is none righteous, no not one'' (Rom. iii. 10).

(3) The corruption of the whole nature. The whole nature of man is depraved by sin. The will did not escape this depravity, as Arminians teach.

(4) Actual transgressions in the case of adults. By our actual transgressions we made ourselves far worse than the fall left us, and when the Spirit convinces of sin, it is of actual transgressions. He convinces first—" He told me all things that ever I did." This was the confession of the woman of Samaria, and when Christ met Saul of Tarsus He convinced him of his actual transgressions, and especially, of his persecution. All this is a heavy load which makes the convinced sinner groan under it, but there is more than this in the load. There is misery in it, for sin brings misery along with it. We shall enumerate the miseries into which the fall brought mankind, as these are spoken of in the Shorter Catechism :

(1) By sin we lost communion with God.

(2) We are under His wrath and curse.

(3) We are liable to all the miseries in this life.

(4) We are liable to death. It was sin that caused that men must die. If man had not sinned there would not be such a thing as death. God told Adam that in the day in which he would sin he would die.

(5) By sin we made ourselves liable to the pains of hell for ever. " Death is the wages of sin." Spiritual, natural, and eternal death. Surely this is a heavy load.

(b) Those invited are described as labouring. They are labouring to get rid of their burden. There are many ways in which men labour for this purpose. Many are labouring to get rid of it by denying the existence of God and everlasting punishment. Why do atheists deny His existence? Just because they are afraid of God, to Whom all men are responsible for their actions,

F

and because they are afraid of the everlasting punishment which they deserve for their sins. It is in this world only that men can be atheists; there is no atheist in eternity among the innumerable number of human beings there.

Others labour to get rid of their burden or load by indulging in sinful pleasures such as the theatre, the dance, and the vain song. "They have forsaken Me, the fountain of living waters, and hewed them out cisterns, broken cisterns, that can hold no water" (Jer ii. 13) What an amount of labour people have in building theatres, picture houses, and dancing halls, to seek to fill up the void caused by God leaving their souls on account of sin. But there is no lasting pleasure to be found in these places of amusement. They are broken cisterns that can hold no water, that can afford no true happiness to an immortal soul.

Others labour to get rid of their heavy load in a religious manner. They labour to get rid of it by the works of the law. They think they can find peace with God by doing all they can to satisfy God's law for their sins. Saul of Tarsus laboured much in this way before his conversion. He did this in ignorance of God's way of salvation. Others under conviction of sin are labouring in the same way till they find out, as Paul found out, that by the deeds of the law no flesh can be justified in the sight of God, but none of those whom God purposed to save will be left always to labour in that way. They shall be taken off from their own labour, and brought to look to Christ's soul travail, and rest entirely for salvation on His finished work.

II. *The invitation.*

There are several things in the invitation.

(1) " Come unto Me," Christ says. In the context Christ speaks of Himself as the Saviour and Mediator between God and men, to whom the Father delivered all the blessings we need in order to be saved. " All things are delivered unto Me of My Father, and no man knoweth the Son but the Father; neither knoweth any man the Father save the Son and he to whomsoever the Son willeth to reveal Him" (v. 27). Therefore the first thing in the invitation is to come to Christ. You cannot get rid of your load until you come to Him, and you are invited to come to Him as you are a guilty sinner, dead in trespasses and in sins, just as the fall left you and as you yourself left you seven times worse than the fall left you. Someone may say, If I were better than I am I should be encouraged to come to Christ. If I repented of my sins. If I had faith I would come, but the Gospel call is addressed to you as you are without repentance, without faith, and without good works. It is true that you will not and cannot close with Christ in the offer of the Gospel without saving faith, but as already stated, it is just as you are you are invited to come to Him.

(2) The second thing in the invitation is, " Take My yoke upon you." We understand by the yoke, a yoke of service. No sooner you come to Christ and close with Him in the offer of the Gospel than you are called upon to engage in His service. You leave off the service of sin and you begin the service of Christ. Not only is it the case that you are commanded to serve Him, but, because of the grace of God in you, working in you a new disposition, you are naturally inclined from your new nature to do this. His service is called a yoke, not a yoke of bondage but of true liberty and delight. In a yoke there is more than one person. We read of a yoke

of oxen. Oxen are used in ploughing, and there are two oxen yoked together in that work. In like manner the believer is not alone bearing the yoke of service, and who is with him in the yoke? Christ is with him, for "without Him we can do nothing." When Christ sent forth His Apostles to serve Him in the Gospel He said, "Lo, I am with you alway, even unto the end of the world" (Matt. xxviii. 20). The Church is with him. Paul speaks of a fellow labourer and calls him "a true yoke-fellow," and speaks of others as labouring with him in the Gospel. If you engage in Christ's service Christ is with you and all God's people are with you. Not only those whose duty is to preach the Gospel, but those who are not in the office of the ministry are with you, helping you by their prayers and in all other scriptural respects.

(3) The third thing in the invitation is, "And learn of Me, for I am meek and lowly in heart." If you come to Christ and take His yoke upon you, you are to learn of Him. He is both the teacher and the lesson taught. "They shall all be taught of Him," and "He left them an example that they might follow in His footsteps." As He is meek and lowly in heart, they are to learn of Him to be so also. They are not only to be found in Him, but also to be conformed to Him. This is their own desire and hope, as the Apostle John, speaking as the mouthpiece of the Lord's people, says, "We shall be like Him" (1 John iii. 2). Not like Him as God, but like Him in His human nature. It was in human nature Christ, as the second Adam, bore the image of God, which was lost by sin, and not only is it the case that they shall be made like Him in soul, but they shall also be like Him in body, as the Apostle Paul says: "Who shall change our vile body, that it may be fashioned like unto His glorious body,

according to the working whereby He is able even to subdue all things to Himself" (Phil. iii. 21).

There is a burden spoken of which those coming to Christ are to take upon them. As we have spoken of the yoke as a yoke of service, we understand by the burden sufferings for Christ. These sufferings are sometimes spoken of in Scripture as the cross, and in this sense every believer has to take up the cross that is peculiar to him or the sufferings he may have to endure in connection with his professing and following Christ according to His Word. No sooner did the Apostle Paul believe in Christ and begin to serve Him in the Gospel, than he met with opposition and sufferings. He suffered much from the Jews, but knowing that he suffeerd for Christ's sake he did not complain but patiently bore the burden allotted to him. And Christ, in another part of Scripture, says, " If any man will come after Me, let him deny himself, take up his cross and follow Me" (Matt. xvi. 24). We are not to make a cross for ourselves, but we are to take up the cross the Lord has assigned to us in His holy providence, and then we may be assured that the Lord will support us under it. Christ did not conceal from His people that in this world they should have tribulation, but He commanded them to be of good cheer even in tribulations, because He had overcome the world. He took the sting out of all their troubles by His own sufferings and death, so that those adversities cannot do them any harm any more than a dead lion can injure the passer by. The yoke which is grievous to graceless men is easy to the true Christian, and the burden which is heavy to carnal men is light to the renewed soul. Paul calls it " a light affliction which is but for a moment." Any suffering for Christ's sake is much lighter than sin, so that the Lord's people would prefer to suffer than to sin.

III. *The promise: " I will give you rest."*

The first thing that is in the rest, that Christ promises, is peace with God, or reconciliation. Of this peace the Apostle Paul speaks in Romans v. 1: " Therefore being justified by faith we have peace with God through our Lord Jesus Christ." This peace is perfect, without any change in all the vicissitudes of life.

(2) The second thing in this rest is, peace of conscience, a peace which flows, as an effect, from peace with God. Although peace with God is unchangeable, peace of conscience is changeable. Sin on the conscience changes it, but after death peace of conscience shall be as unchangeable as peace with God.

(3) The third thing in this rest is peace of full satisfaction with Christ, as the Saviour of sinners. Those who take up with any Saviour but Jesus Christ cannot have full satisfaction in the object in which they trust for salvation.

(4) Rest of hope. A man without hope for eternity cannot have rest if he is alive to the importance of his soul's salvation. Judas lacked this rest, was driven to despair, and committed suicide.

(5) Lastly, perfect rest in heaven, which shall never be disturbed to all eternity. " Blessed are the dead which die in the Lord from henceforth. Yea, saith the Spirit, that they may rest from their labours and their works do follow them" (Rev. xiv. 13).

In conclusion. We have been speaking of the universal call of the Gospel, which is addressed to all sinners who come to hear the joyful sound. If it is addressed to all, as it certainly is, every individual present in the church to-day is invited to come to Christ, and, if you refuse the invitation, you shall carry with you going home an additional guilt—a guilt which if you persist in till death makes your salvation impossible, for it is a sin against the remedy which God provided for sinners such as you are. If you die without Christ it were better for you that you had never been born.

How thankful we ought to be that Christ invites us to come to Him as we are to save us from sin and misery, and if we have come to Him how thankful we ought to be for giving us grace to make us willing to comply with the invitation. We ought to be praising Him continually without ceasing day and night during our time in the world, and calling upon others to join us in His praise, like the Psalmist in Psalm xxxiv. : —

> God will I bless all times, His praise
> My mouth shall still express.
> My soul shall boast in God, the meek
> Shall hear with joyfulness.
> Extol the Lord with me, let us
> Exalt His Name together ;
> I sought the Lord, He heard, and did
> Me from all fears deliver. AMEN.

XVII.

Christ Drawing all Sorts

" And I, if I be lifted up from the earth, will draw all men unto Me."—John xii. 32.

CHRIST spoke the words of our text in answer to what two of His disciples told Him—namely, " that there were certain Greeks among those who came up to the feast at Jerusalem who desired to see Him." These Greeks were Gentiles. The fact that He began to speak of His death implied that seeing Him by the bodily eye only would not benefit them in order to salvation, for many saw Him in that way that did not believe in Him. They would require to see Him by the eye of faith, and to know Him, not only in His divine Person, but in His atoning work, which He finished by His death. He, in effect, intimated that these Greeks were the first fruits " of the great multitude of them, which no man could number, that would be saved," but in order to this He must be lifted up on the Cross and die; for, by His death, the middle wall of partition between Jews and Gentiles was to be broken down, and the Gospel, which was so long confined to the Jewish nation, was to be extended to all the nations of the world.

In meditating upon the subject of our text, we shall notice :

I. The Person that was to be lifted up.
II. The uplifting of this Person.
III. The effect that would follow.

I. *The Person:*

There is an emphasis laid on the personal pronoun
" I." It does not merely say, " if I be lifted," but,
" I," the Person that I am, " if *I* be lifted up." In
speaking of this Person, we are to speak of Him according to the revelation given of Him in the Scriptures.

(a) In the Scriptures we find that He is God, the
same in substance with the Father, equal with Him in
power and glory. The Apostle John begins his gospel
history by speaking of His Godhead, the other evangelists begin their history of Him by speaking of His
humanity ; but John, as already stated, begins his
history thus :—" In the beginning was the Word, and
the Word was with God, and the Word was God." In
this description of the Saviour we have His eternity, His
personality, and His Godhead, and then the Apostle
proceeds to speak of His humanity : " The Word was
made flesh, and dwelt among us," or tabernacled in
our nature. The unbelieving Jews could not deny that
He was man, but they denied that He was God ; and
the Unitarians deny this also. These have no Saviour,
and therefore they die, generation after generation, in
their sins, and perish eternally. Our authority for
saying that they perish is Jesus Christ Himself, for He
said to the Jews, " If ye believe not that I am He (the
Person that I claim to be), ye shall die in your sins "
(John viii. 24). All that die in their sins are lost. As
John speaks of Him as being with the Father, he intimates that He is a distinct Person from the Father.
When you say that a fellow-creature is with you, that
means that that man is a distinct person from yourself.
Although there is but one God, there are three Persons

in the Godhead, the Father, the Son, and the Holy Spirit. It was neither the Father nor the Spirit that suffered and died for sinners, but Christ, the second Person. As God, the Apostle John speaks of Him as Creator, without whom " nothing was made that was made."

He is called the " Word " as the revealer of the Father. He revealed what was in the mind of the Father in His purpose of salvation. No creature knows what is in your mind till you express it in word or some other outward sign. In like manner, no creature, man or angel, knew the Father's gracious purpose of saving sinners till He was revealed by Him who is called the " Word." " No man hath seen God at any time : the only begotten Son, who is in the bosom of the Father, He hath declared Him " (John i. 18). Every revelation given of the Father's purpose of salvation was given by Him who is the Mediator between God and men. We believe that even the first promise given of a Saviour was given by Christ Himself.

(b) The Person to be lifted up was, and is, not only God, but man also. " The Word was made flesh." When He became man He did not cease to be God. It was God the Father that prepared human nature for Him—" a true body and a reasonable soul." " A body hast Thou prepared for Me" (Heb. x. 5). Not a body without a soul. How did the Father prepare human nature for His Son ? Not by ordinary generation, but by an extraordinary generation. The nature of man was so much ruined by sin that it was necessary to create it again in Him who was to be the Saviour of those whom He purposed to save. The human nature of the Son of God was created by the Holy Spirit in the womb of the virgin Mary without sin. The first mention we have in Scripture of His human nature is called a *heel*, but a heel implies a body, for every man that has a heel has a body. Satan was to bruise the Saviour's heel, that is, he was to cause suffering to the human nature of Christ, but he was not to touch His Godhead. Although it was the Father that prepared human nature for His Son, it was the Son's part to assume that nature and unite it to His divine Person, so that He is now God-Man. In this union of the human with the divine, there is a great deal to be learned. When we see that man, that was separated from God by sin, is united to God again in Christ, we conclude that it is God's purpose to bring him nigh to Himself again, however far he went astray. And our conclusion is correct when we consider that as Christ's human nature, which He took to Himself, was never separated from His divine Person, so all those who are united to Christ shall remain in that union for ever. It is an everlasting union, and this is the teaching of Scripture, although Arminians teach that a man may be united to Christ to-day and may totally and finally fall away from that union before the end of his time on earth. Moreover, when we see from the testimony of Scripture that Christ took His human nature to heaven, this teaches that He will bring all whom He unites to Himself to heaven also.

In order that Christ might work out everlasting redemption for His people, it was necessary that He should do so in their nature. It was man that sinned, and it is in his nature that sin must be atoned for. It is remarkable that every time Christ appeared to men, under the Old Testament dispensation, it was in the

form or shape of man He did so, although He did not
actually assume the nature of man till the Word was
made flesh. .

(c) Not only was the Saviour God and man, He was
also appointed by the Father in a threefold office as
Prophet, Priest, and King. Why was this necessary?
It was necessary to meet our threefold need :

(1) By sin we lost the knowledge of God. So great
is our ignorance of Him, that the fool in our heart says,
'' There is no God.'' It is Christ as Prophet that
removes our ignorance, and restores the knowledge of
God which man had before his sin and fall. He does
so by His word and Spirit. In the new creed adopted
in 1892 by an erring church, it is stated that man, after
his fall, possessed knowledge of God and of his duty, but
that is not according to Scripture or the experience of
sinners when they are convinced of their fallen condition. It is always safe to go by the rule of Scripture,
and God's curse is upon those who depart from that
rule. '' To the law and to the testimony, if they speak
not according to this word, it is because there is no light
in them'' (Is. viii. 20).

(2) We are not only ignorant, but we are also *guilty*.
We are guilty because we have sinned, and we cannot
atone for our guilt by anything we may do or suffer.
But God appointed Christ as Priest to satisfy Divine
justice, and to reconcile us to God, which He did by the
once offering up of Himself as an atoning sacrifice. The
work of a priest was not only to offer up sacrifice, but also
to pray for the people. So in like manner Christ ever lives
to make continual intercession for His people. This
work of intercession He began on earth, as you may see

in the 17th chapter of John, and He continues it for ever in heaven.

(3) We are not only ignorant and guilty, but also rebellious. Our rebellion is so great that we cannot subdue it ourselves, nor can any creature, man or angel, do it ; but God, who knew our great need and impotency in this respect, appointed Christ as King, who is able to do what man cannot do. In the execution of His office as King, He, as stated in the Shorter Catechism, subdues us to Himself by the effectual work of the Holy Spirit, rules us by the law of His word, defends us from all dangers, restrains and conquers all His and our enemies. In order to accomplish this, the Father gave Him power over all men. Yea, " He has given Him all power in heaven and in earth."

II. *The uplifting of this Person:*

Although the uplifting here signifies His being uplifted on the cross on which He died (ver. 32), yet we shall speak of several ways in which He was lifted up.

(1) He was lifted up before the eyes of men in the first promise given of Him in Scripture. He was lifted up there as the Saviour who was to bruise the head of the serpent—-the devil. He was to do this by His death. He died, not as conquered, but as a conqueror. Satan thought that if he succeeded in inciting men to put Christ to death he would be the conqueror, and that none of the human race should be saved, but he discovered, to his great disappointment, that it was Christ by His death that gained the victory, and not he. " He led captivity captive, and received gifts for men : yea, for the rebellious also, that God the Lord might dwell

11

among them'' (Ps. lxviii. 18). The first promise was renewed again and again for four thousand years, until at length it was fulfilled. It was a rich promise, including in its compass all the Gospel promises we find in the Bible. It was the one great Gospel text that the Old Testament prophets preached from for that long period. Some might say that many would get tired at hearing a sermon from that one text for so long a time, but the Gospel is always new to, and welcome by, the Lord's people ; they never get tired of hearing the Gospel.

(2) He was lifted up in the bloody sacrifices and other types in the ceremonial law. Although some looked no further than the blood of bulls and of goats and other animals, believers looked by faith to the blood of Christ which was to be shed in due time. Abel did so, of whom it is said that '' he offered up unto God a more excellent sacrifice than Cain'' (Heb. xi. 4). Cain did not understand the way of salvation by the blood of Christ ; he thought he could be saved by his own works, as many do in every generation. But without the shedding of blood there is no remission (Heb. ix. 22). Those who expect to be saved on any other ground than the blood of Christ, shall find out that they are sadly deluded.

(3) He was lifted up in His incarnation, when He was born into the world. He was God manifest in the flesh, and no longer manifested in types and shadows. He was lifted up in this respect that His own people beheld His glory, '' the glory as of the only-begotten of the Father, full of grace and truth '' (John i. 14).

(4) He was lifted up in His death. This was a very solemn way in which He was lifted up, but it was for this end that He came to the world. He was lifted up

between heaven and earth, nailed to the cursed tree, and was crucified. Crucifixion was not a Jewish but a Roman way of putting malefactors to death. It was under the Roman government that Christ was put to death. He was condemned by a Roman judge, who, although He found no fault in Him, yielded to the cry of the people, and delivered Him to be crucified. It was to His crucifixion Christ referred when He said, " As Moses lifted up the serpent in the wilderness, even so must the Son of Man be lifted up, that whosoever believeth in Him should not perish, but have eternal life" (John iii. 14, 15).

(5) He was lifted up from the grave in His resurrection. For the sins of His people He was brought to the dust of death ; but the Father raised Him from the grave as an evidence that He who died fully satisfied the demands of law and justice in room and stead of His guilty people.

(6) He was lifted up from the earth in His ascension to heaven, where He is now glorified with " the glory which He had with the Father before the world was " (John xvii. 5).

(7) He is still lifted up in the preaching of the Gospel. In the preaching of the Gospel, Jesus Christ and Him crucified is lifted up before the eyes of men, and the joyful sound is proclaimed in their ears. It is not themselves but Jesus Christ that His ministers preach, as the Apostles did. " We preach not ourselves, but Christ Jesus the Lord, and ourselves your servants for Jesus' sake " (2 Cor. iv. 5) ; or, as he says in another place, " Whom we preach, warning every man, and teaching every man in all wisdom, that we may present every man perfect in Christ Jesus " (Col. i. 28).

III. *The effect of His being lifted up:*

All men shall be drawn unto Him. " I will draw all men unto Me." " All men " here does not mean every individual of the human race, for in the past it is evident that many of the human race have not been drawn to Christ. The promise is absolute, there is no condition to it, and therefore it shall be fulfilled without fail. By " all men " here we are to understand—all sorts of men, Gentiles as well as Jews. The context leads us to this view. There were certain Greeks, or Gentiles, who desired to see Jesus, and He told the two disciples, Philip and Andrew, that after His death, and resurrection, He would draw all sorts of men throughout the world to Him, black and white, bond and free, sinners of every description, even the chief of sinners. He would draw to Him all for whom He died. Those who hold the larger hope quote this passage of Scripture in support of their error. They hold that those who died in their sins, and were cast into hell, shall, after a period of suffering, be brought from the place of perdition and brought to heaven by Him who says, " I will draw all men unto Me." I heard a minister pray, who said in the course of his prayer, " All spirits are united to God, and He will bring all these to be with Him in heaven." Those who hold the larger hope say, not only that men who are in hell, but also the devil and his angels, shall be brought to heaven by Christ; but these false teachers shall never be in heaven unless they are brought to repentance during their lifetime on earth. Their larger hope shall then disappear, and everlasting despair shall take its place. In drawing sinners to Him there is a forthputting of effectual power on the part of Christ, and a willingness on the part of those drawn.

He does not say that He will drag them against their will, but that He will *draw* them. He will renew their will, and make them willing in the day of His power to come to Him. The drawing of sinners to Christ is ascribed to the Father as well as to the Son, as He told the Jews who would not come to Him, "Murmur not among yourselves. No man can come unto Me, except the Father which hath sent Me draw him " (John vi. 43, 44). There are many attractions in Christ calculated to draw sinners to Him. " He is the brightness of the Father's glory, and the express image of His Person." " He is fairer than the sons of men, chief among ten thousand, and altogether lovely." He is merciful and gracious, and His wonderful condescension in dying for sinners ought to melt the most callous sinners, and constrain them to come to Him.

In drawing sinners to Him, He quickens them by His Spirit, for no dead man will come to Him. He draws them to Him, not only by the effectual work of the Spirit, but also by means of the word of the Gospel. The word of the Gospel is necessary to the salvation of adult sinners. None such can or will come to Christ, although some say, without Scripture warrant, that the heathen may be saved without the word of the Gospel. Faith in Christ is necessary in order to be saved. The Apostle Paul shows the impossibility of believing in Christ without hearing of Him in the word of the Gospel. " How shall they believe in Him of whom they have not heard? and how shall they hear without a preacher? and how shall they preach except they be sent?" And he concludes his argument by saying: " Faith cometh by hearing, and hearing by the word of God" (Rom. x. 14, 15, 17). In his Epistle to the

Ephesians, 2nd chapter, he reminds those to whom he writes of their condition before the word of the Gospel came to them, that they were then without hope, and without God in the world (ver. 12). In his first Epistle to the Thessalonians—that is, to men who were originally heathen, but were now true believers in Christ—he tells them that the change was effected by means of the word of the Gospel which came to them. " For our Gospel came not unto you in word only, but also in power, and in the Holy Ghost, and in much assurance " (1 Thes. i. 5). The effect of the Gospel coming to them in this manner was that " they turned from idols to serve the living God." It is the testimony of missionaries who went to preach the Gospel to the heathen, who never heard the Gospel before, that they never saw the heathen turn from idols to serve the living God before they heard the Gospel. We are therefore warranted to conclude that the Gospel is necessary as a means of drawing sinners to Christ.

Christ will draw all men He saves (1) into union with Himself, (2) into conformity to His image, (3) into fellowship with Himself, and (4) to be with Him where He is in heaven. This was His last petition in His intercessory prayer on earth : " Father, I will that they also, whom Thou hast given Me, be with Me where I am ; that they may behold My glory, which Thou hast given Me ; for Thou lovedst Me before the foundation of the world " (John xvii. 24).

In conclusion : What think ye of the glorious Person that was lifted up from the earth in the several ways in which we have spoken of His being lifted up ? Have you been drawn unto Him, or are you still as far away from Him as you have been before the Gospel came to you ? If you continue to the end in that deplorable condition, you will perish for ever. We are all hastening on to the world of eternity. There are two places in that world—heaven and hell. Those who have been drawn to Christ shall go to heaven when they leave this world ; while those who die without Christ shall be cast into hell, to be tormented for ever, with the devil and his angels. A good number of the Lord's people were removed by death from our congregation during the last thirteen years. These are now, so far as their souls are concerned, with Christ where He is, and their bodies, though in the grave, being still united to Christ, shall be raised up at the resurrection, glorious bodies, reunited to their souls, to be made perfectly blessed in the full enjoyment of God to all eternity. O, how they shall ascribe in a sweet song the glory of their salvation to the Son of God who died for them, and to the Father who sent His only-begotten Son to redeem them by His humiliation unto death, and to the Holy Spirit who quickened them when they were dead in trespasses and sins, and who worked faith in them to believe in Christ. They shall sing their song of praise under a deep sense of their obligation to Father, Son, and Holy Spirit, one God. AMEN.

XVIII.

The Gospel Day

"And it shall come to pass in that day, that the light shall not be clear nor dark.

"But it shall be one day which shall be known to the Lord, not day, nor night, but it shall come to pass that at evening time it shall be light."—Zech. xiv. 6, 7.

IN this chapter the prophet speaks of New Testament times as he does in the preceding chapter when he speaks of the smiting of the Shepherd (Christ). When Christ came the prophet tells that His feet would stand on the Mount of Olives. This passage of Scripture is quoted by pre-millenarians in support of their view of the coming of Christ to reign in human nature on earth for a thousand years, forgetting that when Christ came first to His state of humiliation on earth this Scripture had been already fulfilled, for His feet stood on the Mount of Olives several times. According to their view, Christ would come to this world three times, whereas Scripture speaks of His first coming to work out everlasting salvation, and His second coming to judge the world at the last day. In speaking from the words of our text we shall notice:

  I. The day spoken of.
  II. The kind of day it was to be.
  III. The wonderful change that was to take place
    at the evening of that day.

I. *The day spoken of :*

Every day has a beginning and an end, so has this day. When did it begin? It began at the resurrection of Christ. The Old Testament day came to an end when Christ died and was laid in the grave. The sun of that day set when He was buried, and when He rose the sun of the New Testament Church rose to give light to the w rld. It is the sun that makes the day. The sun of the New Testament Church that rose at Christ's resurrection is still shining in the firmament, and shall continue to shine to the end of the world.

We have spoken of the beginning of the day, and shall now speak of its end—how long the day shall be. Though we cannot speak with certainty of the future— that is to say, how much of the day is yet to come before its end, we are sure of how much of the day is past. There are now nearly two thousand years since it began, and we learn from Scripture that it shall last for more than a thousand years yet to come. The day of the Old Testament Church was long—four thousand years—but the day of the New Testament Church, though brighter in many respects, shall not be so long as that, but we are sure i; shall last to the end of the world. Then the sun shall go down never to rise again in this world. It shines in heaven and never sets there, which makes heaven an everlasting day.

II. *The kind of day it was to be.*

" The light shall not be clear nor dark"—there is a mixture of light and darkness. If we look to the history of the Church in the past we shall see that the day was such with regard to the ministers in the visible church. There were ministers who were enlightened by the Spirit themselves, and there were others who were not con-verted but still in the darkness of a state of nature.

(1) In the time of the Apostles this was so, and after the Apostles had been removed from the Church by

death, the light of the day was so much darkened that one would be doubtful as to whether it was day or night; still there was so much light that it was day.

(2) The day was such with regard to the professing members of the Church—there were wheat and tares, as we have in the parable on that subject—and although the disciples of Christ noticed that there were tares among the wheat, they were allowed to grow together till the harvest came, when they should be separated by the Judge of all.

(3) This was the kind of day in the visible church with regard to truth and error. There was the light of truth and there was also the darkness of error, and in the darkness of the middle ages, the darkness prevailed so much in the Church that one could not call it either day or night; still it was day because there was the light of truth in the Church, though clouded by the prevalence of error.

(4) This was to be the kind of day in the experience of the Lord's people. There was light in them and there was darkness in them. There was grace in them, and there was sin in them, so that often they could not call it day and were afraid that they were still in the darkness of a state of nature, but notwithstanding all the darkness that they saw in themselves it was day in their case in the sight of the Lord. It was such a day in the experience of God's people in regard to joy and sorrow. They have during their time in the world a mixture of both. The light of joy is not clear nor dark, and the darkness of sorrow is not so dark but that it is still day with them.

(5) It was such a day with regard to peaceful and persecuting times in the Church. There were times when the Church was allowed to carry on the Lord's work in peace, and there were other times when she had

to suffer persecution in doing the Lord's will. One has only to read Church history in proof of this. In times of peace the light of prosperity was somewhat clear, but in times of persecution the darkness of adversity was great indeed. Still it was day, and some found it to be a bright day, inasmuch as they enjoyed more of the Lord than when they were left at ease. Some of the martyrs were singing the praise of God in the flames, so that it seems their bodies did not feel the heat of the fire. When the Lord's people are left at ease without persecution, they are apt to get formal and lukewarm in their devotions, and the Lord on that account permits enemies to trouble them that they might be aroused from their lethargy, as the Lord says through the Psalmist, "Slay them not, lest My people forget" (Ps. lix. 11).

III. *The wonderful change that was to take place at the evening of that day.*

"At eventime it shall be light." The evening of this day was to be the brightest part of the day of the New Testament Church. In the evening of the day the sun was low in the firmament, and according to appearance ready to set and disappear, but the sun that rose at the resurrection of Christ never set since that event. It gave light to the Church, however dim at times. The Lord never left His Church to descend into the darkness of midnight, nor did He allow any particular believer or member of the Church to fall into the darkness of despair, however low that person might come. "Light is sown to the righteous" (Ps. xcvii. 11), and that light will arise to give light when he is in darkness. If you saw the natural sun in the evening so low in the horizon that you were thinking that it would soon disappear and leave you in the darkness of night, and the next time you looked you saw the sun rising in the east as if it were the morning of the day, would you not say that that was a wonderful sight? Now this is how it shall be at the evening of the day spoken of in our text. It is in the evening of this day the millennium shall begin, and the light shall be so clear and so bright that none who has the sight of his eyes can have any doubt but it is day and not night. It looks more like the morning than the evening. As the natural sun rises and advances to its meridian height, so does the spiritual sun in that glorious period. The work of enlightening all the nations of the world shall begin on a small scale, and shall go on gradually "till the earth is full of the knowledge of the Lord as the waters cover the channels of the deep." It may be asked, by what means shall this be brought about? We answer, by the preaching of the Gospel, and by the effectual working of the Holy Spirit in the hearts of men through the Word preached. The first to be converted are young men who are to become ministers in the Church. We find that this was the case in Christ's personal ministry on earth. He converted those whom He afterwards commissioned to go into all the world and to preach the Gospel to every creature. At the millennium there shall be a great multitude of such ministers, and it is not at all probable that there shall be any unconverted minister in the sacred office of the ministry then. If an unconverted man were asked to study for the ministry, he would refuse, saying, " I am no prophet, I am an husbandman, for man taught me to keep cattle from my youth" (Zec. xiii. 5), or some other occupation. The millenium will begin first in the pulpit, then it shall proceed to the eldership. It is not likely that there shall be any unconverted man holding that office, whereas previous to that glorious period graceless men who were wealthy and in high positions in society were put in that office. The light of the millennium shall descend to the pew, and it is not likely that any unconverted person shall be admitted to Church membership, or that any such shall dare ask to be admitted to the Lord's Table. The good work shall go on apace till all the nations of the world are enlightened by the Gospel. The Jews, who had been so long under the veil of unbelief, shall be converted to the Christian religion. They shall be brought in, in connection with the fulness of the Gentiles, and those of them who shall be ministers shall be the greatest preachers of the Gospel since the days of the Apostles. The Mahomedans shall be converted and shall believe in Christ as their Saviour. The Papists shall be converted and cast off their superstition and worship and serve God only. The Hindoos, the Chinese, and all other nations shall become Christians. Although we have no warrant that every individual in the world then shall be converted, we may safely say that the unconverted shall be very few. As nations shall be converted, kings shall be converted too. During a thousand years probably all kings will be godly and will give of the revenue of their kingdoms towards the maintenance of the Church. Kings shall be nursing fathers and queens shall be nursing mothers to it (Is. xlix. 23). Satan shall be bound for a thousand years, and the Church shall have peace during that long period ; there shall be no persecution from without or discord within the borders of the Church ; there shall be no war among nations, no training of soldiers. " They shall learn war no more" (Is. ii. 4). There shall be no need for sword or spear - these instruments of war shall be turned into plough-shares and pruning hooks. They shall be used, not as

now, to tear the flesh of their fellowmen, but to tear or
till the earth in order to yield food for man and beast.
There shall be no famine or pestilence, for God's wrath
is turned away from the world, and He bestows an abundance of spiritual and temporal blessings on the inhabitants of the earth. Men shall live long—the most of the
diseases that now cause death shall be unknown. There
shall be no need for doctors, no need of medicine, and
a chemist's shop shall not likely be seen in the world.
" There shall be no more thence an infant of days, nor
an old man that hath not filled his days, for the child
shall die an hundred years old'' (Isaiah lxv. 20).

One may ask when is the millenium to begin? Many
students of unfulfilled prophecy are strongly of the
opinion that it shall begin at the end of the two thousand
years of the Christian era. There are yet eighty-three
years of that period to run, and this is, to say the least,
very probable, for something very remarkable took place
at the end of every two thousand years since the beginning of the world. At the end of the first two thousand
years from the creation, Abraham, in whose seed all the
families of the earth were to be blessed, was called.
And at the end of the second two thousand
years Christ came in human nature to this world, and as
the millennium is a remarkable event it is very probable
it shall begin at the end of the third two thousand years
since the creation of the world. If it will begin then,
there may be babes now born who shall see at least the
dawn of it, for there are some who live for eighty-three
years and more, but as there were dark days and troublous times before the coming of Christ as a light to lighten
the world, so we have very dark days and troublous and
perilous times at present which portend the near approach
of the millennial dawn. In the Churches we have the

darkest day since the Reformation, and the same may be said of the state in our own nation, and in all the other nations to which the Reformation brought the light of the Gospel. It is said that the darkest time of the night is a little before the dawn of day.

In the chapter in which we have our text it is said "that there shall be one Lord and His Name one"—that is, God shall be acknowledged by all nations as the one Lord whom they shall serve, and as His Name is one there shall not be different opinions about Him, or different modes of worship—all shall worship Him according to the rule of His Word, whereas there are now different denominations in the visible Church. There shall then be only one denomination. There shall be no room to ask to what church do you belong, for there is but one Church, as was the case in the days of the Apostles, and as there is but one Church there is but one creed, and we believe that the creed shall be that which is contained in the Westminster Confession of Faith, and we are sure that the Church shall be Presbyterian in her government, doctrine, and discipline. We are sure of this because the Church in the days of the Apostles was Presbyterian. Peter calls himself a presbyter (1 Peter v. 1). It was parting from the order of things in the time of the Apostles that caused different denominations among professing Christians, but at the millennium there shall be a return to that order; and on that ground we conclude that the Church shall be Presbyterian in her government. The great battle of Armageddon shall precede the millennium. The kings of the earth and the whole world join in that great battle. In the present war almost all nations take part in it, and more nations are gathering to engage in the conflict, so that before the end of it, it looks as if all kings and nations will be involved in it. If it is the Armageddon, the Papacy, at whose instance the war began, shall be destroyed. The war is between Christ and Antichrist, and we are sure that Christ shall gain the victory. The Turk, with his host of Mahomedans, shall be overcome and conquered also, for Scripture foretells that the river Euphrates, the source of his strength, shall be dried up, and this is already to a great extent fulfilled, and the complete fulfilment is only a matter of time, and according to appearance only a short time, and then we may look for the dawn of the millennium. "Watchman, what of the night? The watchman said, The morning cometh, and also the night" (Is. xxi. 11). The night has come, and we may look for the coming of the morning soon.

In conclusion: (1) A word to the Lord's people. Looking back to the time in which "God who commanded the light to shine out of darkness, shined in your heart to give you the knowledge of His glory in the face of Jesus Christ," you found out by experience that your day has been like the day spoken of in our text—"neither clear nor dark"—so that you were often afraid that it was not day at all with you. If this was your experience you may look for a clearer light at the evening of your life on earth. This was the case of some of the Lord's people who had been for the most part of their time in the wilderness, doubtful about their interest in Christ, who when they came to die were so full of light that they had no doubt that they were now leaving the world to be with Christ where He is.

(2) A word to the sinner. Spiritually you never saw the light of day. It was night with you since you were born, and except you are born again you shall have a

never-ending night in eternity; but if you cry to God for mercy He may turn you from darkness to light and from the power of Satan to Himself.

(3) When the millennium shall come, God's will shall be done in earth as it is done in heaven. There shall be no Sabbath-breaking or open transgression of His law. The power of godliness shall be so great and universal that the few who are not converted shall be found walking in the ways of His commandments outwardly, so that one would think that they were godly persons. They would feel ashamed if any of the Lord's people would see them breaking God's commandments. The Gospel shall have a moral influence on these that they do not desire to trample upon God's law. What a contrast to the present time when so many transgress His law without shame; and worse than that, in order to grieve the Lord's people who rebuke them for their sins; but at the millennium even those that are not converted shall respect the Lord's people and thank them for their good advice.

May the Lord add His blessing to his own Word. AMEN.

XIX.

Prisoners of Hope

"Turn you to the strong hold, ye prisoners of hope : even to-day do I declare that I will render double unto thee."— Zech. ix. 12.

THE prophet in this chapter refers to the coming of Christ. In the 9th verse he calls upon the Church to rejoice: "Rejoice greatly, O daughter of Zion; shout, O daughter of Jerusalem : behold, thy King cometh unto thee. He is just, and having salvation; lowly and riding upon an ass, and upon a colt, the foal of an ass." You remember when, shortly before He suffered, He went to Jerusalem, that this Scripture was fulfilled. He rode upon an ass though He was King. The ass was not used in war, but horses were so used. Asses were used in time of peace to ride upon, and for other purposes. "He shall speak peace to the heathen, and His dominion shall be from sea even to sea, and from the river even to the ends of the earth." He comes for deliverance, although the deliverance here mentioned may refer to the deliverance from Babylon; yet, seeing that the prophet speaks of the coming of Christ in the flesh, we must think of the deliverance in a more comprehensive sense than merely a deliverance from the Babylonian captivity. It means specially the deliverance of sinners from a state of nature to a state of grace, and this brings us to the words of our text, which may be divided into the following heads : —

    I. The prisoners.
    II. The exhortation.
   III. The promise.

I. *The prisoners :*

Good people may be in prison, but, as a rule, it is guilty people that are imprisoned, and it is a just thing to imprison them. If they be not imprisoned, there will be no protection for life or property from law-breakers. All the human race, descending from Adam by ordinary generation, are law-breakers, and guilty, and have been imprisoned by God, though many are not aware of it. Some children may have been born in a literal prison, but it is true that all the posterity of Adam have been born in prison, and remain there till they are delivered out of it by Christ.

When a man is imprisoned, he is stripped of his own raiment and clad with prison clothes. In like manner when we had sinned and were imprisoned, God stripped us of our original righteousness in which we were created, and the garment we have on now is our own righteousness, which is made up of filthy rags. No sensible person could boast of a raiment made of rags, and not only rags but filthy rags. Yet man in his ignorance boasts of such clothing, as the Apostle Paul did before his conversion. A prisoner also gets prisoners' food, and not the good food he had when he was at liberty in his own home. What is the food of the prisoners spoken of in the text? Not the bread of life, but something to satisfy their carnal lusts. Some live on novels, others on the world, and others on grosser sins. It is to be borne in mind that it was not God that provided that food for them, but on account of their sins he judicially gave them over to it, and as long as they are in prison they will take no other food.

A prison is a place of suffering—a dungeon. When Paul and Silas were in prison, their feet were put in the stocks, until their blood was oozing out freely. The prisoners we speak of are liable to all the miseries of this life—to death itself, and to the pains of hell for ever.

It is also a dark place. Sinners in a state of nature are in darkness, and doing the works of darkness, that cannot bear the light of day. A prison is, moreover, a place of confinement. The windows are barred, and the door locked, so that the prisoners cannot get out, till they are delivered in a just way.

The prisoners spoken of in the text are " prisoners of hope." There are prisoners spoken of in Scripture who are without hope, that is, those that are in hell. Their prison is a place of everlasting despair. They know that they never can get out of it. Although some of them when they lived in this world might have believed in the larger hope, yet when they were cast into hell they found out that there was no room for the larger hope there, but they found that out too late. But so long as sinners are in this world—though prisoners—they are prisoners of hope. There is hope set before them in the Gospel, therefore do not despair, if you seek salvation. Seek the Lord while He may be found, call upon His name while He is near. Receive Christ in the offer of the Gospel.

The ground on which the Saviour brings sinners out of prison is His own atonement, by which He rendered full satisfaction to all the requirements of God's law which we have broken. Justice would require to be satisfied before any of the prisoners could be set at liberty. The Rev. John MacRae, (big MacRae, as he was commonly called), made a supposition that Christ pitied the prisoners, and came to the door of the prison, and asked justice, who held the key and stood at the door, to let the prisoners out. Justice shook its head, and said, I must get satisfaction for their guilt before they are let out, but when Christ paid the price of their redemption, justice most cordially handed the key to Him. Christ opened the door and proclaimed liberty to those within the prison, but, notwithstanding that the price was paid, and a proclamation of liberty made, no one was willing to leave their place of confinement, so that power was required to bring them out as well as price. Hence the need of the work of the Holy Spirit in order to our accepting of liberty, as well as of the atoning work of Christ to merit liberty for us, although Arminians are of a different view. These hold that they have ability of will to believe and repent whenever they like, but both Scripture and the experience of God's people are opposed to their erroneous view of man in a state of nature.

II. *The exhortation.*

" Turn ye to the strong hold." There is no such exhortation to those in the prison of hell, but, in this world, we are exhorted to turn to the stronghold for protection, and the exhortation follows us till death, although we might live a hundred years. What is the stronghold? Christ, whose name is the only name given among men under heaven by which we can be saved. " His name is a strong tower, and the righteous flee unto it," and find safety in Him. He is a strong tower or fortification. In times of war belligerents have strong towers or fortifications to which they flee when they are hardly pressed, but these fortifications which are built by men are not impregnable, and they are often bombarded and levelled to the ground, but the stronghold to which we are exhorted to turn is so strong that no enemy, not even Satan himself, can break it down. However numerous and mighty the enemies might be, they

G

cannot succeed in overthrowing it. Its walls consists of
God's Being and attributes, of which justice, as satisfied
by the blood of the covenant, is a most powerful part.
Christ, the Angel of the Covenant, "encampeth round
about them that fear Him and delivereth them." They
are as safe in that stronghold as Christ Himself is, so
that Christ may say to the believer as David said to
Abiathar when the latter was afraid of his life : "Abide
thou with me, fear not; for he that seeketh my life
seeketh thy life : but with me thou shalt be in safe-
guard" (1 Sam. xxii. 23). This is Almighty safety ; and
God's people will not go to any other place of
safety. If they cannot say in the full assurance of faith
that they have a saving interest in Christ, they can and
will say : "To whom shall we go? Thou hast the words
of eternal life. And we believe and are sure that thou
art Christ, the Son of the living God" (John vi. 68, 69).
This is the language of faith. When Christ brings sinners out of this prison, God the Father takes off them their
prison garment of filthy rags, and clothes them with the
white garment of Christ's righteousness, which he imputes
to them, and is received on their part by faith alone.
What a great and glorious change of state ! They do
not any longer live on prison food, but they live on
Christ, the true bread that came down from heaven, of
which, if a man eat, he shall never die. They are also
changed in their nature, so that they are not disposed to
be law breakers when they are set at liberty. Among
men there are some prisoners, and, as soon as they are
let out of prison, they begin law-breaking again, and
that because their nature was not changed. But, as for
God's people, sin is the evil that they would not—
although they are not perfect in their nature. They
love righteousness and hate iniquity. They are now

made free by Christ, and therefore they are free indeed. Once out of prison, they shall never enter into it again. They may in their own experience be in prison as the Psalmist was when he cried: "Bring my soul out of prison, that I may praise Thy name" (Ps. cxlii. 7); but that was not the prison in which he was when in a state of nature.

III. *The promise.*

"Even to-day do I declare that I will render double unto thee." What is the double? In Gaelic, we preached from the text, "As Moses lifted up the serpent in the wilderness, even so must the Son of Man be lifted up: that whosoever believeth in Him should not perish, but have eternal life" (John iii. 14, 15). This text explains what the double is. One part of the double is according to this text, that believers shall not perish. It is a great blessing not to be cast into hell. It is a dreadful thing to think of those in hell. I dread to think of ministers and others who professed the Christian religion and died unconverted to be lost for ever. I cannot bear to think of it, but it is a fact; but those who turn to the stronghold, at the Saviour's command, shall never go to the place of everlasting perdition. They shall never perish, and this is one great part of the double promised. But great as that part is, the other part is far greater, namely, "they shall have eternal life." Many would be satisfied if they would escape the punishment of the lost in hell, without any desire to be with Christ in heaven. At times of spiritual revival in Scotland many were awakened to concern about the salvation of their souls, and when examined by ministers it was found that some were moved by fear of eternal punishment and others were made afraid that they would be separate from Christ in eternity. Those who were moved by the fear of God's wrath fell back to their old habits, while those who were afraid that they would be separate from Christ in time and in eternity turned out to be true and bright Christians and persevered to the end. It is he that endures to the end that shall be saved. No man or angel can express the blessedness of those saved. Another double is that they shall get grace on earth and glory in heaven. The redeemed shall have tribulation in this world, for that is promised, but however great their tribulations may be, they may say with the Apostle Paul: "I reckon that the sufferings of this present time are not worthy to be compared with the glory that shall be revealed in us" (Rom. viii. 18). We are utterly unworthy of this great double portion, but it is worthy of the Giver.

Take those words with you and pray over them Many lose their souls by giving their heart to the lawful things of the world, to the neglect of their precious soul's salvation. It was no sin to the rich man in the parable to have his riches, if he got his riches in an honest way; but, when he made a god of it, then he lost his soul.

Others lose their souls in the pursuit of pleasure and amusement, such as the dance, the theatre, and the vain song. These are broken cisterns in which there is no water—that is, no true comfort or satisfaction to an immortal soul, which needs God Himself for true and lasting comfort and pleasure. Seek first the kingdom of God, and His righteousness, and all you need in your journey in this world shall be added unto you. Solomon, when God requested him to make his choice, asked wisdom, and God gave him with wisdom riches and honour above many. See then that you seek wisdom, which is the beginning of the fear of God. All destitute of this fear are fools, and if they continue till death without the fear of God it shall be said to them, as it was said to another man, " Thou fool, this night thy soul shall be required of thee"—to be punished throughout eternity.

O, the need of the power of the Spirit from on high, to awaken the careless. There are generations of God's wrath, and it is to be feared that this generation is such. In such a generation it will be a miracle of grace that any should escape everlasting damnation. The generation in Noah's time was a generation of God's wrath, and they were swept off the face of the earth by a terrible flood, and after the flood God began a work of spiritual revival and reformation. In the present European war, which is a work of divine judgment, many are swept off the face of the earth by the sword, and it is to be feared that the most of these are lost for eternity, though we have clear evidence that some of our soldiers killed are of those to whom death is gain. I have read a letter, recently written by a young soldier belonging to our Church, and which he wrote to his widowed mother the day before he was killed. It appears from his letter that he anticipated that he would be killed in action the following day when a battle was fixed to take place. From the letter it appears that he was a true Christian whose hope was in Christ alone, resting upon His finished work as the only but all-sufficient ground of his salvation. The name of the young soldier was Angus Cattanach, from Kingussie, a grandson of the late godly Alexander Cattanach, Badenoch. The letter will appear in the Free Presbyterian Magazine, and readers of that periodical will see it for themselves.

It is to be hoped that after this war, in which the great majority of the soldiers are killed to be lost for ever, the Lord will begin a work of spiritual revival which shall spread and go on increasingly till all the kingdoms of the world shall become the kingdoms of the Lord and of his Christ. Then the inhabitants of the earth shall learn war no more, for a thousand years. There shall be no soldiers as such, for there shall be no wars, except in the sense of fighting the good fight of faith. All the nations of the world shall be like brethren living in amity and peace. There shall be no wicked Kaiser there—no wicked king—no wicked minister. The Gospel of Peace preached in all nations shall bring this to pass. The Jews shall be converted, and the ministers among them will be perhaps the greatest preachers of Christ and Him crucified since the days of the Apostles. There shall be no preachers of idolatry, no priests of Baal. There shall be no theatres, no places of dancing, or the vain song. There shall be no Sabbath-breakers, a sin which is now so common and for which God punishes the nations of Europe in the present awful war. There shall be no novels, no newspapers printed on Sabbath. There shall be no shinty or football matches. The earth shall get rest from these nuisances. There shall be no lapsing in any congregation throughout the world. All shall flock to the house of God, and although all the inhabitants of the earth shall not be godly, the godless shall be few, and the Gospel shall have such moral influence on these few that one would think that they were godly people.

The exhortation in our text shall be complied with by all the nations of the world willingly and readily. We shall now finish this discourse by repeating the text—" Turn ye to the stronghold, ye prisoners of hope: even to-day do I declare that I will render double unto you." AMEN.

XX.

The Strait Gate

"Enter ye in at the strait gate : for wide is the gate, and broad is the way, that leadeth to destruction, and many there be which go in thereat :

"Because strait is the gate, and narrow is the way, which leadeth unto life, and few there be that find it."—Matt. vii. 13, 14.

OUR text is part of the sermon that Christ preached on the mount. That sermon begins with the fifth chapter and ends with the 7th chapter of Matthew. There was a great multitude in the audience. His own disciples were there, and many others who were still in a state of nature. Christ gave the first part of His sermon to His disciples, calling them several times blessed—"Blessed are the poor in spirit," etc. After addressing His own disciples, He began to speak to the unconverted, the great majority of whom composed His hearers. He did not neglect in His preaching those in a state of sin and misery, and thus set a good example before ministers of the Gospel who are to preach not only to the Lord's people but to others also. Let us take up our subject thus :

I. The gate.
II. The exhortation.
III. The reason to enforce the exhortation.

I. *The gate.*

The Gate is Christ. "I am the door." "I am the way." It is "a strait gate." How is Christ "a strait

gate''?   (1) Negatively: He·is not strait in His power
to save.   "He is able to save to the uttermost all that
come unto God by Him."   He is not strait in His invi-
tations to sinners.   "Look unto Me and be ye saved all
the ends of the earth."   "Him that cometh unto Me, I
will in no wise cast out."   All to whom the message of
salvation comes are invited to Him.   (2) Positively: (1)
Because all who enter in by Him must leave their sins
outside the gate: "Let the wicked forsake his ways."
Although Jesus saves His people, He saves them, not in
their sins but from their sins.   (2) Because He will not
admit any who will not leave outside his own righteousness.   He will admit the sinner, but not his filthy rags—
self-righteousness.   The gate is so strait that that cannot
enter in by it.   Many would give up the practice of sin
in order to be saved, but would not renounce their own
righteousness, and be indebted entirely to Christ for
salvation.   Such will find the gate too narrow for them
when it is too late.   They shall find themselves shut out
from God and from heaven.

The strait gate is the door of entrance to the narrow
way.   Christ is the gate, and if we would enter that
gate we must be "born again."   The gate is so strait
that no unregenerate man can enter in thereat.
"Verily, verily, I say unto thee, except a man be born
again, he cannot enter the kingdom of heaven."   Christ
is the door to that kingdom, and, if we would enter the
kingdom of glory in the other world, we must enter the
kingdom of grace in this world.   When a soul believes
in Christ, he enters in the way that leads to everlasting
life in heaven.

That way is a "narrow way."   It is hedged on both
sides by the law of God.   The believer, though delivered
from the law as a covenant of works, is not delivered

from it as a rule of life. "Teach me, O Lord, the way of Thy statutes; and I shall keep it unto the end. Give me understanding and I shall keep Thy law" (Ps. cxix. 33, 34). It is a narrow way, and it is a strait way— "The law is holy, and the commandment holy, and just, and good" (Rom. vii. 12).

The way that leads to death or destruction in the world of eternity is a broad way. It is also a crooked way. It is not the same course of sin that all in this way practise and follow. Some follow one course, others another. But they are all in the same broad way, and though the way winds hither and thither in innumerable zig-zag directions, to suit the various inclinations of the great multitudes that throng it, they shall all meet together at the end, for at all the terminuses there is destruction. Christ knew this, and warns sinners of the danger. The broad way is downhill, and is easy to travel for those who walk after the flesh, and for those who take up the form of religion but deny its power. It is not only the irreligious that are found in the way— many professors of religion are found therein. It is like a river running downwards which carries along its course the dead fish without a struggle on their part. All in the broad way are spiritually dead, and they are easily carried along with the current of the river, and when any are quickened by the spirit, they begin like living fish to struggle against the stream.

There are many in the broad way. By nature all the fallen human race are in it. There are some taken from it, but as yet the most are in it. Christ's flock is a "little flock." Satan's flock is a large one—very large. Some people boast of having a majority, so may Satan; as yet he has the majority of men in the world. He is their father, they are his children; he is their master,

they are his servants. Those in the broad way say,
Satan is not our father; God is our father. So said the
Jews, but Christ said to them, " Ye are of your father
the devil," and we know that what He said is true.
It is not what you, that are in the broad way, may say
about yourselves that is true, but what Christ says about
you. You will never leave the broad way till you first
come to realise that you are in it. May the Lord open
your eyes to see where you are, sinner, before it is too
late! All who are now in the narrow way that leads to
life were convinced that they were by nature on the
broad way that leads to destruction. They believed this,
and then they began to strive to enter in at the strait
gate. They by grace entered in, and they pity with all
their heart their fellow sinners who are still in the broad
way from which they themselves had been taken by Him
who " came to seek, and to save that which was lost."
They are entirely indebted to Jesus Christ for this merciful translation. O, the blessed Jesus! Let all that is
within me be stirred up to praise His holy name, and let
my tongue be as the pen of a ready writer to recommend
Him to my fellow sinners!

II. *The exhortation:*

The exhortation is addressed to sinners who are still
in the broad way that leads to destruction. It is a part
of Christ's sermon on the mount when multitudes gathered to hear him. His own disciples were there, but the
great majority of the audience were in a state of sin and
wrath, and to the latter he addresses this exhortation.
It may be objected, How can sinners in a state of nature
strive to enter in? Christ addresses them as rational and
responsible creatures, and they are bound, at the risk
of perishing for ever, if they neglect this duty, to strive

that they may be saved. "Secret things belong unto the Lord, revealed things belong unto us and to our children." This is a revealed duty, and is pressed on us by Christ. He says: "Strive to enter in at the strait gate." You cannot extricate yourself from the duty He enjoins. You may neglect it, but it is still a bounden duty, and if you are saved you will strive to enter in. Do you ask, How am I to strive that I may be saved? what means to use, what efforts to put forth in the use of the means? In striving for obtaining any good thing we need in this world, there are means to be used, and if these means are neglected that good cannot be obtained. In like manner in striving to be saved, there are means that must be used, or you cannot possibly be saved. These means are not the devices of men, but the ordinances of God. He gave you the Bible, which reveals that all have sinned and have come short of His glory, and you are one of this all that have sinned, and the Bible also reveals that Christ came " to seek and to save that which was lost." If you would strive to enter in, search the Scriptures, for they are they which testify of us as sinners, and of Christ as the Saviour. We have no warrant to believe that any who neglect to read and search the word of God, as the great means of salvation, can be saved. Prayer is another means of salvation. " Seek and ye shall find, knock and it shall be opened to you," is one of the exhortations of the Saviour with respect to the duty of prayer. If you neglect the means of grace, you cannot enter in at the strait gate. The sacraments—baptism and the Lord's Supper—are means of grace; but they are not essential to your entering in at the strait gate. They are outward symbols and seals of the covenant of grace, but you may enter into God's favour although you had not been baptised or been

a communicant. These are then the means you are to
use if you would be saved. The way you are to use
them is to strive. This is Christ's exhortation, " Strive
to enter in." It indicates the manner in which you are
to use the means prescribed in the Word of God.   To
strive is not to engage in the duty in a careless and an
indifferent manner, not to be half-hearted in your endeavours to enter in.   It is to use all diligence, to
exhaust all your energy, like those running in the race
that they might obtain the crown at the end.   It is to be
in agony, like a dying man striving to retain life.   The
importance of the matter at stake—the salvation of your
precious soul—calls for the utmost endeavour on your
part for striving that you may enter in at the strait
gate—that you may believe in Christ, and be found in
Him not having your own righteousness.   But you may
object : Can I strive with success without God working
in me by His Spirit—changing me from a state of nature
to a state of grace? No, but it is not what God will
work by His Spirit in all that are saved that Christ
speaks of, but your duty, and the duty of every sinner
to whom the Gospel comes.   God, and He alone, can
effect the change that is necessary to salvation, but that
does not exempt you or me or any other sinner from our
own duty.   You fail in your striving if you do not
earnestly, and in God's way, pray that He may be
pleased to give you His Holy Spirit to convince you of
your sin and lost condition by nature, and so to change
you as that you will indeed enter in at the strait gate.
You will never enter in without this change, but this
calls you to strive the more that He may work it in you.
It is God's part to bless the means of grace, but it is our
duty to make diligent use of the means.

III. *The reason to enforce the exhortation:*

" For wide is the gate, and broad is the way that leadeth to destruction, and many there be which go in thereat. Because strait is the gate, and narrow is the way, which leadeth unto life, and few there be that find it." You will see from these words of the Saviour that there are two things—or two considerations—which ought to make you strive that you may be saved : (1) There is the consideration of the many sinners who through the wide gate and the broad way go to everlasting destruction. The gate of entrance into the way to destruction was opened in this world by sin. That gate is so wide that all men thereat enter into a state of sin and misery. The way is a broad way, and all men are in it in a state of nature. It is so broad that it contains all classes of sinners, and that it holds all manner of sins without overcrowding it, and without the prospect of any sinner being expelled from it, however far he may give the reins to his sinful nature in the practice of sin. There is plenty of room there for the formal professor of religion, the self-righteous and the prayerless. There is room for the Sabbath-breaker, the swearer, and the drunkard ; there is room in it for the unclean and the murderer, the infidel, and the atheist. In short, the leader at the head of all those in the broad way gives them licence to live as they list. There is no prohibition except that which warns sinners against trespassing out of that way. This way is congenial to the natural man, but it leads to destruction, and Christ brings it forward in His sermon as a solemn consideration to enforce His exhortation : " Strive to enter in at the strait gate." He tells us that " many there be who go in thereat"—that is, go to destruction in the other world. All who remain in the broad way till death shall find

13

themselves, in eternity, in the place of everlasting destruction; for Christ, and not man, be it observed, says that that way leads to destruction.

(2) The other consideration is the fewness of those who find the way that leads to life. As there is a way, as we have seen, that leads to death, there is a way that leads to life—life eternal in the other world. That way is the way of holiness, and is a narrow way, and the gate to it is Christ, and that gate is a strait one in the sense we have indicated. Christ tells us that they are few that find the narrow way that leads to life. Why are there so few that find this way? (1) Because it is the few that think at all of the all important matter of salvation. Many, many are like Gallio, caring nothing about the matter. They are careful about their worldly concerns and neglect the one thing needful. (2) Because many who may now and then think about the matter do not consider it of present concern. They think they can afford to postpone it till a more convenient season, as if the disposal of the accepted time and the day of salvation were in their own hands.

(3) Others do not find the way because they do not wish to come to it by the strait gate—Christ. They think they can come to the way by some other gate— such as the sacraments. If they are baptised they think that that is the gate leading to this way. If they sit at the Lord's table, and eat and drink the outward symbols of Christ's broken body, and shed blood, they imagine that that is the gate to the narrow way. Thousands and tens of thousands miss the way by taking these methods to get at it. But there is no entrance to it but Christ. '' I am the way . . . no man cometh unto the Father but by Me.'' He says, in effect, The consideration that it is few that find the way that leads to life ought to urge

you to strive with more earnestness and more diligence that you may be one of these few.

Few in number as they are in every generation, there are those who found the way that leads to life. It was not in them by nature what would lead them to this way; but God taught them by His Spirit and word. By His teaching they discovered that they were by nature in the broad way that leads to destruction, and they learnt that Christ, and He alone, was the door to the way of life. They came to Him by the teaching and guidance of the Spirit, and accepted Him as He is offered to us in the Gospel. In Him they found an open door for sinners who are out of the way; in Him they found life, and as living and renewed creatures they are now in the way of holiness that leads to eternal life in heaven. That way, though a narrow way, is not too narrow for the new man that is created after the image of God, in righteousness and true holiness, and if the old man is still in them, as it is, it is being crucified with its affections and lusts, and in due time it must, by the sanctifying work of the Holy Spirit, give up the ghost, and then it shall find a grave in the waters of Jordan, never to have a resurrection. If you ever find the way of holiness, you must strive to enter in by Christ, and if you enter in by Him you must strive all your lifetime here below that you may be made meet for the inheritance of the saints in life. " Work out your own salvation with fear and trembling, for it is God who worketh in you both to will and to do of His own good pleasure."

In conclusion: Let us (1) seek to realise the awful fact that all men are by nature in the broad way that leads to destruction in eternity.

(2) Let us admire and appreciate the love and grace of God in providing a Saviour to deliver sinners out of

that state into which sin brought us. Angels desire to look into this mystery with wonder. How much more ought we to look into it?

(3) Let us deplore the indifference of many of our fellow sinners in Gospel lands concerning the momentous matter of the salvation of their immortal souls, and if we have found grace to enable us to come to God through Christ, let us press the exhortation, "Strive to enter in at the strait gate," upon the many who still walk in the broad way that leads to destruction. This is the duty of ministers in a special manner.

(4) Let us who are brought to the narrow way be careful to walk in it. Though narrow, it is a pleasant way. "I delight in the law of God." "How great is the peace of them that love Thy law." The honey of the heavenly Canaan is found in this way. The hidden manna is found in it. The fellowship of God is enjoyed in it. "Enoch walked with God" in it. If we would keep up fellowship with God, let us be careful to keep in this way. Antinomians think that they can enjoy God out of this way, but theirs is a delusion. It is in this narrow way He can be enjoyed. "The ways of the Lord are right, and the just shall walk in them, but the transgressors shall fall therein." "Make me to go in the way of Thy commandments, for therein do I delight."

I am now many years in His service as an ordained minister, and I would like to be young again to begin anew to preach Christ and Him crucified to perishing sinners. I feel as if I did nothing for Him in the past. I am thirsting to serve Him in what remains of my life on earth. He is precious to me, and I would wish to proclaim His preciousness to others. My time in this world may not be long, and my desire is that every moment should be spent in His sweet service. Many in this degenerate age despise the ministry of the Gospel. But if I were to come back to the world after I am away, I would prefer to serve Christ as a minister to being crowned king over the whole world. But I shall not come back. O, for grace to redeem the time—to be up and doing for Christ while it is day, for the night cometh when no man can work in this world! The night cometh, but the morning of the day of glory shall shine on those that are in Christ, never, never to be succeeded by night. Amen, so let it be!

XXI.

The Good Work begun

" Being confident of this very thing, that He which hath begun a good work in you will perform it until the day of Jesus Christ."—Phil. i. 6.

THE Apostle Paul had a special call to visit Philippi, because God had work for him to do there. In a vision, he saw a man from Macedonia saying to him, " Come over, and help us," and he readily complied with the call, and found there a few who gathered together to worship God. These might be represented by the man from Macedonia, inasmuch as that they felt their need of a man of God to teach them more perfectly. Lydia was one of these, and she profited by the teaching of Paul. The first man there of whose conversion we have an account, and *that* through the instrumentality of the Apostle, was the jailor, and thus the good work began at Philippi.

The Apostle writes this epistle, in company with Timothy, when he was a prisoner at Rome. He was imprisoned there for the Gospel's sake. The only reason why he was now shut in confinement in Rome was that he preached the Gospel. He therefore calls himself " a prisoner of Jesus Christ." This epistle was written some twelve years after he had been called in the extraordinary manner already referred to to preach the Gospel at Philippi (Acts xvi. 9). His preaching was then blessed to some. The good work was begun there, and the Apostle in this epistle assures the Church planted there by his instrumentality that that good work should be carried on and brought to perfection.

In endeavouring to speak from this text, let us consider three things: —

      I. The good work begun.

      II. The certainty there is that this work shall be carried on to perfection.

      III. The time when the good work is completed— " The day of Jesus Christ."

I. *The good work begun*: It is the work of the Spirit in the application of redemption to believers. This is a work, and not an act. An act is complete at once, but in a work there is a beginning and a going on with it till it is finished.

The Spirit of God is the Author of this work, for it it a work *in* them. Christ did a work outside of us, but the Spirit does a work in us. The Spirit is the sole Author of this work. As the work of redemption was done from beginning to end by Christ alone, and there was none of the people with Him, so the work of applying Christ's redemption to believers from beginning to end is the work of the Holy Spirit, and there is none of the people with Him. Let us consider how the Spirit does this work.

(1) He quickens to life the dead sinner. The whole soul is quickened to life—the understanding, the memory, the conscience, and the will. We are all spiritually dead by nature. The first thing, then, the Spirit does is to quicken the dead. Nothing good can be done to the dead till they are brought to life. You cannot feed and clothe them as long as they are dead. The Spirit

quickens the dead sinner by means of the word of truth. He comes to the grave of the dead and cries, " Awake thou that sleepest, and arise from the dead, and Christ shall give thee light." When the Spirit quickens the dead sinner, He then opens his eyes, and the awakened soul sees where he is. He sees that he is in a state of sin and misery. " Adam, where art thou ?" Well, he is in a lost condition.

(2) He convinces him of his sins, which brought him into that state. He convinces him, first, of his actual transgressions. He begins with the last act of sin the sinner committed, as in the case of Saul of Tarsus— " Why persecutest thou Me ?"—and from that sin He brings him back on the whole course of his life, to his childhood, and to the fountain from which his actual transgressions proceeded—the sinfulness of his nature. Memory is revived, and is very active in reproducing to the soul his sins. Some complain of a bad memory, but under conviction of sin there is no reason for that complaint. There is nothing the sinner remembers so well as his sins. The omniscient Spirit that searches the heart and the life has begun His work. Formerly the sinner may have asserted that he was a sinner, but now he is convinced of it. So long as you have any doubt about anything, you are not convinced of it: you wait for more light on the subject. But when you are convinced of it, you say : " I see it now ; you need not use any further argument to convince me that the thing is actually as you say. I see it clearly now." So it is in the work of the Spirit in convincing of sin. God tells us, in His word of truth, that we are sinners, and such sinners as He describes us to be ; but until the Spirit begins the good work in us, we are not convinced of it.

Those who think of themselves otherwise than according
to what God says of them in His word are not convinced
of their sins, and are not subjects of the saving work of
the Holy Spirit. But all in whom He begins the good
work are convinced of their sins. They see it clearly;
they have no doubt about it. They may have many
doubts that they shall be saved, but they have no doubt
as to their being sinners. They may have doubt that
it is the good work of the Spirit, but they have no doubt
as to God's testimony concerning themselves. They set
to their seal that God is true.

(3) The convinced sinner, not yet knowing the way
of salvation, begins to seek to be saved by the works of
the law. It may be asked, Is it the work of the Spirit
that makes him to try to be saved that way? I think
we may say that it is. He purposely permits it. All
men are by nature under the covenant of works, and we
think that the Spirit *permits* the convinced sinner to try
the works of the law, not that he may be saved by these
works, but that he may find out by experience that " by
the works of the law no flesh can be justified in the
sight of God." Christ sent the young man that asked,
what he should do to obtain life, to the law. " Thou
knowest the commandments." So does the Spirit also,
at least by way of permission. The impossibility of
being saved by the law is a lesson to be learned by the
teaching of the Holy Spirit. Those who think and
teach that man can be saved in whole or part by his
own works have not been taught by the Spirit of God,
but by the spirit of delusion. No work can be the
ground of salvation but the work of Christ. This is
clearly taught in Scripture, but we must be taught it

also by the Holy Spirit, and He teaches it to all in whom He begins " the good work."

(4) When the sinner is convinced that there is no salvation by the works of the law, then He enlightens his mind in the knowledge of Christ—in the knowledge of His divine Person as the second Person of the Trinity; of His two natures, as God and man; and of His threefold office, as Prophet, Priest, and King—the one Mediator between God and men, the only name given under heaven among men by whom we can be saved. However long or short be the time which the sinner may take in coming to a saving knowledge of the only Redeemer in these aspects, he in whom the Spirit begins " the good work" is taught to know Him.

(5) In this good work there is a new creation. There is a new nature—" All things are made new." All the faculties and powers of the soul partake of this new creation. The mind, the will, and the affections undergo a radical change. The Spirit, who is the Author of the work, dwells in all His graces in the new nature. Faith, which implies knowledge of Christ, is the first grace that comes into exercise in receiving Christ in the offer of the Gospel. The soul that receives Christ by faith is effectually called. The effectual call embraces the work of the Spirit from the first awakening of the dead soul till he is united to Christ by faith. The call that comes short of this is not effectual. The other graces act also—love, hope, repentance, etc., have their appropriate exercises.

(6) Sanctification is an important part of the good work, and follows regeneration. An unregenerate soul cannot be sanctified. It is those that are regenerated that the Spirit sanctifies. The standard of sanctification

is full conformity to the image of Christ. Believers
must grow up to the full stature of a perfect man in
Christ. There are no dwarfs in the family of God in
heaven. Nor are there children there, in the sense of
being imperfect; they are all of the same stature—
perfect men in Christ. It is this work the Apostle is
confident has begun in those to whom he writes.

II. *The certainty there is that this good work shall
be carried on to perfection:*

It is reckoned that the Philippian believers were now
twelve years professing Christians. The good work had
hitherto gone on, and the Apostle assures them that it
shall be carried on to perfection. There are some who
teach that the work of grace may begin and yet not be
finished. There is not, however, any ground for this
opinion in the word of God. Paul knew better. The
Apostle says that he is confident that it shall be performed. Confident here means to be fully assured.
There is no room for doubt in this matter. Paul uses
the same term in the 8th chapter to the Romans, when
he says, " I am persuaded that neither death nor life
. . . . . shall be able to separate us from the love of
God which is in Christ Jesus our Lord" (Rom. viii.
38, 39). There are several stable grounds of this
assurance : —

(1) It was God who began the work. His work is
perfect. Man may begin a work which he can never
finish, but it is not so with God. He began the work
of creation, and finished it. He, in the Person of His
Son, began the work of redemption, and He said on the
cross, " It is finished." And, in like manner, God,
the Spirit, will perfect the good work which He has
begun. He also will say, " It is finished."

(2) There is adequate provision made for the completion of the good work. He counted the cost before He began. There is enough in the merit of Christ. It is at the expense of Christ, the Spirit begins the good work. It is vain to ask Him to begin it on the ground of man's works—He will not do it. But He works it on the ground of Christ's merit.

(3) God's eternal purpose of salvation makes it sure. That purpose is unchangeable; it shall be fulfilled.

(4) The Holy Spirit undertook to do it. He will without fail make good that undertaking.

(5) It is the nature of grace to grow. Grace may seem sometimes to be under a decay, but it shall never die. It is an incorruptible thing; it will spring up again and come to maturity. It will ripen into glory.

(6) The means of grace makes it certain. These were instituted by Christ in the Church for this very end, and they shall answer the ends for which they were set up.

(7) Providence is another ground of assurance. " All things work together for good to them that love God "—adversity as well as prosperity. " Our light affliction, which is but for a moment, worketh for us a far more exceeding and eternal weight of glory."

(8) The mystical body of Christ must be complete. All the members must be gathered to Christ, who is the Head, and be made conformable to Him as the pattern.

This good work shall be perfected at the day of Jesus Christ. That is the last day, when He comes to judge the world. So far as the souls of the redeemed are concerned, they are made perfect in holiness at death, and do immediately pass into glory. But their bodies lie in the grave till the resurrection. Their bodies are still imperfect, but at the resurrection they shall be made perfect in holiness, like their souls. They shall be raised up in glory. So the Apostle extends the good work begun to " the day of Jesus Christ." And this brings us to our third head:—

III. *The time when the good work begun shall be completed:* " *The day of Jesus Christ.*"

This is the day when He shall come again. The good work shall go on till that day. It shall then be completed. The bodies of the saints shall be made perfect, and the number of the redeemed shall be complete. No more sinners shall be invited to Christ. The Gospel call shall cease. The door of the Church and heaven shall be forever closed against the impenitent. No place any longer for such but hell. " Depart from Me, ye cursed, into everlasting fire, prepared for the devil and his angels." The redeemed shall be invited to heaven in the words of Christ, the Judge: " Come, ye blessed of My Father, inherit the kingdom prepared for you before the foundation of the world." The wicked, on the left hand, shall go into everlasting damnation; but the righteous, on the right, shall go into everlasting life. The day of Jesus Christ is coming. Seek now to be found in Christ. " Now is the accepted time, now is the day of salvation." " Seek ye the Lord while He may be found; call ye upon Him while He is near."

(1) All days are the days of Jesus Christ, but this day is in a particular sense His. He gave us many

days, but reserved this day for Himself. Men claim this day as their own, thinking that their sentiments will decide it. It is not theirs, but the day of Jesus Christ. It is—

The day of His revelation, the day in the which He shall come again. '' The Lord Jesus shall be revealed from heaven.'' It is the day of His second advent. (Matt. xxv. 31-46 ; 2 Thes. i. 7-10).

(2) It is the day in which He shall raise the dead— the day of the general resurrection. The great trumpet shall be sounded, and all that are in their graves shall hear the voice of the Son of God, and they shall go forth out of their graves.

(3) It is the day of final judgment. All shall be judged then—ministers and congregations, parents and children, masters and servants, kings and subjects, all nations shall be gathered before the judgment seat of Jesus Christ at that day. The day is His : all the speaking is His, all the work of the day is His. All men who took the work of this day into their own hands while in the land of the living shall find out, to their sad disappointment, that Christ is Judge at that day, and not they.

(4) It is the day of the destruction of this world. "The heavens shall pass away with a great noise, and the elements shall melt with fervent heat, the earth also and the works that are therein shall be burnt up'' (2 Peter iii. 10).

(5) It is the day in which the wicked shall be punished with eternal punishment. Many men now

deny that there is such a thing as eternal punishment, but these presumptuously usurp the place of Christ, the Judge, and shut their eyes to the plain teaching of Scripture. They imagine that the day of judgment is theirs, and that they should judge. But it is not theirs. It is the day of Jesus Christ, the Judge of the quick and of the dead. The wicked shall be on that day punished with everlasting destruction (not annihilated) from the presence of the Lord, and from the glory of His power (2 Thes. i. 9).

(6) It is the day in which ·the good work begun shall be completed. Although the souls of believers are made perfect in holiness at death, yet their bodies lie imperfect in their graves till the resurrection. Then they shall be raised up in glory, re-united to their souls, and their vile bodies made conformable to the glorious body of Christ. The good work of the Spirit, begun at conversion, shall then be completed. The Spirit will then cease His work among men ; the means of grace shall cease ; the door of the Church on earth shall be closed for ever—no preaching of the Gospel, no invitation to sinners, no more warnings to flee from the wrath to come. It is no longer the accepted time, and the day of salvation. It is " the day of Jesus Christ"—the day of final reckoning, the day in which the eternal destiny of all the human race, from Adam downwards to the last of his posterity, is unalterably and for ever fixed. A solemn day it is ! A day of everlasting joy to the Lord's people—a day of everlasting sorrow and misery to the wicked.

The good work shall be carried on till this day. Sinners shall be converted from generation to generation, and believers shall be built up in their most holy faith till Christ shall come again at the last day. It was a good work begun in and among them. The work of the Spirit had respect not only to the subjects of His work in that age, but also to the subjects of His work to the end of time.

XXII.

Justification

" Being justified freely by His grace through the redemption that is in Christ Jesus : Whom God hath set forth to be a propitiation through faith in His blood, to declare His righteousness for the remission of sins that are past, through the forbearance of God."—Romans iii. 24, 25.

IN this chapter the Apostle shows that all men, Jews and Gentiles, are sinful, and condemned. He also shows God's way of salvation, which we shall consider in the following discourse.

In speaking from the text, we shall notice :

    I. The moving and efficient cause of justification —*i.e.*, the free grace of God, without any merit or worthiness in man.

    II. The meritorious cause—*i.e.*, the redemption of Christ : the price He paid by His atonement.

    III. The instrumental cause—*i.e.*, Faith.

    IV. The blessing involved in justification.

    V. That this way of justification and salvation in Christ has been set forth by God in types and shadows, and in the declaration of the Scriptures of the Old and New Testaments. " Whom God hath set forth to be a propitiation through faith in His blood."

14

I. *The moving and efficient cause of justification:*

This cause is not in men, but in God. The cause is the free grace of God. " Being justified freely by His grace." The grace of God here means His favour, His love, which is the source of salvation. Justification, as described in the Shorter Catechism, " is an act of God's free grace." In Ephesians ii. 8, the Apostle says, " By grace are ye saved." Grace there means grace in the fountain, and not grace in the stream, as communicated to believers. Grace in God is the efficient cause of justification, and the whole of salvation, without any merit or worthiness in men to deserve it. Works done by men are excluded from having any share in the cause of salvation. " Not of works, lest any man should boast " (Eph. ii. 9). Because the cause of justification is in God Himself, and nothing in sinners to merit it, it is stated in our text that sinners are justified *freely*. " Being justified freely." This is good news to sinners who have been convinced by the Holy Spirit of their sin, unworthiness, and helplessness to save themselves. But it is not appreciated by the self-righteous. They are too proud to be debtors to God's free grace.

II. *The meritorious cause of justification:*

It is Christ's redemption : " Through the redemption that is in Christ Jesus." Christ is called the Redeemer. When an Israelite lost the inheritance, his next-of-kin had the right of redemption. If he undertook to redeem the lost inheritance, he had to pay a certain price for it, and, when he thus bought it, he restored it to his poor brother free. In order to be our kinsman—

" a Friend that sticketh closer than a brother "—Christ
assumed our nature—free from sin—and paid in full
the price of our lost inheritance by His obedience unto
death, and He now restores all to His people. Although
lost by sin and the fall, it is now free to them. If one
heard an Israelite for whom his friend bought the
inheritance say afterwards, " I paid for it, at least
partly, myself," when he did not in fact contribute a
penny towards its purchase, one would say that the man
was a liar, and most ungrateful to his benefactor. But
none of those for whom Christ paid the redemption price
will thus act towards Him. They will thankfully
acknowledge their indebtedness to Him, and ascribe
to Him the glory of their privilege. And those who
think that they merit salvation, in whole or in part,
have no saving interest in Christ's purchase. The
atonement of Christ is the only but all-sufficient ground
on which God justifies the guilty sinner. And as
Christ by His atonement satisfied all the requirements
of justice, so " God is just, and the justifier of him
that believes in Jesus."

III. *The instrumental cause of justification* :

It is faith—" Through faith in His blood." No
man is justified in the sight of God till He receives
Christ by faith. Faith, that is, saving faith, is one of
the graces of the Spirit, and implies a change of nature,
which in Scripture is called the new birth (John iii. 3).
This faith is not to be found in the natural heart; it is
wrought in the soul by the Holy Spirit in those who are
regenerated and born again. The first act of the
regenerated person is to receive Christ by faith as He
is freely offered in the Gospel, and, having received

Him, he rests on Him alone for salvation.   It is a
person that receives Christ, and faith is like the hand,
the instrument by which he lays hold of Him.   So Paul
speaks to the Colossian believers: " As ye have, therefore, received Jesus Christ the Lord" (Col. ii. 6).
Although the believer receives Christ in all His offices,
yet justifying faith has respect to Him as *Priest* in
particular.   So it is said in our text: " Faith in His
blood."   It is as a guilty sinner he is justified, and he
sees in Christ's atonement what satisfied divine justice
and meets all his guilt, and he cordially closes in with this
gracious way of justifying the ungodly.

IV. *The blessing of justification:*

The description given in the Shorter Catechism of
justification includes all that has been said on the
subject.   " Justification is an act of God's free grace,
wherein He pardoneth all our sins, and accepteth us as
righteous in His sight, only for the righteousness of
Christ imputed to us, and received by faith alone."
Here we have the efficient cause of justification, the
free grace of God ; the meritorious cause, the death of
Christ : the instrumental cause, faith ; and the blessings
of justification, the forgiveness of all our sins, and the
acceptance of our persons as righteous in His sight.   It
is the blessing of justification we have to consider now.
The blessing is twofold—pardon and acceptance.   All
our sins, past, present, and future, are pardoned.   It is
to be noted that it is the *guilt* of our sins that is pardoned—blotted out as a thick cloud.   And the guilt
being removed, the liability of the believer to punishment is cancelled.   Although the believer needs and

asks, pardon after justification, yet in the eye of the law all his sins, past, present, and future, are forgiven, inasmuch as Christ satisfied justice for all his sins, that is, all the sins God foresaw he would commit during his time in the world. This is no encouragement to sin, but quite the reverse. Sins committed after justification are more heinous in the sight of God, and more lamented by the believer, than sins committed before justification. Such sins are not, however, visited by God with the punishment they deserve, but with fatherly chastisement. '' If his children forsake My law, and walk not in My judgments; if they break My statutes, and keep not My commandments; then will I visit their transgression with the rod, and their iniquity with stripes. Nevertheless My loving-kindness will I not utterly take from him, nor suffer My faithfulness to fail '' (Ps. lxxxix. 30-34). These sins will not cause God to withdraw His act of justification, but He will by severe chastisements bring His children to repentance, to hate sin the more, and to watch more carefully against temptation to sin. They shall, moreover, have the effect of shutting them up to salvation by grace more entirely, giving all the glory to God.

Acceptance of their persons as righteous in the sight of God is the second part of the blessing of justification. Justification is a change of *state*. We are fallen in our nature, and in our state. Salvation in its application is a restoration of fallen man to his original condition, as he came forth from the hand of God, perfect in his nature, and perfect in his state, and thus qualified to answer the great end of his being—to glorify God, and to enjoy Him.

H

We have already spoken of a change of nature. We have now to notice a change of state. Both are necessary in order to be saved. A change of nature precedes, in the order of nature, a change of state. The former is effected by the Holy Spirit by means of the word of the Gospel, which is the incorruptible seed by which God's children are born again (1 Peter i. 23); the latter is the act of God as Judge, pronouncing a sentence of acquittal from guilt. God justifies them on a just ground—the righteousness of Christ—which is imputed to them, as all their guilt was imputed to Christ as their substitute and surety, who fully satisfied the justice of God in their room and stead by His obedience unto death. God now accepts of their persons as righteous in His sight, just as if they had never sinned against Him. Justification is an *act* which is done once for all, never to be repeated, and never to be reversed. They are complete or perfect in their justification the moment they are justified; as perfect as they will be at the day of judgment. It is on this account justification is called an act, to distinguish it from sanctification, which is a work that has a beginning, a progress, and finishing at death. It is to be noted that it is not in the bulk that God justifies sinners, but as individuals. Every one that is justified is brought to the bar of God, charged with guilt, and pleads guilty before the Judge; but at the same time, apprehending the mercy of God in Christ, pleads for mercy and pardon in the name of Christ, and on the ground of His merit, and on that ground only. For those justified are taught to know the way of salvation by Jesus Christ.

V. That this way of justification and salvation has been set forth by God since the time He revealed Himself to our first parents in the garden of Eden as the God of Salvation:

Our text states that God the Father has set forth His Son Jesus Christ to be a propitiation through faith in His blood, and *that* for the remission of sins, which is one of the blessings of justification. In the Old Testament dispensation the way of justification through the mediation of Christ was set forth in types and shadows, and plain declarations of Scripture; and in the New Testament, which is the complement and fulfilment of the Old, the way of justification is more plainly set forth. There was but one way of justification under both dispensations—the Old and the New. The Apostle, in the fourth chapter of this epistle, proves this. To show God's way of justification under the Old Testament dispensation, he brings forward Abraham as an instance. The Jews, having rejected the Messiah, looked for justification on the ground of their own works. Paul discusses the matter with them. He says: " If Abraham were justified by works, he hath whereof to glory, but not before God " (Rom. iv. 2). Then he proceeds to prove that Abraham was not justified by works, but by faith. He believed God's promise concerning the Messiah, on the ground of whose atoning sacrifice he was justified, as that atonement was set forth, not only in promise, but also in bloody sacrifice.

Having proved by clear and convincing arguments, drawn from the Old Testament Scriptures, that Abraham was not justified by works, but by faith in Christ, the Apostle proceeds to show that it is in the same way believers under the New Testament dispensation are justified: " Now it was not written for his sake alone that it was imputed to him (Abraham) ; but for us also, to whom it shall be imputed" (that is, Christ's righteousness), " if we believe on Him that raised up Jesus our Lord from the dead ; who was delivered for our offences, and was raised again for our justification" (Rom. iv. 23-25). Here we have again the meritorious cause of justification set forth—Christ's death. The following passages in the New Testament are to the same effect:—" Be it known unto you therefore, men and brethren, that through this Man (Christ) is preached unto you the forgiveness of sins: and by Him all that believe are justified from all things, from which ye could not be justified by the law of Moses " (Acts xiii. 38, 39). " Knowing that a man is not justified by the works of the law, but by the faith of Jesus Christ, even we have believed in Jesus Christ, that we might be justified by the faith of Christ, and not by the works of the law: for by the works of the law shall no flesh be justified " (Gal. ii. 16). Many other Scripture proofs might be given in support of our contention that there is but one way of justification under the Old Testament dispensation and under the New, but let those given suffice.

In conclusion: '(1) In preaching the Gospel and showing God's way of salvation to sinners, it is the duty of ministers to point out and refute false views on the subject, as the Apostle does in this epistle. As all men are by nature under a covenant of works, and ignorant of the Gospel, they are prone to seek salvation by works. The Jews, being ignorant of God's righteousness, went about to establish a righteousness of their own, in order to be saved. Paul himself did this before his conversion. But when he was taught of God, he renounced his own righteousness, and closed with all his heart with God's way of salvation by Jesus Christ, as he tells in the third chapter of his Epistle to the Philippians. Luther, in the time of his ignorance, strove hard to merit salvation by his own works and sufferings. But when he was converted by God's grace, he accepted of God's way of salvation, and began to proclaim it to others. He, like Paul, preached the doctrine of justification by faith in Jesus Christ, without the works of the law. Wherever you see men seeking salvation by their own works, you may conclude that they are not converted to God, that they are still in a state of nature, and, if they die in that condition, that they are lost in eternity.

(2) Although salvation by works is ingrained in the hearts of all men in their natural state, yet the error is confirmed in them by false teachers, who preach the covenant of works as the way of salvation. These "leaders of the blind" shall have an awful account to render at the day of judgment. The blood of those whom they led astray shall be required of them, and they shall be punished with greater severity than those they were the means of leading to hell.

(3) People who have the word of God contained in the Scriptures of the Old and New Testaments are left without excuse if they remain ignorant of the way of salvation, clearly set forth in these Scriptures, although none can know that way in a saving manner without divine teaching.

(4) How thankful to God we ought to be for giving us His precious word of truth, in which He revealed Himself as the God of salvation, reconciling the world to Himself, not imputing their trespasses to them.

(5) What a glorious work Christ's ministers have in proclaiming, in the preaching of the Gospel, God's gracious provision of salvation for perishing sinners, in which provision they see an all-sufficiency for their own salvation and the salvation of their hearers! When preaching this to others, they feed and feast upon it themselves. Preaching time is then to them a feasting time. We are accustomed to hear of the phrase, " A diet of worship." Well, God's ministers when preaching, and His people when hearing, the Gospel feed upon Christ—" the bread of life."

(6) A word to the Lord's people: You were by nature the children of wrath, even under condemnation as others. But there was a day in your past history when God convinced you of your woeful condition. Then you began to ask, like the jailor of Philippi, " What must I do to be saved?" As you were then ignorant of God's way of salvation, you began to seek salvation by the covenant of works; and you continued that work till God convinced you that by the works of the law no sinner can be justified in His sight. Then He showed you a more excellent way. He revealed to you, in the word of the Gospel, that Christ is the end of the law for righteousness to every one that believes (Rom x. 14). At that stage your great concern was how to believe in Christ. You were like a blind man. He had the organ of sight, but he could not see because he was blind. Ask the blind man to see this object or that object, and he will tell you that you ask him to do

what is impossible for him to do. He can speak and cry, but to see he cannot. No creature, man or angel, can open his eyes. God only can do that. Say, then, that God opened the eyes of this blind man. It was now as easy for him to see as it was difficult, yea, impossible, for him to see before he received his sight. Tell him now not to see, and he will tell you that he cannot but see unless he shuts his eyes. So it was with you. Till God lovingly enlightened your mind in the knowledge of Christ, and renewed your will, you found that you could not believe in Christ. But when He did this work in you by His Spirit and word, you found it the easiest thing to believe in the Lord Jesus Christ, to cordially embrace Him as He is freely offered in the Gospel. You felt sweetly drawn to Him in a manner you cannot explain to others. It is such a mysterious thing that one must learn it for himself or herself by believing in Christ. It comes by hearing or reading the Gospel, as the Apostle Paul says, " So then faith cometh by hearing, and hearing by the word of God " (Rom x. 17).

May the Lord add His blessing. AMEN.

XXIII.

Christ made Wisdom, etc.

"But of Him are ye in Christ Jesus, who of God is made
unto us wisdom, and righteousness, and sanctification, and
redemption."—1 Cor. i. 30.

THE Apostle Paul was never done of speaking of Christ.
The late Rev. Donald Macdonald, Shieldaig, told us
that he once had a dream, in which he dreamt that he
was at a question meeting. After several had spoken
to the question, he was asked to speak, and, in doing so,
he said: "The question you have is very dark; I will
leave it yourselves, and go to Christ." I said,
"Although you were awake you could not do better."
I said to him, on another occasion, "You cannot
preach, without speaking of Christ?" "No," he said.
"What would you do, if Christ was not in your text?"
"If Christ was not in my text, I would bring Him into
it through a back door." There is no consolation without Christ. The Lord's people cannot do without Him,
and ministers will be praying for a text to preach from,
and when they are in great need, the Lord will give
them a text where Christ is. So it was with the Apostle
Paul; he felt his need of Christ, and he would preach
Him to others.

He writes this epistle to the Corinthians, and
addresses it to believers in the Church at Corinth: "To
them that are sanctified in Christ Jesus, called to be
saints, with all that in every place call upon the name
of Jesus Christ our Lord, both their and ours " (ver. 2).

The epistle was meant for other believers besides those at Corinth. He prays for them as well as preaches to them: " Grace be unto you, and peace from God our Father, and from the Lord Jesus Christ " (ver. 3). Mark the order of his petition—grace first, and then peace. There is no true peace without grace. He thanks God that He bestowed grace upon them, which changed them from the state in which they had been by nature. " I thank my God always on your behalf for the grace of God which is given you by Jesus Christ " (ver. 4). It is a cause of thankfulness to know that there are others who received grace, and are in a state of salvation. The source from which they received grace is God the Father and the Lord Jesus Christ, in whom all the fulness of grace dwells. Then he acknowledges with thankfulness that they are " enriched by Him in all utterance, and in all knowledge " (ver. 5). After this he gives them a kind of rebuke for their divisions. They were not divided with regard to the doctrines of the Gospel, but with regard to the ministers of the Gospel. Some preferred this one, others preferred that one. Some preferred to hear Paul preach, others Apollos, and others Cephas or Peter. " I am of Paul, and I of Apollos, and I of Christ " (ver. 12). Without disparaging the true ministers of the Gospel, we should remember that Christ Himself is greater than all. There is a kind of an allowance for preferring some ministers to others, but the Corinthians were going too far, for this caused a division among them. They were not to look to ministers as their Saviour, but to Christ. " Is Christ divided ? was Paul crucified for you ? or were ye baptized in the name of Paul ?" (ver. 13). He thanks God that he baptized none of them but Crispus

and Gaius, and the household of Stephanus, lest he
should be thought to have baptized in his own name.
Paul's chief work was to preach the Gospel, which is
more important than to administer the two sacraments
—'' baptism and the Lord's Supper.'' Some put these
sacraments before preaching, and hold that none can be
saved without being baptized and partaking of the
Lord's Supper; but these sacraments are not necessary
to salvation.   There are many in heaven who were
never baptized, and who never sat at the Lord's table.
That is not to say that these ordinances may be
neglected.   The Jews required a sign, and the Greeks
sought after wisdom, and considered themselves wiser
than others; but the Apostle tells them that not many
wise after the flesh, not many mighty, not many noble
are called.   '' But God hath chosen the foolish things
of the world to confound the wise, and God hath chosen
the weak things of the world to confound the mighty ''
(ver. 27).   A godly lady, reading these passages of
Scripture, thanked the Lord that it was not said '' not
any noble are called,'' but '' not many.''

In speaking from our text, we shall notice : —

I. The Person spoken of.
II. What this Person was made.
III. Who made Him this?
IV. For whom was He made wisdom, righteous-
ness, sanctification, and redemption?

I. *The Person spoken of*: The Person is Jesus
Christ, the second Person of the glorious Trinity,
who is in nature the same with the Father and
the Spirit, and equal with them in power and
glory, the Creator of all things, and our Creator.

" All things were made by Him, and without Him was not anything made that was made " (John i. 3). He is spoken of as the only Saviour, that they might not look to ministers for salvation, but to Him alone. Ministers, however great, are only instruments and channels, through which God speaks to us.

II. *What He was made.*

He was made wisdom, righteousness, sanctification, and redemption—all that we stand in need of in order to be saved. He is made so as the one Mediator between God and men. There is no Mediator in heaven or in earth but Christ, who is God and man, and is thus able to lay His hand on both parties—God and sinners, who are at variance—and bring them together in peace and agreement.

(1) He is made wisdom: The Greeks were seeking wisdom, but they could not find it without Christ, who is the wisdom and power of God. He is made wisdom as Prophet to make us wise unto salvation. By nature we are all foolish. " O ye simple, understand wisdom; and ye fools, be ye of an understanding heart " (Prov. viii. 5). In order to be made wise we need to be taught, though there are some fools that cannot be made wise by teaching; it is God only that can make us wise unto salvation. Christ teaches His people by His word and Spirit, and makes them who were by nature foolish, wise to make choice of Himself and of eternal life. In order to be made wise we must be made fools in our own estimation. The Apostle Paul, before his conversion, thought he was very wise; but, when Christ began to teach him, he discovered that he was a fool, and on the wrong way to eternity. But God purposed to save him.

and taught him that Christ was the way, the only way to heaven, and from that moment Paul changed his course, and was made wise to make choice of Christ as the only way to the Father. And the same is true of all the Lord's people. There are none so wise as the Lord's people, though they are reckoned fools by the world. God, who is the fountain of all wisdom, made them wise. Christ, as Prophet, convinces sinners of their sin and misery, and enlightens them in the knowledge of Himself, in order to be saved. It is a miracle to be saved, when you think of many you know left to perish in their sins.

(2) He is made righteousness: He is made righteousness as Priest. It was as Priest He wrought out the righteousness on the ground on which we are saved. In Scripture He is called Jehovah our righteousness. Come to Him, not only for wisdom, but also for righteousness. The moment you receive Him by faith, His righteousness is imputed to you as your own. His righteousness is the robe by which the prodigal was clothed when he returned to His father's house. It is a white robe, upon which you cannot put a black spot. You may put a spot on the robe of your own profession, but you cannot put a spot on this robe. It gives you a right to grace and glory, and all the blessings of salvation. How important to seek an interest in Him! Though it cost a great deal to Christ, it is freely offered to you. It cost Him the pouring out of His soul unto death. We are all clothed in respect of our bodies, but we paid something for that clothing. Some will ask, " What did that dress cost you?" and you will tell that it cost so much. But if you ask the believer, " What did that robe by which you are clothed cost you?" he will

answer, " It cost me nothing, but it cost my Saviour a great deal." It cost Him His humiliation unto death. By grace are ye saved; it is not of works, lest any should boast. Those who look for salvation by their own works are greatly deceived, and when we hear of their death it leaves us sad, because we know that they are lost. There is no work meritorious but the work of Christ. A good man went to see another good man of whom he heard a good report as to his godliness. In the course of conversation, the visitor, in order to test this man, said that sinners were saved by works, and the other man said that they were not. And after a long discussion on the subject, in which he drew out of his friend many precious things, he said, " I meant the work of Christ," and then both were agreed on the ground of salvation. All are saved on that ground, and therefore there is no room for boasting. Abraham, the father of the faithful, has no more room to boast than Manasseh, Mary Magdalene, and Saul of Tarsus, because all are saved on the same ground. Paul called himself the chief of sinners. When did he call himself so? When he was almost ripe for heaven. In the history of the Apostle, we find three stages of growing in grace. The first stage is when he compares himself to the other apostles, and considers himself the least of them. The second stage is when he compares himself to saints, and reckons himself less than the least of them; and the third stage is when he compares himself to sinners that are saved, and calls himself the chief of sinners. " This is a faithful saying, and worthy of all acceptation, that Christ Jesus came into the world to save sinners, of whom I am chief " (1 Timothy i. 15). He was nearest

15

heaven when he called himself the chief of sinners. There was a good minister, at Kiltarlity, called Ronald Bain, and he would be disputing with the Apostle about some points. One point was that the Apostle called himself the chief of sinners. Walking in his room alone, he was heard saying: " You, Paul, call yourself the chief of sinners, but I cannot agree with you, for I am a greater sinner than you have been. If you mean that you are the greatest sinner that was saved, I do not agree with you, for I am a greater sinner than you have been; but if you mean that every sinner saved is the greatest sinner in his own estimation, I agree with you." Grace humbles as well as exalts; it brings down its subjects to the dust. Abraham, in pleading with the Lord for sparing Sodom, called himself, dust and ashes (Gen. xviii. 27). The Lord's people, when praying in secret, say many things concerning themselves as sinful and unworthy that they would not say in public prayer. The son of a godly catechist said, " It is not the same way that my father prays in private as he does in public. He is more free in private in confessing his sins "; which reminds me of what I heard told of a godly woman who had a cruel husband, who hated the Lord's people, and accused his wife of sins of which she was not guilty. She was one day praying in a barn, and her husband, who was passing, heard her voice, and he stood listening. He heard her putting down herself as a great sinner. The most of her prayer consisted of confession of sin. When he heard this, he opened the door and said, " You cannot now deny that you are a great sinner, for I heard you confessing it."

(3) He is made sanctification: All that shall be communicated to you for sanctification is in Christ as

the fountain, and He sanctifies His people by His word and Spirit. He is the fountain which contains all the purity and holiness of which they are made partakers. He is also the pattern to which they shall be conformed. When the Lord commanded Moses to build Him a tabernacle, He showed him a pattern, and charged him to make everything in the tabernacle according to that pattern. The first Adam by sin lost the image of God in which he was created ; the second Adam restores it, and may say, " I restored that which I took not away " (Ps. lxix. 4). We cannot get to heaven without perfect holiness. There are two reasons for which the Lord's people are left in the world—(1) They are left till their work for Him is finished ; and (2) till His work within— the work of sanctification—is completed. When this is done, they shall be left no longer upon the earth. They shall depart to be with Christ, which is far better ; for a perfectly holy man could not live in this world.

(4) He is made redemption : The word redemption here means the redemption or deliverance of the body from the power of death and the grave at the resurrection. In Romans viii. 23, the word redemption is used in this sense : " Even we ourselves groan within ourselves, waiting for the adoption, to wit, the redemption of our body." He is the resurrection and the life, and will raise the bodies of His people from the grave, to be glorified with their souls in heaven, and will conform their vile bodies to His own glorious body. And we have reason to believe that their glorified bodies shall shine as the brightness of the firmament (Dan. xii. 3). What a glorious transformation as compared with the state of their bodies on earth, where they were liable to

many troubles, and disease, and sin in their members, which made them vile indeed.

III. *Who made Him wisdom, righteousness, sanctification, and redemption?*

God. It was the Father that found out, appointed, and made Christ all this for the salvation of sinners. We are thus indebted to God the Father as well as to Christ for the provision of grace, and we ought to praise and thank Him for His wonders done for the children of men.

IV. *For whom was Christ made wisdom, righteousness, sanctification, and redemption?*

The Apostle says, for us—that is, for His people, whom He had elected from all eternity to eternal life. Some deny the doctrine of election, but these forget that God was not under any obligation to save any of the human race. He might have left them to perish like the fallen angels, for whom He made no provision of salvation. You cannot know whether you are elected or not, or whether you are among the number for whom Christ was made wisdom, righteousness, sanctification, and redemption, till you are effectually called by the Holy Spirit. It was after Paul was effectually called that he was able to say, " For us." If you have a right to say that you are of that number, and when you are able to say it, you will be in a happy frame of mind, and say with the Psalmist, " What shall I render to the Lord for all His benefits towards me ?" (Ps. cxvi. 12).

We have been speaking of election, but, if you are still in a state of nature, it is not with election you have to do at first, but with the call of the Gospel, inviting you to Christ as a lost sinner. There are some Christians who teach that you must know that you have been elected before you can have a warrant to comply with the Gospel call, and if these men heard me preach the universal call of the Gospel, they would say that I was preaching error. If I am preaching error in this respect, they must charge Christ with preaching error, for He preached the universal call of the Gospel. " Look unto me, and be ye saved, all the ends of the earth " (Isaiah xlv. 22). The call of the Gospel is to you as a sinner. As the fall left you, and as you yourself made you seven times worse by your actual transgression than the fall left you, you are called. If you are still in a state of nature, be not at ease in that state. Cry to God for mercy, and for grace to bring you out of that state, and to make you a new creature in Christ Jesus. He is the hearer and answerer of prayer. He hears the cry of the poor and needy. He heard the publican when he cried, " God, be merciful to me, the sinner." Cease not crying to Him till He comes to pluck you as a brand out of the fire.

What a glorious work it is to preach Christ, as the Apostle Paul did, and what a glorious change it makes on people to whom it is blessed. The Corinthians were heathens, ignorant of the true God, and very corrupt in their manners, but now the Apostle characterises them as rich in knowledge, and as saints. May we then prize the Gospel, and seek that it may be blessed to ourselves and to others. AMEN.

J

XXIV.

The Betrothal

" And I will betroth thee unto Me for ever ; yea, I will betroth thee unto Me in righteousness, and in judgment, and in lovingkindness, and in mercies. I will even betroth thee unto Me in faithfulness : and thou shalt know the Lord."—Hos. ii. 19, 20.

HERE is a promise given to the children of Israel that notwithstanding that they had forsaken the Lord who had brought them into a covenant relation with Himself, He will bring them into a covenant relation which cannot be broken—I will betroth thee forever.

In speaking from the text we shall notice,

I. The betrothal.
II. The manner in which it is to be made.

I. *The betrothal*: Although to betroth means to enter into a contract with a view to marriage, here it signifies to marry. So it is rendered in the Gaelic translation. It is in this sense we are to use it. We shall notice :

(1) The parties to be betrothed. Among the human race parties marry who are of equal rank in society, but it is not so in this case. There is an infinite difference in rank between the husband and the spouse. The former is infinite in His being and attributes, while the latter is a creature whose creator is God. " Thy Maker is thine husband ; the Lord of Hosts is His Name ; and thy Redeemer the Holy One of Israel. The God of the whole earth shall He be called" (Is. liv. 5). What a glorious husband the Church has : there is none like

Him, none so good, so powerful, and so wealthy. " The earth belongs unto the Lord and all that it contains" — for supplying all the temporal needs of His Church, and he has unsearchable riches of grace for supplying her spiritual needs. The party to be betrothed is not only a creature but a sinful creature. This is true of all the human race by nature. "All have sinned, and come short of the glory of God." They were shining in the beauty of holiness as they came forth from the hand of the Creator, but are now by sin uglier than any creature on the earth. As it was to the Jews the promise was primarily made, it is a wonder that God would betroth them to Himself, for they were guilty of spiritual adultery. The Lord was their first husband, but they forsook Him, broke the marriage covenant and married another husband—a false god. " If a man put away his wife, and she go from him and become another man's, shall he return unto her again? Shall not that land be greatly polluted : but thou hast played the harlot with many lovers ; yet return again to Me, saith the Lord" (Jer. iii. 1). This is a wonder indeed, but the God of all grace deals thus with sinners. What a wonder that the Lord God would look upon such sinful creatures and bring them into union with Himself. The Church, in her natural condition, was not only sinful but miserable, liable to all the miseries in this life, to death itself, and to the pains of hell forever. If the husband was rich, she was poor. She lost all the riches given her in her first creation. Nothing belonged to her in her fallen condition but sin and death, yet this is the very person to whom God says, " I will betroth thee." Like the Jews, we as a nation were brought into a covenant relation with God, but we broke the covenant, forsook our good Husband who did great things for us, and married a cruel husband who cannot do us any good but much evil. We joined ourselves to idols, yet He calls us back by the word of the Gospel to betroth us to Himself, if we return to Him with faith and repentance. We ought to wonder at this, but all His works are works of wonder.

The consent of the woman is necessary to marriage. What way or ways did God take to gain the consent of His intended spouse? (1) He hedged up her way with thorns and built a strong and high wall which made it impossible for her to take any further steps after her lovers. When the Lord begins to bring sinners to Himself He makes this world a wilderness to them, so that they find by sad experience that it will not yield to them the happiness they expected to find in it He convinces them by His Spirit of their sin and misery. He uses His Word and Providence in dealing with them, and reminds them that it was He Himself and not their idols that gave them the temporal mercies they enjoyed. " For she did not know that I gave her corn, and wine, and oil, and multiplied her silver and gold, which they prepared for Baal. Therefore will I return and take away my corn in the time thereof, and my wine in the season thereof, and will recover my wool and my flax given to cover her nakedness. And now will I discover her lewdness in the sight of her lovers, and none shall deliver her out of my hands. I will also cause all her mirth to cease, her feast days, her new moons, and her Sabbaths, and all her solemn feasts. And I will destroy her vines, and her fig trees, whereof she hath said, These are my rewards that my lovers have given me; and I will make them a forest, and the beasts of the field shall eat them. And I will visit upon her the days of Baalim, wherein she burned incense to them, and she decked herself with her earrings and her jewels, and she

went after her lovers, and forgat me, saith the Lord"
(vv. 8-13). This way of dealing with her had the effect
of making her see the vanity of idols, and the bitterness
of the sin of idolatry, and of commending God to her as
the giver of all good. Like the prodigal, she, finding
herself in the miserable position into which she had
brought herself by forsaking God, and remembering that
even the servants in the heavenly Father's house were
better off than she—she by the teaching of God's Spirit
resolved to return to her first Husband whom she had
foolishly deserted. " I will go and return to my first
Husband; for then was it better with me than now"
(v. 7). Her consent was gained at last, she was " made
willing in the day of God's power."

Who performs the work of betrothal? Ministers join
parties in marriage, but it is God only that does this
work; for He says, " I will betroth thee." If you are
united to God in spiritual marriage it is He that did it.

II. *The manner of the betrothal*: There are seven
things in the manner.

(1) It is forever. In marriage the covenant relation
lasts till the death of either party or both. It is of the
law of marriage that the Apostle Paul speaks when he
says, " The law hath dominion over a man as long as
he liveth" (Rom. vii. 1.), but, in the case of the spiritual
marriage, neither party ever dies. This is true not only
of God, but it is also true of the Church. " He that
believeth in Me hath everlasting life" (John vi. 47). If
you come to-day to receive Him, and be brought into
covenant relation with Him, that relation shall be everlasting. " Who shall separate us from the love of
Christ? Shall tribulation, or distress, or persecution,
or famine, or nakedness, or peril, or sword? Nay, in all

these things we are more than conquerors through Him that loved us" (Rom. viii. 35, 37).

(2) In righteousness. It is a righteous or just thing of God to save sinners and bring them nigh to Himself. " He is a just God and a Saviour." He is as just in saving as He is in punishing. He does it in righteousness also inasmuch as the bride is not only accepted on the ground of Christ's righteousness, but because it is with the white robe of Christ's righteousness she is clothed.

(3) In judgment. The betrothal takes place not rashly, without previous consideration ; everything in it was well considered and arranged in the court of God's will, and in the covenant of grace, which is well ordered in all things, and sure.

(4) In lovingkindness. In the Gaelic translation the word lovingkindness is rendered into two words, *caoimh-neas* agus *caomhgràdh*—that is, kindness and tender love. Kindness is a disposition to be good to another person or persons, and is the effect of love. The love of God is the great source of salvation and the cause of all the kindness that He shows to His people. David loved Jonathan so much that he showed much kindness to his son Mephibosheth on Jonathan's account. In every right marriage there is love, mutual love in both parties. Here there is love on the part of God, and there is love on the part of the Church. It is the love of God that is meant here which is the cause of her love to Him.

(5) And in mercies. Mercy has respect to misery. The Church before her betrothed was in misery, but the Lord had mercy on her. " But after that the kindness and love of God our Saviour toward man appeared, not by works of righteousness which we have done, but according to His mercy He saved us" (Titus iii. 4, 5).

Mercy in God flows forth to sinners through the atonement of Christ.

(6) In faithfulness. In keeping the marriage covenant fidelity or faithfulness is required. Faithfulness here signifies (1) truth. The betrothal was to be accomplished not in a mere outward profession but in reality and truth. (2) Faithfulness in fulfilling all that He promised to do to His Church. " Faithful is He that calleth you, who also will do it " (1 Thes. v. 24).

(7) Knowledge of the Lord is necessary in order to the betrothal. " Thou shalt know the Lord." No sensible woman marries a man of whom she is ignorant as to what kind of a man he is. Although the Church was in the state of nature ignorant of God, she is taught by the Spirit and Word to know Him ; her mind is enlightened in his knowledge as He revealed Himself in the Old and New Testaments. " For God who commanded the light to shine out of darkneess hath shined in our hearts, to give the light of the knowledge of the glory of God in the face of Jesus Christ" (2 Cor. iv. 6). In her time of ignorance, she could make no distinction between the true God and Baal, but now she knows the Lord, and, not only so, but she is able to realise her relation to Him, and to call Him " Ishi," or " My Husband." Although she may not be able at all times in the full assurance of faith to say this, yet there are times in which she has no difficulty in saying it, and when she cannot say it in words her conduct speaks for her. After her betrothal she renounces for ever Baal, who was formerly her lord and husband. His names are taken out of her mouth by her new Husband. " For I will take away the names of Baalim out of her mouth, and they shall no more be remembered by their name" (v. 17). Those who keep up the memory of false gods or goddesses prove by their conduct that the living and

true God is not their husband.   There are many in our
day who celebrate the memory of Easter, a heathen idol
that was worshipped by those who were ignorant of the
true God.   It is lamentable that in this 20th century this
false goddess is still worshipped in the land of the Gospel,
and is worshipped even in Dingwall at a time which they
call Easter, but which they cannot find in the Word of
God.   The term Easter is indeed found in Acts xii. 4, but
it is a mis-translation of the original.   The word in the
original is *Pascha*, which means Passover and not Easter.

Concluding remarks: The promise of betrothal includes Gentiles as well as Jews. " I will have mercy
upon her that had not obtained mercy" (v. 23).   The
Apostle Peter applies this to the Gentiles, " Which in
times past were not a people, but are now the people of
God; which had not obtained mercy" (1 Peter ii. 10).
The Apostle Paul speaks of this as a mystery " which in
other ages was not made known unto the sons of men,"
that the Gentiles should be made fellowheirs, and of the
same body, and partakers of His promise in Christ by
the Gospel (Eph. iii. 5, 6). How thankful we ought to
be that the Gospel came to us who are of the Gentiles.
And if it has been blessed to us in bringing us into the
covenant relation with God of which we have spoken, we
have still more reason to thank the Lord and praise Him
for His goodness to us. In our state of nature we were
not His people, and, in that state, we had no right to
call Him our God and our Husband, but if we obtained
mercy we are His people and He is our God. Before
parties marry they have thoughts about it, and this is
true of the spiritual marriage. God had thoughts about
it from all eternity, and the sinner who is betrothed had
thoughts about it previous to the day of his espousals.
He began to think about it when he was awakened to a

sense of his need of Christ revealed in the Gospel. He was by nature married to the law as an husband; but when he broke the law it began to curse him, and he found out that he could not by anything he might do or suffer come to peaceable terms with that husband, but having been informed by the Gospel that Christ the Son of God died that sinners might be saved, his thoughts were directed towards Him, in the hope that He might bring him into saving union with Himself.

Parties intending to marry not only think about the matter, but they speak of it. God spoke of it and still speaks of it in the Scriptures, and the sinner spoke of it also, especially in prayer, saying, "God be merciful to me, the sinner," or, "Oh, that I might be found in Christ, not having mine own righteousness which is of the law, but the righteousness of Christ, the righteousness which is of God by faith." Many were thinking and speaking of marrying that never married, but that is not the case with those that are saved. They in God's good time believed in the Lord Jesus Christ, and were saved. Their new Husband broke down the tie between them and their old husband, the law, so that they are no longer under it as a covenant of works.

Every time the Gospel is preached sinners are invited to come to God that He might betroth them to Himself. We now invite you to come as you are, sinful, miserable, and lost. What response are you prepared to give to His gracious call? If you refuse to comply with the invitation, and continue to refuse to the end of your life, your punishment shall be greater than that of the heathen who never heard the Gospel. Hearken, O daughter, and consider, and incline thine ear, forget also thine own people, and thy father's house (Ps. xlv. 10).

XXV.

The Feast of Fat Things

" And in this mountain shall the Lord of hosts make unto all
people a feast of fat things, a feast of wines on the lees, of fat things
full of marrow, of wines on the lees well refined."—Is. xxv. 6.

THE prophet begins this chapter by speaking to God.
He praises Him for the wonders He had done, for His
counsels of old, which are faithfulness and truth. All
that He does in time are the effects of the counsel of His
will. The prophet praises the Lord for His works of
judgment as well as for His works of mercy. He praises
Him for overthrowing and making an heap of the city of
His enemies. He made a heap of many cities in Old
Testament times, such as Babylon and other cities, but,
as our text speaks of New Testament times, we understand by the city here the city of powerful enemies that
oppose and seek the destruction of the kingdom of Christ,
which shall be destroyed in connection with the setting
up of the kingdom of Christ in the world. This is a
cause of praise and thankfulness to God. The city of
pagan idolatry was destroyed by the introduction of the
Gospel and also by terrible works of judgment, and
in the present terrible war the Lord is destroying many
idolatrous cities, and He will continue to do so till all
of them are made a heap of ruins. But the prophet
especially praises the Lord for the provision of salvation
of which he speaks in our text.

In speaking from the text we shall call your attention
to the following particulars : —

The feast spoken of.

II. The Person who made the feast.

III. The place where the feast was made.

IV. Those for whom the feast was made.

I. *The feast* : The feast means the provision which God made in Christ for perishing sinners. Solomon speaks of a feast when beasts were killed to provide a feast, but in this feast it was not a beast that was killed, but the Son of God in our nature. He is the feast, for He says, " My flesh is meat indeed, and My blood is drink indeed." In a feast there is an abundance and a variety of the best things full of marrow. The marrow is within the bone, and in order to get at the marrow the bone must be opened up, and, although no bone of Christ was broken, yet by His awful sufferings He speaks of all His bones being out of joint, and they were opened up by the sword of justice, so that the fat things full of marrow are now on the feast table. In order to feed on the marrow of the Gospel, the Scriptures must be expounded or opened up to us, as Christ did to the two disciples going to Emmaus on the day of His resurrection. He expounded to them in all the Scriptures the things concerning Himself, and in order that they might understand the Scriptures He opened their understanding also. We are commanded not only to read the Scriptures but to search them, so as to find Christ in them and to feed upon Him.

The feast is not only made up of the best food, but also of the best drink—wines well refined. Under the Old Testament the death of Christ was set forth in types and shadows, but under the new it is set forth without these types and shadows, and therefore His blood is typified by wine well refined, and, as He said Himself, it is drink indeed. As wine cheers the heart of the sorrowful, so the blood of Christ cheers and comforts those that mourn in Zion. '' And wine that maketh glad the heart of man'' (Ps. civ. 15). If literal wine has this effect, how much more the wine of the Gospel? Solomon says that wine makes one forget his poverty and to remember his misery no more (Proverbs xxxi. 7). This is indeed true of those who drink of the wine spoken of in the feast.

There is in this feast spiritual food and drink for the whole soul of man. There is food for the mind which requires knowledge to satisfy it. All men labour to feed their mind in some way. The most careless about the salvation of their souls do so. Some try to feed their souls by reading novels, and that because they are ignorant of Christ; others by a variety of other things, such as pleasures and amusements, which are but as husks upon which swine feed. This is what the prodigal did before he returned to his father's house. But there is nothing that can truly satisfy the mind of man but the knowledge of God and of Jesus Christ whom He has sent, as Christ said, '' And this is life eternal that they might know Thee the only true God, and Jesus Christ, whom Thou hast sent'' (John xvii. 3). That satisfies the mind of the believer.

There is food and drink for the conscience of man. The only thing that can satisfy an awakened conscience is the blood of Christ which satisfied all the requirements of the law of God. The conscience of the believer is as satisfied with the blood of Christ as the law of God is. Many try to satisfy their conscience by other things, such as their own endeavours to satisfy the law by their own works or sufferings. If you are a true believer you are fully satisfied in your conscience with Christ's atonement. Some would ignore Christ's atonement as necessary as a ground of reconciliation with God, and would substitute in its place the following of Christ's example. A student who often visited the widow of the late Professor Smeaton, Edinburgh, called on her on a certain day after the death of her husband. In the course of conversation she, among other advices she gave him, advised him when he began to preach to give a prominent place in his sermons to Christ's death, but the student, who imbibed the new ideas that began then to be taught in the Colleges, said to her that they thought more of His life than of his death. She replied, so did Peter at one time, for Christ said to him, " Get thee behind me, Satan." The late Professor Drummond was of the same opinion as this student regarding the meritorious ground of salvation.

There is food in the feast for the affections, for the affections require food, and desire it. Love is the chief part of the affections, and love hungers and thirsts after some object to satisfy it. God was the object on whom the love of man was set before he sinned and fell, but after the fall man ceased to love God and began to love the world. But this love is forbidden in Scripture : " Love not the world, neither the things that are in the world. If any man love the world the love of the Father is not in him" (1 John ii. 15). When the sinner is savingly changed in his nature and united by faith to Christ, then his affections are withdrawn from the world, and set upon God again. The love of God is shed abroad in his heart by the Holy Spirit, and as an effect he loves God because God loved Him first, and gave the greatest manifestation of His love in sending " His Son to be the propitiation for the sins of His people." If we love God we shall manifest our love to Him by an endeavour to keep

16

His commandments. If we love Him we love His Word, His people, and His cause in the world and seek His glory and the coming of His kingdom by every scriptural means. This much on the first head.

II. *The Person that made the feast*: " The Lord of hosts." It was not we that made the feast, but Jehovah, nor did He consult us or any creature, man or angel, in making it. He knew all our needs in our fallen condition, and He made the provision of salvation to meet all our requirements in the state to which we have brought ourselves by sin. The feast that man makes is like himself. If a poor man makes a feast for his friends, he cannot be expected to provide a rich feast, but when a king makes a feast the feast will be such as is worthy of a man in his high position. Although we are utterly unworthy of the Gospel feast, the feast is worthy of its Maker and the glory of the provision is due to Him alone, and will be ascribed to Him by all who partake of it. They say with the Psalmist, " Not unto us, O Lord, not unto us, but unto Thy Name give the glory, for Thy mercy and for Thy truth" (Ps. cxv. 1).

III. *The place where the feast was made*: " In this mountain." What is this mountain? If we mean a literal mountain, it may be said that it was made on Mount Calvary, where Christ was crucified. But we may say that the feast was made in the Church which is spoken of in Scripture as a mountain, as you may see in Micah iv. 1: " In the last days it shall come to pass, that the mountain of the house of the Lord shall be established in the top of the mountains, and it shall be exalted above the hills, and people shall flow unto it." It was not made outside the Church in heathen lands, but within the visible Church, of which the Jews were members. It was within that Church and by that Church Christ was put to death, and as Christ is the sum and substance of the feast, His death was accomplished according to the determinate counsel and foreknowledge of God, as you may see in Acts ii. 23 : " Him being delivered by the determinate counsel and fore-knowledge of God, ye have taken, and by wicked hands ye have crucified and slain." Inasmuch as it was for the sins of His people He was put to death, it may be said that all the redeemed had a hand in putting Him to death, for it is said that they shall look upon Him whom they have pierced and mourn for Him (Zech. xii. 10). Although this is primarily spoken of the Jews, it has a wider application. It applies to all who are brought to repentance to the end of time. If you look to Christ by faith, and mourn for your sins, you will see and feel that you were the cause of His death. As it was in the Church that Christ was put to death, it is in the Church by the preaching of the Gospel the feast is set forth before you. It is set before you on the Gospel table. When a feast is placed on a table it is set in several dishes filled with a variety of food to suit the needs of every individual of the guests, and to satisfy the hunger and thirst of all. The dishes are the promises of the Gospel, and Christ in all the aspects in which He may be viewed as God's provision of salvation, is set before us in these promises, as He is made by Him for His people wisdom, righteousness, sanctification, and redemption. In these promises there is the sincere milk of the word for new-born babes that they may grow thereby, and there is strong meat for them who are of full age, even for those who by reason of use have their senses exercised to discern both good and evil (Heb. v. 13, 14).

IV. *Those for whom the feast was made:* "Unto all people." Under the New Testament dispensation it is extended to the Gentiles throughout the whole world, and, in order that all the nations of the world should partake of the feast, the Apostles were commanded by the Head of the Church to go into all the world, and preach the Gospel to every creature of the human race to whom they had access. They were to begin their work at Jerusalem, and to give the first offer of the Gospel to the Jews, who had their hands red in the blood of Christ, by putting Him to death. Peter in his sermon on the day of Pentecost charged them with the awful sin of crucifying Him. This pricked them in their hearts, and they thought that on account of their great wickedness there was no mercy for them, but they were the first to whom Christ was freely offered in the Gospel, and by the grace of God the first to receive Him as their Saviour. If they were great sinners, as they really were, Christ is a great Saviour—the only Saviour. And as all the redeemed are saved by grace, salvation is as free to the chief of sinners as it is to those who were not so guilty in their actual transgressions. The blood of Jesus Christ, the Son of God, cleanses us not from some sins only, but from all sins, though they might be as scarlet and red like crimson (Is. i. 18). This was verified in the case of those who were guilty of the great sin of crucifying the Lord of glory, and is an encouragement to great sinners to the end of time, but although the Gospel, which is the power of God to salvation to everyone that believes, began to be preached at Jerusalem, in New Testament times it did not stop there, but was extended to the Gentiles, for the feast was made for all people, Jews and Gentiles. As the Lord of Hosts prepared a feast for all people, He will prepare for it all who shall partake of the feast, as you may see in the context: " And He will destroy in this mountain the face of the covering cast over all people, and the veil that is spread over all nations" (v. 7). There is a veil of spiritual blindness and unbelief on all by nature, but, in the case of all that are saved, that veil is destroyed, and removed, so that they shall see their need of salvation and come to know Christ as able to save to the uttermost all that come to God through Him. This work of preparing guests for the feast is effected by the Holy Spirit in their effectual calling, and by the instrumentality of Gospel ministers whom God uses as He used the Apostle Paul, " in turning sinners from darkness and from the power of Satan unto God" (Acts xxvi. 18).

All to whom the Gospel is preached are invited to come and partake of the feast. Christ said, and still says, " Come unto Me all ye that labour and are heavy laden, and I will give you rest" (Matt. xi. 28). " Look unto Me and be ye saved, all the ends of the earth" (Is. xlv. 22). We in the name of Christ invite every individual sinner present here to-day. Some one may say, " I am afraid that I am not invited. If Christ mentioned my name, it would encourage me to come to Him." Well, He mentions your name—your name is a sinner. The publican understood that that was his name, and he prayed, " God be merciful to me the sinner," and Christ saved him, and if you will cry to Him like the publican He will save you. The publican also understood the ground on which sinners are saved, and that ground is the propitiation of Christ. "Be merciful to me" might be rendered, according to the original, be merciful to me on the ground of the propitiation made by Christ. " And He is the propitiation for our sins" (1 John ii. 2). If you feel your need of Christ and are satisfied with Him as all

K

your salvation and all your desire, then you may conclude that " Christ is yours and that you are His." But
you who are indifferent about the salvation of your
never-dying soul, it is high time for you to awake out
of your sleep and out of your slumber, lest death should
soon sweep you away into eternity, where you shall be
fed for ever by the wrath of God. The late Hector Jack,
who was for many years a faithful witness for Christ in
Strathconon, when brought under conviction of sin,
would not taste food for his body for days, and when
urged to take food he would say, " No, I shall soon be
fed with the wrath of God throughout eternity"—but he
was enabled to come to Christ and found in Him a feast
for His needy soul. If you come to Him you shall never
perish but have eternal life.

May the Lord add His blessing to our remarks on
this great subject. AMEN.

XXVI.

The Shepherd and the Flock

" My sheep hear My voice, and I know them, and they follow Me :
And I give unto them eternal life ; and they shall never perish, neither
shall any man pluck them out of My hand."—John x. 27, 28.

JESUS CHRIST spoke these words after telling the Jews,
who believed not in Him as the Messiah, that they were
not His sheep. They blame Christ, not themselves, for
not believing that He was the Messiah. They came to
Him and said, " How long dost Thou make us to doubt"
(v. 24). He said to them that He told them, but they
believed not. He referred them to the works which none
but God could do. The question about His Messiahship
was hypocritical. If He confessed that He was the
Messiah, they would make that a charge against Him as
blasphemy and as deserving of death. Indeed, that was
the thing for which they put Him to death. It was in
this connection that He told them they were not His
sheep. He meant by that that they were none of those
given Him by the Father in the everlasting covenant.
That was the cause of their not believing in Him. All
that the Father gave Him in that Covenant will certainly
believe in Him. After declaring that fearful saying,
He comes to speak of His own people, even those given
Him by the Father.

In speaking from our text we shall call your attention
to the following particulars : —

    I. Christ's property in His people, called here
       " sheep."

    II. The marks He gives of them.

    III. The promise He makes to them.

I. *His property in His people* : Before we come to speak of Christ's property in His people we may make a remark on their being called sheep.   At the day of judgment all the human race are divided into two classes —sheep and goats. The redeemed were never goats, they were always sheep, even when they were in a state of nature like others, for so Christ speaks of them : " And other sheep I have which are not of this fold : them also I must bring, and they shall hear My voice ; and there shall be one fold and one shepherd" (v. 16). The other sheep who were to be brought into His fold were the Gentiles, who would in due time be brought to believe in Him by means of the word of the Gospel.

Christ's property in His people is indicated by the possessive pronoun " My." How are they His?

(1) They are His as given Him by the Father from all eternity, in the everlasting covenant of grace. " Thine they were, and Thou gavest them Me" (John xvii. 6). They were the Father's in His eternal purpose of salvation.   They were viewed as in a lost condition when they were given to Christ. If you give a gift of what is your own to a friiend, the gift is his by all rights.   He may justly say, It is now my property. Oh what a wonder that Christ would accept of sinners in whom no good thing dwelt, but He accepted of them willingly. This shall be a wonder to the Lord's people in time and in eternity.

(2) They are His by purchase. What you buy is your own ; no one could justly dispute your right to it. Christ bought His people at a great cost. An Apostle speaking to the redeemed said, " Ye are not your own, ye are bought with a price ; therefore glorify God with your bodies and spirits which are His."

What was the price Christ paid for them ? Not silver or gold, but His own precious blood, as the Apostle Peter

said : " Forasmuch as ye know that ye were not redeemed
with corruptible things, as silver and gold, from your vain
conversatioin received by tradition from your fathers ;
but with the precious blood of Christ as of a lamb without
blemish and without spot" (1 Peter i. 18, 19). He means
the same thing in the present context when he says,
" I lay down My life for the sheep" (v. 15). He began
to pay the price when He entered into His state of
humiliation, and finished His work of redemption at the
end of thirty-three years when He cried on the Cross,
" It is finished." He bought them all by the one sacrifice of Himself to satisfy justice and to reconcile them
to God, but although He bought them He did not take
actual possession of them all at that time. When a sheep
farmer buys a flock of sheep he does not ordinarily take
them away with him at once ; he leaves them on the
ground till a certain date and then he comes to take them
with him to his own place. But though the farmer ordinarily takes with him all the flock he bought, when he
take any at all, without leaving any behind, Christ does
not do so. He takes them, it may be, one at one time
and thousands at another time, as for example on the
day of Pentecost. The farmer buys only sheep that do
actually exist, and never buys those that may exist in
a future time, but Christ bought many sinners who had
not yet been born into the world, and this makes it
impossible that He should have brought them into His
fold even when He bought them, nor does He bring them
into His fold when they are born after the flesh.
Although the great majority of them in every age are
converted when they are young, there are others left in
a state of nature till they attain to the maturity of man-
hood, and some are left to old age, but before the end
of the world they shall all be brought in and saved.

K*

(3) They are His by a willing surrender of themselves to Him. This will take place in the day of His power. " Thy people shall be willing in the day of Thy power" (Ps. cx. 3). If you have been given to Christ by the Father, and if you were bought by price, and if you are His by a willing surrender of yourself to Him in an everlasting covenant, there was a day in your history in which you gave yourself to Him. The wife that gives herself in marriage to a husband is his. The husband can justly say—she is mine; the relation is mutual, as the Church says, " My beloved is mine, and I am His." Did you ever offer yourself to Christ? You may say that you are afraid He will not accept of such a great sinner as you are, but He assures you that He will not reject you on that ground. " Him that cometh unto Me I will in no wise cast out."

(4) They are His in service. All that believed in Christ have changed masters and service. In their state of nature Satan was their master, and his will they did, but now Christ is their Master and they endeavour daily to do His will. They endeavour to glorify Him with their bodies and spirits, which are His.

II. *The marks Christ gives of His sheep:*

(1) They have an ear mark. " My sheep hear My voice." A sheep farmer puts a mark on the ears of his sheep to distinguish them from the sheep of his neighbour, so that if they wander or mix with other sheep he can claim them as his by the mark on the ears. Christ's sheep bear this mark. " They hear His voice." Although the voice of Christ may be heard in His work of Providence, it may be heard especially and more particularly in the word of the Gospel. They delight to hear His voice there and to obey it. The word in the

original—rendered " to hear"—means also " to obey."
They know Christ's voice in the Gospel. They know not
the voice of strangers—that is, they do not own or
acknowledge the voice of these, but they know the voice
of Christ because they know Himself personally. When
a dear friend with whom you were acquainted comes to
your door and speaks, before you open the door you will
say, It is such a person. You will even say, I am sure
it is he, for I know his voice. The Church said, " It is
the voice of my beloved," although He spoke outside
when the door was shut. If you know Christ personally
you will know His voice in the Gospel. We were speaking of an ear mark. In the context Christ speaks of the
thief who comes to steal, to kill, and to destroy. The
thief among men has a mark on the ears of his own sheep,
and we were told that the mark was that he cut off both
ears to the root—his object in this was that he might
easily put his own mark on all the sheep he stole. Satan,
the great thief, put this mark on many in all ages, and
in this age also. He virtually cut off their ears to the
root so that they will not hearken to Christ's voice in the
Gospel. They will listen to almost any error proceeding
out of the mouth of Satan and his servants. Through
false teachers their ears got turned away from the truth
to fables. " For the time will come when they will not
endure sound doctrine, but after their own lusts shall
they heap to themselves teachers having itching ears.
And they shall turn away their ears from the truth
and shall be turned unto fables" (2 Tim. iv. 3, 4).

(2) They have a foot mark. Whether sheep farmers
put a mark on the feet of their sheep or not, Christ put
a mark on the feet of His own sheep. " They follow
Me." and that perseveringly to the end. There were
some who followed Christ for a time, but " they went

back and walked no more with Him'' (John vi. 66). It is he that endures to the end that shall be saved. The Lord gives to His people not only converting grace, but also the grace of perseverance, so that they shall endure unto the end. They follow Christ as their leader and the captain of their salvation. They follow Him according to the rule of His Word. They do not take the lead themselves; they are satisfied to leave the leadership with Christ, and they follow Him. There are many who are wise in their own conceit, and they take the lead themselves and imagine that Christ will follow them. As leaders they make new laws and new creeds, and in their blindness no creature, man or angel, can convince them that Christ is not following them or with them in their private or public devotions, but sooner or later, in mercy or in judgment, they shall discover that they have been deceiving themselves.

(3) Some sheep farmers put a mark on the nose of their sheep by a red-hot iron, which makes the mark prominent and lasting. Believers have this mark, and therefore feel a sweet savour not only of the person of Christ but even of His garment, in proof of which we may quote the words of the Church: '' All Thy garments smell of myrrh, and aloes, and cassia, out of the ivory palaces, whereby they have made Thee glad'' (Ps. xlv. 3). They cannot be long in the company of those who have been anointed by the unction of the Spirit without feeling a sweet savour of them, while on the other hand they feel a nauseous smell of the wicked. They feel this smell of their own language and their actions.

(4). There is another mark on sheep that distinguishes them from other animals, namely, that they chew the cud. This was a mark of distinction in Old Testament times between clean and unclean animals. The Lord's people may be said to chew the cud.   What is it to chew the cud?   It is to meditate upon the Word of God which they read or hear, and from which they receive food for their souls.   The sheep chew what they had formerly eaten; what they had eaten comes up again into their mouth and they feed upon it a second time.   The Lord's people by meditation feed a second time on the word of the Gospel, or on Christ in the Gospel, so that they receive a twofold benefit.   Sheep are liable to a disease by which they lose the power of chewing the cud, and unless they are cured of that malady, it will cause their death.   A certain shepherd found out a cure, and by the application of that cure he was successful in saving many sheep from dying.   The cure was this: he brought the sheep that had that disease to another sheep he saw chewing the cud, and took with his fingers a part of that which the sheep was chewing out of her mouth and put it in the mouth of the other one, and soon she began to chew the cud as well as ever.   The use we make of this illustration is this: The Lord's people sometimes lose the power of meditating on God's Word, but when they are brought into the company of their fellow Christians who were able to meditate upon the Word and speak out in express terms, they are soon cured of that disease. They can now meditate and, so to speak, chew the cud as well as the rest.

(5) Another mark they have is that of taste.   It is said of sheep that in chewing the cud they will throw out of their mouth any unwholesome thing they had swallowed along with the grass upon which they fed. This is true of believers.   If they had unguardedly or without due consideration swallowed the least error along with the truth, on reflection and meditation they shall cast it away and adhere to the sincere milk of the Word.

They tasted that the Lord is gracious, and call upon others to taste and see that He is good. "O taste and see that the Lord is good: blessed is the man that trusteth in Him" (Ps. xxxiv. 8). They have spiritual discernment to know the distinction between truth and error. Although some of these marks are not in our text, we deemed it proper to refer to them because they are in the Bible, and are marks of the Lord's people.

III. *The promise*: There are two things in the promise—(a heaven)—life and safety.

(1) Life. "And I give unto them eternal life." Life eternal means all the blessings of salvation, grace, and glory. He gives this life to them not on the ground of their following Him, but on the ground of His own merit. He does not say, I sell it to them, but I give it as a free gift. "The gift of God is eternal life through Jesus Christ our Lord" (Rom. vi. 23).

Our life on earth is not everlasting, it shall come to an end. What we need is the life that is everlasting, because our souls are immortal and shall exist for ever. This is the life that Christ promises and gives; it begins on earth and is everlasting in its being and nature, and continues during their time on earth, and grows to its fulness in heaven. "The Lord will give grace and glory, no good thing will He withhold from them that walk uprightly" (Ps. lxxxiv. 11).

(2) Safety. "They shall never perish, neither shall any man pluck them out of My hand." It is a great blessing not to perish in eternity. Many would be satisfied if they escaped eternal punishment, but believers would not be satisfied with that only. What would satisfy them is to have Christ as their portion, and to be conformed to His image and to be with Him where

He is. They are in Christ's hand and are as safe as if they were now in glory. No man or any creature is able to pluck them out of His hand. Many would, if they could, pluck them out of His hand. Satan, sin, and especially unbelief would do so, but they cannot. The word " pluck" is significant, and refers to the strong grasp Christ has of them and to their own unwillingness to forsake Him. If an effort is made to take them out of Christ's hand it must be by plucking; neither party, Christ nor His people, will yield to the plucking. It is therefore in vain for any enemy or all enemies to pluck them out of their place of safety. The Apostle Paul challenges all adversaries to separate them from Christ. " Who shall separate us from the love of Christ?" and he enumerates many things and creatures that would be calculated to separate them from Him if they could, such as tribulation, or distress, or persecution, or famine, or nakedness, or peril, or sword, or death, or life, or angels, or principalities, or powers, or things present, or things to come, or height, or depth, or any other creature. He comes to the conclusion that he is persuaded that none of these shall be able to separate them from the love of God that is in Christ Jesus their Lord (Rom. viii. 35-39).

They are also secure in the hands of the Father, and none can pluck them out of His hand. Oh, how secure and safe Christ's sheep are in the hands of the Good Shepherd and in the hands of the Father in the midst of all their doubts and fears, in the howling wilderness through which they are passing in their pilgrimage to their everlasting rest.

In conclusion, we have been discoursing on a great subject. We leave it with you. Examine yourselves as to whether you bear the marks of Christ's sheep. If you do, your end shall be peace, whatever trouble you may have in the world ; but if you have none of these marks, however easy you may get through the world, your end shall be everlasting dispeace if you die without peace with God through our Lord Jesus Christ. Think seriously of this ere it be too late. " Now is the accepted time, now is the day of salvation." " Seek ye the Lord while He may be found, call ye upon Him while He is near. Let the wicked forsake his way and the unrighteous man his thoughts, and let him return unto the Lord, and He will have mercy upon him ; and to our God, for He will abundantly pardon." Amen, so let it be.

XXVII.

Arise, My Love

"My beloved spake, and said unto me, Rise up, my love, my fair one, and come away. For, lo, the winter is past, the rain is over and gone ; the flowers appear on the earth ; the time of the singing of birds is come, and the voice of the turtle is heard in our land."— Song ii. 10-12.

HERE the Church tells what Christ, her beloved, spake to her. While others did not remember anything that Christ said to them in the way of conviction or comfort, the Lord's people did remember many things He said to them. They are like the Psalmist, who " remembered the days of old." The Church here tells others what Christ said to her. The Church spoke often to Christ, and He in response spoke as often to her. He always spoke to her according to need and according to the condition in which she was. It appears that she was in a low condition when He called her to " rise up" and come along with Him.

In speaking on this subject let us notice—

I. The party addressed.
II. The call given to the party.
III. The reason annexed to the call.

I. The party is the Church, and although it is composed of many members, yet it is spoken of here as one individual. He addresses His Church as His beloved. He loved her with an everlasting, unchangeable, free and sovereign love. He loved her because he would love her. According to the Gaelic translation He calls her

17

His beloved wife. Where did Christ find His wife? He must have found her somewhere among the human race. He found her dead in the grave—dead in trespasses and in sin, and if you should be found He must find you in that condition too. Did He marry her in that state? No. No man would marry a dead woman. In order to marriage the consent of the woman is necessary, and she could not give her consent while dead. In order that she might give her consent to marry Him, He quickened her to life and raised her out of the grave. " And you hath He quickened who were dead in trespasses and in sin." He did this by His Spirit and word. Every woman (except Eve) who was married was first born into the world. Those who are married to Christ are born again—a change without which none can see the kingdom of God. We never heard of parties marrying without thoughts on the subject beforehand. Christ thought on the matter from all eternity, and He brought her to think of it in the day of effectual calling when He convinced her of the sin and misery of this life, and enlightened her mind in the knowledge of Himself and made her willing to enter into the marriage covenant with Himself—a covenant that shall never be broken. Women never marry a stranger, and so before she could marry she was brought to behold the beauty of Christ, even as the chiefest among ten thousand and altogether lovely. Not only were there thoughts about marriage beforehand, there was also speaking on the subject by both parties. The speaking began with Christ, who in due time proposed to marry the Church, and there was speaking on the part of the Church too, who was filled with wonder at the King of Glory asking her in her low condition in marriage.

He calls her not only His beloved, but His fair one. She was not fair by nature. He convinced her of this— but He made her fair (1) by the regenerating work of His Spirit; (2) by clothing her with His unspotted righteousness; and (3) by the work of sanctification begun and which will in due time be perfected. She is not perfect, but He does not mention her imperfection, but leaves that to herself to make mention of, which she daily does with grief and desire to be delivered from all sin in her nature and to be made holy as God is holy. She is fair on account of the garment she wears—the imputed righteousness of Christ—the best robe, no spot or wrinkle in it. You cannot put a spot on the righteousness of Christ, so they are complete in Him, and this is the comfort of God's people. They see all the spots in themselves, but none in Christ. So she is fair in the sight of Christ as to her outward garment as well as with her internal garment—even holiness—a new nature-- holy—nothing so beautiful as holiness, and though not perfect, yet He looks on her as perfect. She is fair and beautiful in outward walk and conversation. Though not perfect in this respect, she is fairer than the unconverted, who trample upon God's law, profane the Sabbath, a sin which is very prevalent in this age, and for which the Lord of the Sabbath pours His judgments upon individuals and nations as He manifestly does in the present desolating war. Man was fair and beautiful before the fall—beautiful in creation, and beautiful in conduct, but when he sinned he became ugly in nature and conduct, in thought, speech, and practice. Many profess the Christian religion who belie their profession by their evil practices. See that your conduct be in accordance with your profession.

II. *The call: Rise up and come away.* This implies that she was in a low condition—depressed by many afflictions and temptations, and perhaps afraid of not being saved at all—so He says, Rise up and come away— don't cast away your confidence ; look for the recompense and the reward. Individual believers may be cast down with many doubts and fears, but Christ comes to them to encourage and comfort them, and says, Rise up and come away. It is not go, but come—that is, come with Me. He does not send them away alone. He goes with them and before them. If He said to the Apostles when He sent them forth to preach the Gospel, Go, He promised to be always with them, and without Him they could do nothing. He does not mention whither or to what they are called to come away. It is His to command and to lead, it is hers to obey, and she may trust Him as to her guidance. " My sheep hear My voice and they follow Me." " Follow thou Me." She needs the company and presence of Christ, for without Him she can do nothing. He knows this, and foretold it, and promised that He would never leave her nor forsake her. Then if this be so, and most assuredly it is, she may well comply with the call, and trust her allwise, powerful, and merciful leader with her future course. He calls her to that which shall be for His own glory and for her everlasting benefit. He calls her to enjoyment and comfort. She was needing this, for under the temporary hiding of the Lord's gracious presence she lay dejected, comfortless, and helpless. Ah, my friends, have we ever been brought low by this cause? If not, we are not Christ's " love and fair one." For the Lord's people have often sad experience of the withdrawal of His gracious countenance from their souls. On such occasions they are brought low, and there is nothing that can raise them up and comfort them but the return of Christ to their sorrowful souls to shine on them as the sun of righteousness, with healing in His wings. He then comes to His Church here and says to her, " Arise and come away." Arise from thy helpless condition, for I can and will help thee. Arise from the power of unbelief, be not faithless but believing. Arise from thy sorrow, for thy Comforter is come. Arise from thy bondage, for I am thy deliverer. Arise to behold My glory and to receive of My fulness. " Open thy mouth wide, and I will fill it." When Christ speaks with power to His Church in the time of need, He renews her strength, and she arises to enjoy anew the brightness of His face.

Those that go forth to serve the Lord without being called effectually are in their own estimation independent of God's grace to strengthen them to do His work. But it is otherwise with the Lord's people. Though He changed them by His Spirit—made them new creatures in Christ unto good works, they know and feel that without Him they can do nothing. But the Lord sends none forth at their own charges. When they are weak, low, and comfortless, He comes to strengthen and comfort them, and thus prepares them to do His will. Before He sent Mary Magdalene on a message to His sorrowful disciples, He revealed Himself to her and comforted her; before He asked Peter to feed His sheep and lambs, He healed him and gave him comfort. This is the way still, and it is when He prepares His people thus, their heart is enlarged to run with delight in the ways of His commandments. Their meat and drink is to do His work. " For me to live is Christ."

When He is about to revive His cause in the world He calls her to prayer, and the Spirit of prayer is revived in His people. He calls her to prayer, which is a pre-

cursor of a true revival of religion in the individual and
in the Church. Before the Spirit was poured down on
the day of Pentecost the disciples were praying for ten
days in the upper chamber in Jerusalem. Before the
great revival of religion that began at Cambuslang, the
Lord's people were stirred up to pray for that event,
and so it is still. If the Lord's people in our day got a
revival of the spirit of prayer, they might expect a wide-
spread revival of religion. Some say, We pray, but what
is the use? we don't receive an answer. But He will
answer in His own good time, which is the best time.
Dr Kidd of Aberdeen on one occasion met a man whose
work was to break stones for the road. The Doctor asked
him if he was praying. The man answered that he was
for forty years, but got no answer to his prayers. The
Doctor asked him would he give up prayer because he
got no answer. The man said he could not do that. The
Doctor then advised him to continue praying. Shortly
afterwards the Doctor was sent for to see the man on his
death-bed. Before the Doctor engaged in prayer he
asked the man what was he to ask in prayer for him.
The man answered, " I do not wish you to ask anything
for me, but to praise the Lord for His goodness to me."
He gave him now, facing eternity, an abundant answer
to all the prayers he put up during forty years. The
time of death is a time of great need, and to have light
and comfort then is of great value. Our lately departed
friend, the General Treasurer of the Church, was on his
death-bed full of the Spirit and of the love of Christ, and
preached about that love to his daughter and other friends
present. He told them that he had no fear of death,
which was a wonder to himself, but not to those who
knew him to be a bright Christian for many years. To
God's people, when He Himself is with them, death is not

gloomy, for they have the light of God's countenance shining upon them, and then they do not wish to remain, but to depart and to be with Christ, which is far better. Death is the common lot of the human race, and it shall be an eternity of misery without Christ, and the misery of this life is as a drop in the ocean in comparison to eternal misery. But He receiveth the chief of sinners who comes to Him even at the eleventh hour.

When the Lord's cause is low, He calls the Church by a special call to service in His vineyard. Before the Reformation the cause was very low, and He called the Reformers to rise up to preach the Gospel. It was the set time. He spoke with power, and they rose up to declare His truth and seek the coming of His kingdom. The Lord blessed their labours abundantly, so that we may say that all the countries of Europe, with few exceptions, came under the saving influence of the Gospel. Idolatry was cast out, and the true worship of God was set up in its place, but, alas! there is great need of a second Reformation, which shall surely come, because it is promised in the Scriptures.

Sometimes He calls His Church to suffering, and whether He calls to service or suffering He Himself is with them. He does not say, go, but come with Me. " When thou passest through the waters, I will be with thee; and through the rivers they shall not overflow thee: when thou walkest through the fire thou shalt not be burned; neither shall the flame kindle upon thee" (Is. xliii. 2). He was with the three young men in the fiery furnace seven times heated, and the fire had no power over them nor was an hair of their head singed, neither were their coats changed, nor the smell of fire had passed on them (Daniel iii. 27). This was a miracle which greatly affected even a heathen king.

The last call to rise up and come away is a call to everlasting glory. When His people are ripe for glory Christ will come to them at death and say, " Rise up, My beloved, My fair one, and come away to be with Me in heaven. I will be with thee going through the dark valley of the shadow of death. Fear not the valley, for I am with thee, and therefore it is only the shadow of death to thee. I will bring thee safely through it and put thee in possession of the inheritance, incorruptible, undefiled, and that fadeth not away—where thou shalt never have cause to mourn for want of My gracious presence." It is a call to come to be with Him among friends, and to see nothing but the face of friends, where Satan will harass her no more, and where there will be no more occasion to speak after the manner of David, who feared he would one day fall into the hands of Saul. No, it will be, " Come away from these temptations, trials, and miseries, and be with Me where I am." " Father, I will that they whom Thou hast given Me be with Me where I am ; that they may behold My glory, which Thou hast given Me ; for Thou lovedst Me before the foundation of the world" (John xvii. 24).

III. *The reason annexed to the call* :

The first thing in the reason is that the winter is past and the rain is over and gone. What winter? (1) The winter of God's wrath. Ah, friends, there is no winter so awful as this one. Many are exposed to it who though they have often complained of the severity of natural winters never felt their need of refuge from the wrath of God, under which they are. But this fearful winter is passed for ever with respect to the Lord's people. Whatever afflictions and sufferings they may meet with in the world, they shall not meet with this winter, for Christ, who bore the severity of it in their room and stead, tells His redeemed people that it is passed never to return. The Church needed to hear this from Christ's mouth, and it ought to be enough to comfort her, and to strengthen her faith to arise and come away with her beloved. Jesus, who saved His people from the wrath to come, says, " They shall never perish, neither shall any pluck them out of My hand." (2) The winter of desertion and chastisement. Though the winter of God's wrath is past—never to return in the case of the Church—she is liable to this winter as long as she is in the state of imperfection. She experiences this winter when Christ is absent. In winter the day is short, and the night is long, and the ground hard and barren, the weather cold, and everything is withered. So it is in the experience of believers when under desertion and chastisement. The winter is a season of threatening, of inclement weather. In the spiritual winter, believers are apt to take to themselves the threatenings of God's Word more than the promises. Although the day is short in winter, still there is no winter without a day, however short. The believer is not left to despair. He looks and longs for the lengthening of the day. When Christ comes to reveal Himself to His people this winter is passed, but it shall return again and again so long as they are in this world. All the seasons are useful in their own place. Although winter is not so pleasant as summer, it kills or destroys many noxious elements in the air that would be injurious to man's health. The spiritual winter kills many injurious things in the Lord's people—such as pride, boasting, and self-seeking, and self-confidence, so that it is among the all things that work for good to those that love God. Job had a long winter night. He was cursing the day of his birth. He was pained with trouble and disease, and tempted by Satan.

but he found that it worked for his good. At death this winter is past, never to return. There shall be no winter then. It will be a long summer—an everlasting summer in the case of the redeemed, but in the case of the lost it shall be an eternal winter without a ray of light.

Another thing in the reason of the call is that the rain is over and gone. In winter there is much cold and disagreeable rain. Waters in Scripture are an emblem of troubles and affliction, and in the spiritual winter believers have a large share of these, and when the winter is past these troubles are over and gone till the return of winter again. Then they enjoy comfort and joy unspeakable and full of glory.

Another sign of winter being past is, the flowers appear on the earth. In winter they only appear in hot-houses, but when they appear on the earth you can conclude that the winter is past and gone. The flowers mean spiritually the promises. In winter the Bible is a closed book, the promises are shut up, and the Lord's people derive no comfort from them. There are some natural flowers which close when night comes and open again when the warm sun shines upon them. This is true spiritually, the promises are closed in winter; but, when the sun of righteousness shines upon the soul, then the promises are opened with comfort to believers.

Another sign that the winter is past is that the birds begin to sing. There are singing birds, but they do not sing in winter. But when the winter is past you will hear them singing merrily in trees and bushes, as if praising their Creator. The lark is a singing bird, and when it begins to sing it rises gradually from the earth and mounts up on its wings singing all the time till it reaches a very high altitude, and so it is with the Lord's people, when they are in a singing mood they mount up

to heaven singing praise to God, Father, Son, and Holy
Spirit, for His mercy to them. There are also migratory
birds that leave the country when the cold winter sets
in and do not return till the winter is past; so is the
case with the Lord's people in the spiritual winter.
Although they have the grace of singing, it is silent in
winter, as was the case with the captives in Babylon.
Their enemies mockingly asked them to sing them one
of the songs of Zion, but they replied, " How shall we
sing the Lord's song in a strange land'' (Ps. cxxxvii. 4).
It has been observed that singing birds when a cold day
comes, even in summer do not sing. In like manner the
Lord's people cannot sing always, while graceless people
can sing at all times, but their singing is only lip singing,
and not heart singing.

Another sign of the winter being past is that the voice
of the turtle is heard in our land. The dove is an
emblem of the Holy Spirit. At His baptism the ·Holy
Spirit came down upon Christ in the shape of a dove,
and rested upon Him. Although we have the Scriptures
in our day the Holy Spirit has been grieved by this generation, so that His voice is not heard from the great
majority of the pulpits in our land, as it had been in the
past. False teachers brought winter on this generation.
Many parishes in Scotland that had been in the past
blossoming as the rose are now a spiritual wilderness.
" He turneth rivers into a wilderness, and the water
springs into dry ground, a fruitful land into barrenness,
for the wickedness of them that dwell therein'' (Ps. cvii.
33, 34), but a change for the better is promised when the
spiritual winter shall pass away and the voice of the turtle
(or the Holy Spirit) shall again be heard in our land.
Ministers shall be raised up, taught of God, and the voice
of the Holy Spirit shall be heard by congregations in

their preaching, and the Lord's people will hear the voice of the Spirit and know His voice. Many now are satisfied with the outward form, but not God's people—they need comfort and uplifting by the application of the word of the Gospel preached, by the Holy Spirit. And not only will the Lord's people benefit by the Word preached, but sinners shall be converted and added to the Church. We long for that day, pray for its coming, and it shall surely come. When the Lord comes to build up Zion, then He shall appear in glory and majesty.

Another sign of the winter being past is that the fig-tree putteth forth her green figs and the vine with the tender grape gives a good smell. The Saviour gives it as a mark that the summer is drawing nigh : when the tender branches of the fig-tree putteth forth its leaves ye know that summer is nigh. The fig-tree here may represent anxious inquirers who say with the Greeks, " We would see Jesus." When the winter is past there shall be many such in our land—few as they are now. When the winter is past the vine with the tender grape gives a good smell. Christ Himself is called the vine, and inasmuch as the believer is made like Christ in bearing His image He may be called the vine also. And he is fruitful like the vine—he bears clusters of grapes which are beneficial not only to himself but to others. These grapes are delicious to the taste and refreshing to those who thirst for the water of life. Not only is it that the taste of the grapes is good, but their smell is wholesome. When you go to a vineyard you may feel the smell of grapes, and so there is a good and wholesome smell of the Lord's people, while the smell that comes from the wicked is nauseous to the upright that come in contact with them.

Christ closes His address to the Church by repeating His call to her, " Arise, My love, My **fair** one, and come away." He knew her backwardness on many accounts to obey His call from a sense of her great unworthiness of such a privilege, but notwithstanding this we have no doubt but she rose and followed Christ during her course in the world, and is now with Him in glory. Where he is, the Lamb that was slain feeds her and leads her to fountains of living waters, and that throughout eternity.

May God keep His own people from sinking during their wilderness pilgrimage till He bring them to the rest that remains to them. AMEN.

(Preached on the Sabbath following Mr Andrew Clunas's death, *i.e.*, January 23rd, 1916. He was the first General Treasurer of the Free Presbyterian Church of Scotland).

XXVIII.

Job's Complaint

"Oh that I knew where I might find him ! that I might come even to His seat ! . . . ."—Job xxiii. 3-10.

WE have here an account of Job's sufferings and the happy issue of them. The Higher Critics say that there was not such a man as Job ; but we are told in this book, and in other parts of Scripture, that Job is an historical personage, and we believe that what is recorded of him in the book of Job is the literal truth. We are told where he lived, and some indications are given of the time in which he lived. The Apostle James (v. 11) says, " Ye have heard of the patience of Job, and have seen the end of the Lord ; that the Lord is very pitiful and of tender mercy." Again, in Ezekiel xiv. 14, God says, " Though these three men, Noah, Daniel, and Job, were in it, they should deliver but their own souls by their righteousness." In face of these testimonies of the existence of Job, we cannot believe the Higher Critics.

In speaking from this subject we shall notice—

I. Job's complaint—" Oh that I knew where I might find Him !"

II. He endeavours to find the Lord—" Behold, I go forward, but He is not there ; and backward, but I cannot perceive Him."

III. That which he proposes to do if he find him— " I might come even to His seat ! I would order my cause before Him, and fill my mouth with arguments."

IV. His hope of success in his earnest pursuit—
" I would know the words which He would
answer me."

I. *Job's complaint*: Job had many reasons why he
should complain. He met with uncommonly severe
sufferings and trials, which would be intolerable were it
not for God's sustaining grace, which enabled him to
bear them patiently. He lost, in one day, his great
wealth, and his children, and soon thereafter he was
deprived of his bodily health by a painful and loathsome
disease. Satan was the instrumental cause of all this
calamity. Satan hated Job with a perfect hatred. He
hated him because " there was none like him on the
earth, a perfect and upright man, one that feared God
and eschewed evil"—that is, sin (chap. i. 8). Job's
character as an eminently holy man was the object of
the devil's malice. Satan knows God's people, and, the
more like God they are, the more he hates them. He
went to and fro in the earth, and saw none like Job. He
saw many with whom he was well pleased, because they
were his own dutiful children and his faithful servants,
but he could not bear the sight of this man of God, and
he contrived many fiendish schemes to make him miserable, if he could not destroy him from the face of the
earth. Looking with a malicious eye, to see how he
might bring to pass his evil design, he saw that God put
a wall of protection about Job and all he possessed. He
went to and fro about the wall many a time, but found
there was no gap for him to enter in. He is in perplexity. What is he to do? He sees that he cannot get
at Job without asking permission of God. To approac'
the Most Holy One he has no desire; but such is]
hatred of Job, and his determination to injure him, '

he decides on the hard task. Off he goes, and appears
before the Lord with a guilty eye. He is confronted by
Job's God with the question, " Whence comest thou?"
Satan answered the Lord, and said, " From going to and
fro in the earth, and from walking up and down in it."
As the prince of this world, the evil one intimated, by
his answer, that he has a right to travel through the
earth, and that he had not trespassed on any forbidden
ground. What or who was he in search of? The Lord
knew his errand, and asks him another question, " Hast
thou seen (or considered) My servant Job? I know th.t
thou hast. That man is a perfect and an upright man,
one that feareth God, and escheweth evil (or sin). What
hast thou, Satan, to say against such a holy man?"
Now that liberty is given to the great enemy of God and
His people to speak, he begins his work of accusation.
He cannot deny but Job is the Lord's servant, but he
maintains that he serves Him from worldly motives and
mercenary ends. " Doth Job fear God for nought?
Hast thou not made an hedge about him, and about his
house, and about all that he hath on every side? Thou
hast blessed the work of his hands, and his substance is
increased in the land." He insinuates that it is for
these outward blessings that Job serves God, and, if they
were taken from him, his religion would soon vanish
away like smoke. " But put forth Thy hand now, and
touch all that he hath, and he will curse Thee to Thy
face" (i. 11). Strip him of his great wealth and deprive
him of his children, and his religion is gone. There will
be no more secret prayer, no family worship, no going
to the sanctuary for public worship; on the contrary,
Job will cast off all appearance of piety. He will turn
to be an atheist—he will defy Thee and curse Thee to
Thy face. If Satan were asked, How dost thou know?

he would probably answer, I have seen many who made a high profession of religion in times of prosperity, but when the tide of Providence turned against them, they turned their back upon God and His cause. But he was very much hitherto experimenting on worldly professors of religion; but he will find in the end that Job is of a different character. If he can show that Job, the most pious man then in the world, is a hypocrite, he thinks that he can prove that religion is a sham. But true religion is not a sham, but a reality, and the Lord for His own glory, the good of His people and cause in the world, as well as for the overthrow of Satan's kingdom, allows the matter to be put to the test, though this must bring unspeakable sufferings on His servant. "And the Lord said unto Satan, Behold, all that he hath is in thy power, only upon himself put not forth thine hand" (i. 12). The great adversary, having received this permission, went to work. "So Satan went forth from the presence of the Lord" (i. 13). As he goes along, let us suppose that a number of evil spirits under his dominion met him, and asked, "What news?" "Good news," he would reply, with a fiendish smile on his face. "I got permission to rob Job of all he has." "But how canst thou do that?" "True, I cannot do it in my own person. I am only a spirit, and you cannot do it either." "How canst thou do it, then?" "My dear children, be not troubled about that matter. Don't you remember that, apart from the fact that I have the most of the men of this generation in my service, I have a band of robbers in yonder desert who are professionally fitted for such a work? They have been trained by myself. They know the art of robbery well." "Who are they?" "The Sabeans and the Chaldeans. Besides these instruments, I am the god of fire, and I have the wind at

1

my command—of course, by God's permission.   So
having these instruments of robbery and destruction,
I am sure of success."   "That will do," replied the
evil spirits.   "Let us go to work.   We also hate the
man of thy malice.   Were it not for such men we would
keep possession of the whole world from generation to
generation—there would be no man to rebuke the works
of darkness, and to speak the praise of God whom we
hate."   "You are just at it, my dutiful children," rejoined
the prince of darkness.   "In those parts of the world
where there are none to fear God and eschew sin, we
manage to keep the people, young and old, under our
control and in our service.   In my peregrinations to and
fro in the earth, I find that to be the case.   But enough
of talk, let us proceed to work.   Let a deputation of you
go to the Sabeans, another to the Chaldeans, and I will
command the elements, fire and wind, to do their work."
Orders were obeyed.   The Sabeans, incited by the evil
spirits, after killing the servants that were ploughing—
all except one to carry the tidings to Job—carried away
the oxen, and the asses; the Chaldeans carried with them
the camels, and slew the servants with the edge of the
sword—all except one who carried the tidings to Job.
The sheep were burnt with fire from heaven, and the
arch enemy himself caused a great wind from the wilderness to blow upon the four corners of the house of Job's
eldest son, where all his children were feasting.   Job
was now by this day's work of Satan a poor man—
deprived of all his great wealth, which consisted in sheep,
oxen, asses, and camels, and bereaved of all
his children.   Satan says now, "Surely Job's
religion is gone, his great riches is gone — the
servants that were spared brought him the news."   He
sent one of the evil spirits to Job's house in the evening

to listen at the door, to see whether he had family worship that night. The messenger returned. "What is the news from the hypocrite's house? Had he family worship to-night?" "Yes, and the wonder is, he in his devotions blessed God with such thankfulness as if nothing had happened." "Do you remember anything of what he said?" "Yes." "Tell me." "When worshipping God, he addressed Him thus in the course of his prayer: 'Naked came I out of my mother's womb, and naked shall I return thither; the Lord gave and the Lord hath taken away; blessed be the name of the Lord.'" "Are you sure that you heard him utter these words?" "Yes, quite sure." "Alas! alas!" exclaims the accuser of the brethren, "that is not what I expected. What shall I do?" "Father," replied the evil spirit, "be not discouraged; surely all your devices are not exhausted. You can try another plan to make Job cast off his religion." "But I have exhausted all the permission given me by God. I am chained. I cannot go further to injure the object of my hatred unless I get leave. To my great grief I must confess that I have failed to make out my point—to prove that Job is a hypocrite. But I am not done with him yet. If I get permission to strip him of his bodily health, I think I would succeed in stripping him of his religion. Much as I dislike approaching God the second time, I am so intent on getting the true religion banished out of the world that I shall venture. There is to be a convocation of the sons of God to-morrow, and I shall appear among them, and if God speaks to me that will give me an opportunity of asking permission for a further attack on Job." The appointed time came, the sons of God were met, and Satan comes in among them. And the Lord said unto Satan, "From whence comest thou?" He gave the same answer as on the former occasion. He told the course of his travel, but did not tell the havoc he made on Job. But the Lord knew it. " Hast thou considered My servant Job, that there is none like him in the earth, a perfect and an upright man, one that feareth God and escheweth evil? and still he holdeth fast his integrity, although thou movedst Me against him, to destroy him without cause" (ii. 3). " Thou hast not proved that he is a hypocrite. Thou hast stripped him of his great wealth and of his children, but not of his religion. He still holds fast his integrity. It is as well for thee to give up and to confess that thou art defeated." " Not yet," thinks the evil one.   " I want a little lengthening of the chain of restraint by which my power is limited, and if I got that I think I would make out my point." Many false professors of religion cleave to their profession, while they enjoy health of body, though they lose other outward comforts. " But put forth Thy hand now, and touch his bone and his flesh, and he will curse Thee to Thy face." " And the Lord said unto Satan, Behold he is in thine hand, but save his life. So went Satan forth from the presence of the Lord and smote Job with sore boils from the sole of his foot unto his crown. And he took a potsherd to scrape himself withal, and he sat down among the ashes" (ii. 6-8). His wife pitied his miserable condition, and Satan moved her to advise her husband to put an end to his life by suicide. " Then said his wife, Dost thou still retain thine integrity? Curse God and die. But he said unto her, Thou speakest as one of the foolish women speaketh. What? Shall we receive good at the hand of the Lord, and shall we not receive evil? In all this did not Job sin with his lips" (ii. 9. 10). In all his attempts to prove that Job was an hypocrite, and that there was not such a thing as true religion in the world, Satan failed to prove his point, and had to confess that he was defeated. Let us suppose that the Lord said to Satan : " Have you any more devices to bring affliction upon my servant Job?" He had to confess that he had none, that he went to the utmost degree of his schemes. Then let us suppose that the Lord said—" Stand you aside, Satan, and I will begin to afflict him with a sorer affliction than any you have tried. I will hide My face from him." It was this that brought the bitter cry from his soul, " Even to-day is my complaint bitter, my stroke is heavier than my groaning." " Oh, that I knew where I might find Him." The hiding of God's face swallowed up all the sufferings brought upon him by Satan. He would make no mention at all of these sufferings if the Lord lifted the light of His countenance upon him as in the past in the time of his prosperity. When the Lord hid His face from the Psalmist he was afflicted. The hiding of God's face is the greatest affliction to His people. If they enjoy the light of His countenance they can bear other afflictions, however great, without a murmur.

II. *His endeavours to find the Lord* : He went forward and backward to seek the Lord—he sought Him on the right hand and on the left—that is, he sought Him everywhere where he might expect to find Him. But we shall speak of those places in the following manner : —

What is it to go forward to seek the Lord? It is to go forward in hope to find Him. As Jonah said, " I will yet again look toward Thy holy temple." It is to look to the promises the Lord made to His people that He would manifest Himself to them.

What is it to go backward in seeking the Lord? It is to remember the days of old, as the Psalmist

did when he was in darkness: he remembered
the days of old. This is a way of seeking
the Lord when one is in darkness, and many found Him
by remembering His goodness to them in the past. If
you miss the Lord, seek Him by remembering His lovingkindness to you in the past. Begin at the time when He
awakened you out of the sleep of death. When He convinced you of your sin and misery, when He enlightened
your mind in the knowledge of Christ, renewed your will
and enabled you to embrace Christ by faith in the free
offer of the Gospel; when He pardoned your sins and
made you rejoice with joy unspeakable and full of glory.
If you will do this you will find the Lord again.

Job sought the Lord on the right hand. What is it
to seek Him on the right hand? It is to seek Him among
His people, who are the people of His right hand. Many
found the Lord in this way. When they were alone they
were in darkness, but when they came among God's people
they found Him whom they sought. This has been the
experience of believers on communion occasions when so
many of the Lord's people gather together on the mount
of ordinances. There are not only people of His right
hand, but there are blessings of His right hand—the
blessings of salvation. Read these blessings as they are
set forth in the Bible. Meditate over them, pray over
them, and you may find Him whom you seek. If you
do not find Him there, seek Him on the left hand. What
is it to seek Him on the left hand? We mean God's left
hand. There are people who are yet those of His left
hand. The unconverted are so. If you don't find the
marks of the Lord's people upon you see if there is any
difference between you and the unconverted. On communion occasions there are marks given on the Friday
by the Men speaking to the question—marks both of the

Lord's people and of those who are still in a state of nature. There was a godly woman going home from church along with an unconverted woman. The godly woman was troubled with doubts and fears about her interest in Christ. She asked her companion if she was troubled with an evil heart, and her companion said that she was not, and this was the means of relieving her from her doubts and fears. She saw that there was a difference between her and her companion. Another instance of this may be mentioned. The godly Mr Calder, who was minister at Ferintosh, was often under the temptation that not only was he not a minister of Christ but that he was still in a state of nature. On one occasion he was suffering under this temptation, and he took to his bed, and on Sabbath, when the congregation came to church, the minister did not appear, and some of the elders went to the manse and were told that the minister was in bed. They went to the bedroom door and found it locked. They knocked, but there was no response. Knowing that Mr Calder was suffering from a temptation, one of them took a way to break the temptation by trying to break the door of his bedroom. The minister cried out when he saw that they were doing such work on the Lord's Day, " Are you doing such work on the Holy Sabbath?" a work which he would not do himself. This was the means of relieving him from his temptation. He saw that he had regard for the Lord's Day, which an unconverted man could not have. He rose from his bed, opened the door of his bedroom, went to church, and preached the Gospel with uncommon liberty. This is a way, as already stated, to seek the Lord on the left hand and to find Him. To seek Him on the left hand is to seek Him in His works of Providence. As there

are works of grace, there are also works of Providence, which believers observe in the manner
in which they had not observed when they were
in a state of nature. If they lived near the sea, they
observed with new light the flowing and ebbing of the
sea. They were accustomed from their youth to see this
change in the tide, but never observed that it was the
work of God till they were converted. They saw God in
this. They saw Him also in the revolution of day and
night to which they were accustomed from their youth.
They saw God in all His works of Providence, they saw
Him in removing from this world generation after generation by death. This was before their conversion a
matter of course in which they did not acknowledge God's
hand.

III. *That which he purposed to do if he found Him.*

(1) He purposed to come to His seat. God has a
seat. He sits on a throne, a throne of mercy, and a
throne of judgment. Job had a case to settle, and he
would come to God's seat of judgment to settle that case.
Satan was accusing him of serving God because He was
so good to him in Providence, and his friends who came
to comfort him in his affliction charged him with some
great sin he must have committed to provoke God to
bring affliction upon him, and he would come to His seat
to settle the dispute between them.

(2) He would order his cause before Him, not for the
information of the Judge but for the conviction of his
accusers.

(3) He would fill his mouth with arguments. It is
a wonder that fills us with amazement that we should be
permitted to speak to the Most High. But we have His
own warrant not only to speak to Him but to argue with

Him, for He says, " Come now, and let us reason together, saith the Lord : though your sins be as scarlet, they shall be as white as snow ; though they be red like crimson they shall be white as wool." Job was to fill his mouth with arguments in vindication of his character against the serious charges Satan and men brought against him. There, at God's seat, the righteous might dispute with him. Who is the righteous mentioned here? Some think that it is Christ, but No, it is Job himself. His accusers charged him with being a hypocrite, but he claims, and that justly, to be righteous. He was not only righteous, as a justified person in the sight of God, but he was righteous in his character before men. God Himself, the Judge, tells this to Satan : " Hast thou considered My servant Job, there is none like him in the earth, a perfect and an upright man, one that feareth God and escheweth evil." Notwithstanding all the affliction that came upon him by Satan, men, and God Himself, he retained his integrity. He was thus righteous.

IV. *His hope of success.*

(1) He hoped God would speak in his favour, and that He would know the words which He would answer him and understand what He would say unto him. God speaks to all in His Word in the Bible, but many do not know His voice in the Word, but the Lord's people do. If we benefit by the Word of God, we must understand it. Job hoped not only to hear the words the Judge would speak to him but to understand these words.

(2) He hoped that God would not plead against him with His great power, but that He would put strength in him.

(3) Lastly, he hoped that he should be delivered for ever from his judge. Satan was judging him wrongfully, and men, even godly men, were judging him also, and he hoped that God would deliver him from their judgment, and so He did, and Job went back from the judgment seat of God acquitted from all the guilt with which he was charged by his accusers, and as a token of his sinlessness the Lord made up his loss of property, giving him what he had before his trial twofold.

In conclusion : In Job's sufferings religion was put to the test, and it was proved to the hilt that there is such a thing in the world as true religion, which is denied by atheists and infidels. When Job was tried severely by Satan, God gave him grace to stand the trial, and when He Himself was laying him low by one hand, in hiding His face from Him, He was by the other hand upholding him mightily, or he could not have stood the trial. As his day was, so was his strength, according to the promise : " As thy day so shall thy strength be." And as it was in the case of this man of God, so it shall be in the case of all His people, whatever trial may meet them in this world. We cannot bear the least trial in our own strength. We are weak creatures, but we can bear all trials that the Lord sees fit to lay upon us by His own grace strengthening us, for He says, " My grace is sufficient for thee, My strength is made perfect in weakness." Job, who is in Scripture spoken of as an example of suffering, is now at perfect rest in heaven, and finds there that all his sufferings on earth worked for his good. Believer, faint not, sink not, under the burden of your tribulations. Look to the Lord for support and for the good issue of these tribulations. You shall soon be with Job in the Father's house above, and you will have to confess that the

Lord did all things well in His dealings with you by His grace and Providence while you were in the wilderness. Your sufferings on earth were not indeed meritorious, but they enlarged your capacity for receiving the blessings of glory. Sufferings are not in themselves desirable or pleasant to bear, but they are useful in their own place to prepare the Lord's people for the rest that remains to them. All would like with Baalam to die the death of the righteous who neglect to live the life of the righteous, but without holiness no man can see the Lord. Job desired to come to God's seat, but we must all appear before the judgment seat of Christ. We should therefore seek preparation for eternity that we may be found among the happy people on the right hand of our Judge and not on His left hand among those whose doom is, " Depart from Me, ye cursed, into everlasting fire, prepared for the devil and his angels."

May God in His infinite mercy awaken careless sinners to seek the Lord while He may be found, and to call upon His name while He is near, and may He uphold His own people by His grace during their time in a world of sin and misery. AMEN.

XXIX

Saving Faith

" Now faith is the substance of things hoped for, the evidence of things not seen."—Heb. xi. 1.

In the 38th verse of the preceding chapter, the Apostle says, " The just shall live by faith." In the first verse of this chapter he gives a description of what faith is. Let us go in search of faith to see who has it, not of ny kind of faith but of the faith of the just—the faith of those who are justified, and we are to search for it according to the description given of it in our text. " Faith is the substance of things hoped for, the evide ce of things not seen." In this description one would at first sight be apt to think that the Apostle makes it only more difficult to understand what faith is, but in reality he makes it as clear as possible, and he renders it more easily understood, as he describes it, according to its effects and fruit. You cannot see the being of faith, but you may see its fruit. The Apostle James says, " Show me thy faith without works, and I will show thee my faith by my works " (James ii. 18). It is by its fruit the Apostle speaks of the faith of Old Testament believers in this chapter. He does not mention all these persons, but some of them, as specimens, all of whom are described as to what they did and suffered by faith. He begins with Abel, who by faith offered up a more excellent sacrifice than Cain, and after him he mentions Enoch, who by faith pleased God and was translated to heaven without undergoing the dissolution of the body. Noah manifested his faith by believing what God revealed to him, namely, that He was to destroy the world by the flood, and by building the ark for his own preservation and of his household at God's command. Abraham manifested his faith by obeying God's call to go out into a place which he should after receive for an inheritance. Sara, his wife, showed her faith by believing God's promise that she should have a son in her old age. Isaac by faith blessed Jacob and Esau concerning things to come. Jacob, when he was a dying, by faith blessed both the sons of Joseph. Joseph showed his faith by believing that God would deliver His people out of the bondage of Egypt. Moses manifested his faith by refusing to be called the son of Pharaoh's daughter, and by choosing to suffer affliction with the people of God rather than to enjoy the pleasure of sin for a season, esteeming the reproach of Christ greater riches than the treasures of Egypt. The harlot Rahab manifested her faith by receiving spies that were sent to search the land of Canaan.

After these worthies we read that " Gideon, Barak, Samson, Jephthae, David, Samuel, and the prophets " manifested their faith when " through faith they subdued kingdoms, wrought righteousness, obtained promises, stopped the mouths of lions, quenched the violence of fire, escaped the edge of the sword, out of weakness were made strong, waxed valiant in fight, turned to flight the armies of the aliens."

Others manifested their faith by what they suffered for their religion. They were tortured, they endured cruel mockings and scourgings, bonds, and imprisonment. They were stoned, sawn asunder, tempted, slain with the sword, wandered about in sheepskins and goatskins, being destitute, afflicted, tormented, of whom the world was not worthy; they wandered in deserts and in mountains, and in dens and caves of the earth. "And these all having obtained a good report through faith, received not the promise. God having provided some better thing for us, that they without us should not be made perfect." We have dwelt so long on how Old Testament believers manifested their faith, in order to show that faith—saving faith—is seen by its effects and fruits in doing and suffering. The Apostle does not mention them all, for he says that time would fail him to do so. If we have the faith of the just it shall be manifested in the same manner in doing and suffering for Christ and the Gospel. We shall now proceed to speak of faith according to the description given of it in our text, and

I. *As it is the substance of things hoped for*:

Good things are the object of hope, evil things are the object of fear. We never say we hope that such a calamity will befall us, but we say we hope to receive that which is good for us, for good things are the objects of hope. What is hoped for is not shadows but realities they are things. (1) These things are things revealed in the Scriptures. We have no warrant to hope for anything that God did not reveal in the Scriptures; (2) They are things which God promised. It is in vain to hope for anything that He did not promise. Faith believes the promise and hope looks out for its fulfilment, for faith is implied in hope, and hope is exercised towards good things we have not yet received. "Hope that is seen is not hope, for what a man seeth, why doth he yet hope for? But if we hope for that we see not, then do we with patience wait for it" (Rom. viii. 24, 25). "Faith

is the substance of these things." These things have a
substance, a reality in themselves. How then does faith
give them a substance? It does this in the following
manner:—(a) Although they have a reality in the Scriptures, they are, in the estimation of those who have not
faith, as if they were not. " The natural man receiveth
not the things of the Spirit of God, for they are foolishness unto him, neither can he know them because they
are spiritually discerned" (1 Cor. ii. 14). But when
sinners are changed by the grace of God they believe
them, and in this sense they become real to them, and
their faith gives them a substance which they had not
formerly in their estimation. " He that hath received
His testimony hath set to his seal that God is true"
(John iii. 33). Not only is it the case that faith gives a
substance in this sense to these things as they are revealed
in the Bible, but it gives a substance to them in their
own souls which they had not before, for although it is
the Holy Spirit that communicates them by means of
the Gospel, it is by faith they are received. It is by
faith they receive Christ and the benefits of His
redemption. It is by faith they receive the earnest of
the inheritance, and they hope for the full possession of
it at death. The kingdom of God is within them. You
may be satisfying yourselves by assenting to the truth of
these things as they are revealed in the Bible, but those
who have faith have them in some measure in their souls,
so that they have a substance there which they had not
when they were in a state of nature.

II. *Faith as it is the evidence of things not seen*:

The word evidence here means full assurance. Some
may say if that is so we fear that we have not the faith

of the just, for we have not full assurance of our interest
in Christ. But it is not full assurance of our interest
in Christ that is meant, but full assurance of the doctrines of the Bible. Do you believe that God exists and
that He is what He claims to be in the Scriptures?
Yes, you say, I am so assured of that that I would give
my oath that He is. God is invisible by the bodily eye,
but faith is the evidence of things and persons not seen
by the bodily eye. Those who have not faith cannot
believe or worship a God they cannot see with the bodily
eye. It was the want of this faith that was the origin
of idolatry, of making pictures of God. Do you believe
in the doctrine of sin and the fall of the human race?
You say—Yes, I am so sure of that that I would give my
oath that that doctrine is true. Do you believe that
by the works of the law no sinner can be justified in the
sight of God? You say—Yes, I am so sure of that, that
I would give my oath that it is true. Do you believe
that Christ's atonement is the only ground on which
sinners can be reconciled to God? You say—Yes, I am
so sure of it that I would give my oath that that doctrine
is true. Do you believe that except a man be born
again he cannot see the kingdom of God. You say—
Yes, I am so sure of that that I would give my double
oath as Christ did that that doctrine is true. Do you
believe that all who shall be saved have been foreordained
unto eternal life, and have been given by the Father to
His Son Jesus Christ in the everlasting covenant of
grace? You say—Yes, I am so sure of these things
that I would give my oath that they are true because
they are taught in the Bible. Do you believe that it is
by grace sinners are saved, and not by their own works?
You say— Yes, I am so sure of that that I will give my

oath that it is true. Do you believe that those saved are justified, adopted, and sanctified in this world, and do immediately pass into glory after death, and that there is no intermediate place where they must go for a time before they go to heaven? You say—Yes, I am so sure of that that I would give my oath that it is true. because it is taught in the Word of God. Do you believe that there shall be a resurrection of the bodies of all that are in their graves and that all the human race must appear before the judgment seat of Christ at the end of the world, and that all Christless sinners shall be punished in hell throughout eternity? You say—Yes, I am so sure of that that I would give my oath that it is true. Do you believe that although the redeemed are delivered from the law as a covenant, they are bound to obey it as a rule of life? You say—Yes, I am so sure of that that I would give my oath that it is true. Therefore we say to you that we have full assurance that you have the faith of which we have been speaking, although you might have doubts of your saving interest in Christ, for this is the assurance that is meant when it is said that faith is the evidence of things not seen.

We have been searching for saving faith in the field of God's Word, and in the field of the souls of me . Have we found it? Yes, but not in those who cast doubts upon the Word of God, but in those who believe it with all their heart, and who manifest their faith by its fruits in receiving and obeying God's Word, by doing and suffering for His name's sake.

While we have found faith in some we have not found it in the great majority of those who profess the Christian religion. They are as destitute of it as they had been when born into the world in a state of sin and misery,

19

who, though they may keep up the form of godliness, deny its power in their walk and conversation in the world, and many of them do not keep up even the form itself in their families or in their transactions with their fellow-men in the world, and yet they have a hope of getting to heaven at death. But they shall be sadly disappointed, for without faith it is impossible to please God, and those who do not please God in this world shall be excluded from heaven at death. "Unbelieving" is a part of the description given of those outside that holy city and cast into everlasting perdition. "But the fearful, and unbelieving, and the abominable, and murderers, and whoremongers, and sorcerers, and idolaters, and all liars shall have their part in the lake which burneth with fire and brimstone, which is the second death" (Rev. xxi. 8).

You should examine yourselves and search yourselves as to whether you have the faith of the just, and if you find that you have that faith you may conclude that you are on the way to heaven, but if you have it not you re on the way to hell. But as faith is the gift of God wrought in the soul by the Holy Spirit, you ought to seek earnestly that He would bestow upon you that gift without which you cannot please God.

While it is true that all who have saving faith are fully assured that all the doctrines of God's Word are true, there are some who attain in this life to full assurance of their interest in Christ, and none of us should be satisfied without that assurance. Although this assurance is not of the essence of faith, it is the reflex act of faith by which believers look back to God's dealings with them in their effectual calling, and the more they ascertain that they have been effectually called the more sure they are of their saving interest in Christ. Although their salvation does not depend upon full assurance of their interest in Christ, their comfort depends upon it largely. " Examine yourselves whether ye be in the faith ; prove your own selves. Know ye not your own selves, how that Jesus Christ is in you, except ye be reprobates" (2 Cor. xiii. 5).

XXX.

The Ransomed of the Lord

" And the ransomed of the Lord shall return, and come to Zion with songs and everlasting joy upon their heads : they shall obtain joy and gladness, and sorrow and sighing shall flee away."—Isaiah xxxv, 10.

ALTHOUGH these words may refer to the return of the Jews from that literal Babylon to which in the days of the sons of Josiah they were, on account of their iniquities, carried captive, yet there are such glorious things expressed in the words that the reference cannot be circumscribed to that memorable event. The words must therefore be taken in their ultimate scope as referring to the redemption of God's people by Christ in New Testament times, and their return by faith to the Church on earth, and ultimately to the Church above in heaven. We shall then consider : —

I. The character of the people spoken of—
" The redeemed of the Lord"

II. What is predicted of them : they shall return and come to Zion.

III. The manner of their returning: " With songs and everlasting joy upon their heads."

IV. The blessings they shall obtain at their destination—Zion : " They shall obtain joy and gladness, and sorrow and sighing shall flee away."

I. *The character of those spoken of*—"The redeemed of the Lord."

This implies (1) that they were in bondage. It is those that are in bondage that need to be redeemed. If man had continued in the state in which he was created, he had no need of being redeemed. But he sinned, and brought himself and all his natural posterity into a state of bondage. All fallen men are now in a state of bondage; they are the servants of sin, and under the dominion of Satan. They are also prisoners to the law of God. They transgressed the law, and are therefore under its condemning sentence. They are, moreover, in bondage to spiritual death. They have less power to deliver themselves from the dominion of that death than the people of Israel had to deliver themselves from their bondage in Babylon. The state of man by nature is a state of bondage, and this was the state in which the redeemed were before they were redeemed.

(2) In order to redeem them out of their state there must be a Redeemer. The text tells us who is the Redeemer; it is the Lord. " The redeemed of the Lord." The Lord Jesus Christ is the only Redeemer of God's elect. When a man in Israel lost his inheritance, and sold himself as a slave, there was provision made by the law whereby he might be redeemed, be set at liberty, and put in possession of his forfeited inheritance again. The right of redemption belonged to the next of kin. That friend might, if he had the will and power, redeem or buy his bond brother and his inheritance. The Lord Jesus Christ, that He might redeem His people, took their nature upon Himself. " The

20

Word was made flesh.'' He became their Goël—their next-of-kin. In that nature He paid their redemption price. They were redeemed by the blood of Christ. They were not redeemed by corruptible things, as silver and gold, but with the precious blood of Christ, as of a lamb without blemish and without spot (1 Peter i. 18, 19). The price which Christ paid to the law by the shedding of His precious blood redeemed His people from the curse of the law. He, as their God, satisfied the law in their room and stead ; and so, for them He suffered, the just for the unjust, that He might bring them to God. The price that the Goël in Israel paid was not paid for himself, but for his poor brother, who had nothing wherewith to buy his redemption. So was it with the death of Christ. He died for them who sold themselves as bondmen, and who had nothing to buy their redemption. '' When we were yet without strength, in due time Christ died for the ungodly '' (Rom. v. 6). The poor brother, whose redemption was bought by his friend, received that which he had lost, and which he had no power to recover, as a *free gift*. And so is the redemption purchased by Christ for poor sinners. It is '' without money, and without price '' (Is. lv. 1) ; it is a free gift (Rom. vi. 23).

(3) They are redeemed by power, not, indeed, their own power, for they were '' without strength,'' but by the power of their Redeemer. By His vicarious sacrifice, Christ redeemed His people from the condemning sentence and curse of the law ; by His saving power He delivers them from the thraldom of Satan, the dominion of sin, and the power of spiritual death. '' The prey is taken from the mighty, and the lawful captive delivered '' (Isa. xlix. 24). He who became their

God, undertook to accomplish their deliverance from all the bondage in which they were. He satisfied justice for them, and by His Spirit—" the arm of the Lord " (Isa. liii. 1)—He delivers them from spiritual death, snatches them from the grip of Satan (as David took by his strong arm the poor helpless lamb out of the mouth of the lion), and makes them willing in the day of His power to embrace Himself—their Deliverer—by faith, and to rest upon Him alone for salvation. They are " delivered from the power of darkness, and translated into the kingdom of God's dear Son " (Col. i. 13). They are thus " the redeemed of the Lord."

But (4) their redemption is not completed when they believe in Christ. There is within them and without them what makes them still feel in bondage. They still groan, being burdened (2 Cor. v. 4) ; the flesh is in them, though they are not in the flesh, and that causes them bondage (Rom. vii. 24) ; the devil is after them, though not in them (he has been cast out), and that adds to their bondage, and the world hates and persecutes them, and this completes their bondage. But their Goël undertook to deliver them from their enemies, and He will do it. In the meantime they are the redeemed of the Lord ; they are now the sons of God, and it doth not yet appear what they shall be.

II. *What is predicted of them?*

(1) " They shall return." When the Jews were carried to Babylon, they turned their back on their own land. They willingly turned their back, first on God, and now they are forced to turn their back on their possessions in the Holy Land. But, through God's mercy to them, the time came when they were to turn

their back on the land of their captivity, and return to their own land. Thus it shall be with the redeemed. All that went into captivity did not return, but the redeemed return. It is said in 1 Peter ii. 25 that they *are returned*; here, that they *shall return*. The Lord, by His Spirit working in them both to will and to do, shall dispose them to return, and then, as the effect, they shall return. They shall be made willing to return in the day of His power.

(2) They shall come to Zion. They shall not halt on the way and come short of reaching Zion. In times of awakening, many are moved, but some of them draw back on the way (Lot's wife is such an instance), and never arrive at Zion. But it will not be so with the redeemed; they shall all come to Zion. Zion signifies (*a*) the Church on earth—'' Ye are come to Mount Zion '' (Heb. xii. 22); (*b*) the Church in heaven. When the Jews returned from captivity, they came to Mount Zion; they rebuilt the temple there, and set up the worship of God. In like manner, when sinners return by faith and repentance, they may be said to come to Zion, for they begin the service of God for which they were originally created, and for which they are now created anew in Christ Jesus. It is in the Church on earth they are prepared for the Church in heaven. It is the nursery of glory. When God's children, who are born again, are made meet for the glorious inheritance above, they shall then come also to Zion in heaven. '' They go from strength to strength; every one of them in Zion appeareth before God '' (Ps. lxxxiv. 7). '' The Lord will give grace and glory '' (verse 11)—grace first, glory afterwards. Grace is glory in the bud; glory is grace come to full maturity.

III. *The manner of their returning*: " With songs and everlasting joy upon their heads." This is true in some measure of the Israel of God when they return to Zion on earth. They then sing the song of Moses and of the Lamb. They sing it also after their return from backsliding, and on other occasions. Songs here mean shoutings, such as are made by an army after victory. This is the way in which soldiers express their joy and their gratitude after winning the battle and overcoming the enemy. There is a great victory won at conversion over the devil, the world, and the flesh, and the redeemed shall then exult over the enemy, shout with all their might, giving all the glory to the Captain of their salvation: " Thanks be to God, who giveth us the victory through our Lord Jesus Christ " (1 Cor. xv. 57). But there are many hard battles to face between their conversion and their coming to Zion in heaven. Our life is a warfare (1 Tim. i. 18). The same enemies assail them again. They must therefore put on the whole armour of God (Eph. vi. 17), and be good soldiers of Jesus Christ (2 Tim. ii. 3). They have to fight for their own lives, and in defence of the cause of the King of Zion. In these severe conflicts they are often wounded, but never killed ; " often faint, yet pursuing " ; " often weak," but, " out of weakness made strong," " waxing valiant in fight, turning to flight the armies of the aliens " (Heb. xi. 34).

IV. *The blessings they shall obtain at their destination—Zion*: " They shall obtain joy and gladness, and sorrow and sighing shall flee away."

(1) They shall obtain joy in a larger measure than they enjoyed on earth. Their joy in heaven shall be full

and perfect. It shall be as a crown upon their heads, "even everlasting joy upon their heads." The head is the highest part of man. Their joy on earth did not reach that height. It reached, like the waters that flowed forth from the temple, their ankles, sometimes the loins, but now in heaven it reaches the head, and shall remain at that height forever, for it is an everlasting joy.

(2) They shall obtain gladness. It is said of the disciples that on the day of Christ's resurrection they were glad when they saw the Lord ; how much more glad shall they be when in heaven they see Him constantly, without any interruption throughout eternity.

(3) Sorrow and sighing shall flee away. They had much sorrow and sighing on earth, but when they enter heaven these shall flee away. How shall they flee away ? Just as the gloom of night flees away from the light of the rising sun. As the darkness of night cannot stand the light of day, sorrow and sighing cannot stand the light of glory, where their sun shall never go down. Sorrow and sighing shall flee away, never to return to mar their happiness in heaven. We need not inform the Lord's people that they are often sorrowful in this world on account of indwelling sin, and of the low condition of the Lord's cause in the world, but when they leave the world they shall leave all sorrow and sighing behind them.

In conclusion :

(1) A word to the Lord's people. What a wonderful change shall take place when you enter heaven. A great change took place when you were converted, but

you were imperfect during your time on earth—imperfect in your nature, imperfect in your prayers, in hearing the Gospel, and in all your services; imperfect in your joy, and in all your graces; but in heaven you shall be perfect in all these. How much indebted to Christ you shall feel for redeeming you from your bondage by His own precious blood! You shall see many wonders in heaven, and one of these wonders shall be that you are there yourselves. You will not wonder so much that others are there, but you will wonder at being there yourselves. But by the grace of God you are now what you are, and you will give the praise to Him, and not to yourselves or any other creature. You shall sing, '' Unto Him that loved us, and washed us from our sins in His own blood, and hath made us kings and priests unto God and His Father, to Him be glory and dominion for ever and ever. Amen '' (Rev. i. 5, 6). You are whilst on earth, from a sense of sinfulness, often afraid that you may never get to heaven, but you shall most assuredly return to that Zion of glory, for He that hath begun the good work in you will without fail make it perfect. Live now for Christ, serve Him heartily, for He lived and died for you, and at death He will bring you to be with Himself where He is.

(2) A word to the sinner who is still in a state of nature. You are still ignorant of the bondage into which sin brought all the human race, and you do not feel your need of Christ to redeem you, and you may be thinking, as many do, that you shall get to heaven without being redeemed and changed in your nature; but you are under a delusion. '' Except a man be born

again he cannot see the kingdom of God '' (John iii. 3).
Lay to heart that without that essential change you
must be lost for ever.   Begin now to seek the Lord, and
to pray that He would effect that change in you, and
if so changed, there can be no doubt at all but you shall
be among those that shall return to the Zion of glory
when you leave this world.

May the Lord in His mercy grant that you—even
you—be among that happy people.   AMEN.